14 - organized religion as important ~~instrument~~
arena for ♀ to participate in, and a
recognized impetus to ~~de~~ first wave feminism.
(what about second wave?)
this may even include nearly 19 cent.
                    religious backgrounds of
27 - like Freeman, gives causal weight to state commissions
in creating ♀ networks. Did nothing exist before?

178 - evidence for rel. orgs as abeyance structures
during lull in 1st wave feminism.

last chpt: sees only NWP as heir of suffrage
            movement, while sees lots of multiple
            heirs to 2nd wave -- doesn't mention
            whyever in latter context but easy
            to draw inference. Is it possible to complicate
            picture of NWP as only abeyance structure?
            first by tracing what suffragettes did
            post-1920 and finding roots of 3rd wave
            leaders other than a NWP?

─────────
in 1880s - 51
-51- amend. debated in senate for first time in 1887
52- 1880s sees rise of WCTU + its attention to ♀ rights

Women's Movements
in the United States

Women's Movements in the United States:

Woman Suffrage, Equal Rights, and Beyond

Steven M. Buechler

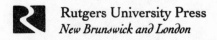
Rutgers University Press
New Brunswick and London

Library of Congress Cataloging-in-Publication Data

Buechler, Steven M., 1951–
Women's movements in the United States : woman suffrage, equal rights, and beyond /
Steven M. Buechler.
    p. cm.
Includes bibliographical references.
ISBN 0-8135-1558-0 (cloth) — ISBN 0-8135-1559-9 (pbk.)
1. Feminism — United States — History.   2. Women — Suffrage — United States —
History.   I. Title.
HQ1426.B8   1990
305.42'0973 — dc20   89-49083
                                                                                    CIP

British Cataloging-in-Publication information available

To Sue

Contents

Preface

While doing research for a previous book on the woman suffrage movement, I was often struck by the parallels between that earlier struggle for women's rights and the contemporary feminist movement. It has become customary to refer to these as the "two waves" of feminism, though like many customs the perception of two unrelated phases of women's activism has been challenged by recent scholarship. Though each "wave" has attracted considerable attention, there have been relatively few attempts to study both phases of women's activism together, and to glean the lessons that such a comparative strategy promises. This book is a contribution to that project.

My work is indebted to all those scholars who have greatly expanded our knowledge about women's movements. This knowledge has grown to a point where no single individual can maintain familiarity with all the material that ideally should inform a comparative study such as this. Through unavoidable ignorance as well as conscious choice, this book speaks more effectively to some questions about women's movements in the United States than others.

My conscious choices have been guided in two major ways. First, I have employed a topical rather than chronological format, giving emphasis to movement origins, organizational forms, ideological visions, classes and races, countermovement dynamics, and endings and futures. The choice of some topics necessarily entails the exclusion of others, though I hope the reader will concur that my choices are worthy of the attention they receive. The topical format brings both advantages and disadvantages. It inevitably risks a certain amount of repetition as similar ground is covered from somewhat different angles in separate chapters. It also risks abstracting important events out of the richer historical context that could be conveyed in a chronological narrative. I have attempted to minimize these risks while building on the main advantage of a topical approach: that it allows for sharper comparisons and contrasts, which underscore the general patterns and illuminate the specific differences in women's mobilization over time.

The second set of choices I have made reflects recent developments in social movement theory within sociology. The newly dominant paradigm of resource mobilization is employed here to illuminate the dynamics of feminist mobilization, but women's movements are also used to critically evaluate the utility of resource mobilization theory. Thus, I expect that some of the questions explored here will resonate most congenially with sociological readers. I have attempted, however, to present the material in a way that speaks to other academic disciplines and is accessible to the general reader. Not all members of these audiences will share my conception of the movements under study, and this reflects the emphases I have chosen as well as the diversity of the subject. There is room for many volumes on the questions examined here.

The research that informs this book has benefited from several sources of support. The National Science Foundation provided a grant to complete my dissertation research on the suffrage movement, while the National Endowment for the Humanities supplied a summer stipend that helped me embark on this comparative study. Mankato State provided two faculty research grants as well as a faculty improvement grant that contributed to this research. I am grateful for each of these sources of support.

Numerous other people facilitated my work in various ways. Eleanor Smeal, Lois Reckitt, and Barbara Hays-Hamilton of the National Organization for Women granted permission and arranged for access to that organization's papers. Eva Moseley and her staff were very helpful at the Schlesinger Library, as was Archie Motley at the Chicago Historical Society. A somewhat earlier round of research benefited from the assistance of Harriett McLoone at the Huntington Library, Elizabeth Shenton at the Schlesinger Library, Roger Bridges at the Illinois State Historical Society, Mary Lynn Ritzenthaler at the University of Illinois at Chicago, Mary Lynn McCree at Jane Addams Hull House, and once again, Archie Motley of the Chicago Historical Society. My thanks to each of these people.

My interpretation of the women's movements analyzed here is especially indebted to the historical work of Ellen DuBois, Nancy Cott, and Sara Evans, as well as the sociological efforts of Jo Freeman, Myra Marx Ferree, and Beth Hess. The manuscript benefited from the comments of several anonymous reviewers, as well as the meticulous reviews and helpful suggestions of Verta

Taylor and Carol Mueller. Their efforts contributed to the strengths of the final product, while its weaknesses remain my own responsibility.

Marlie Wasserman provided the perfect combination of interest, encouragement, support, and prodding that brought this manuscript to fruition at Rutgers University Press. Marilyn Campbell, Kate Harrie, and Barbara Kopel were also helpful in attending to the various details of producing the book. Zulma Davila provided the artwork and designed the cover, while Willa Speiser carefully copy-edited the manuscript. At Mankato State, Karen Purrington diligently kept track of various drafts and stray sections throughout the project.

Throughout my work on this book, I have shared my life with Susan J. Scott, and my dedication of this book to her only begins to acknowledge her support.

Women's Movements
in the United States

Introduction

The contemporary feminist movement has generated intense scholarly interest in women's activism during the last twenty years. As our knowledge of specific women's movements has grown, it has become possible to move to a more general level of analysis that encompasses more than one movement. This book builds upon and contributes to our growing knowledge of women's movements by using the comparative method to identify recurring, enduring, and persistent themes across historical periods as well as to clarify the distinctive, particular, and variable issues that have been inextricably tied to specific socio-historical contexts. By combining an historical consciousness with the sociological imagination, I hope to provide a synthesis of new and existing knowledge about the forms and processes of women's movements in the United States. The synthesis relies on several foundations: extensive primary research on the woman suffrage movement in Illinois; broad familiarity with the secondary literature on the woman suffrage movement throughout the United States; selective primary research into contemporary movement organizations; more general reading of secondary sources on the contemporary movement, and theoretical concerns identified by feminist thinkers and sociological analysts of social movements. Bringing the comparative method to bear on these diverse sources promises a better understanding of both the enduring and variable features of women's social movements.

This study is immediately confronted with some difficult questions about periodizing and defining women's movements. On one hand, it can be argued that there has been a continuous women's movement from the 1840s to the present day, in much the same sense that there has been a labor movement since the beginnings of industrialization. Such a claim may be sustained by pointing to the continuing existence of movement organizations throughout this entire period, beginning with women's rights groups and conventions, followed by woman suffrage organizations, succeeded by the National Woman's Party and the League of Women Voters, followed by the National Organization for Women and other contemporary movement organizations. By reminding us that there has "always" been a women's movement, such a view is an important corrective to the tendency for women to be hidden from history.

On the other hand, it can be argued that there have been a succession of distinct women's movements around particular issues puncuated by periods of dormancy. In this view, the women's rights movement may be dated from 1848 to 1870, followed by a thirty-year dormancy, followed by a renewed woman suffrage movement from 1900 to 1920, followed by another period of dormancy from 1920 to the 1960s, followed by the women's rights/women's liberation movement—which some would argue has yielded to yet another "post-feminist" era in the 1990s. This more finely grained view has the virtue of sensitizing us to historical variations in movement goals, issues, ideologies, strategies, and tactics in each distinct period. It also highlights the question of why women's movements rise and fall in these successive waves, and how such movement life cycles are to be understood.

This study adopts an intermediate position in the debate over periodization. For the purposes of this comparative analysis, the mobilization for women's rights and woman suffrage will be treated as one movement and unit of analysis with a seventy-two-year life span from the Seneca Falls convention of 1848 to the ratification of the Nineteenth Amendment in 1920. This conceptualization is not meant to deny the obvious and important changes that this movement underwent over time; it is meant to frame this issue precisely as a transformation in a single movement rather than a transition between separate movements. Conventional wisdom suggests that after 1920, feminist activism disappeared altogether. This picture is being modified by recent scholarship, which is revealing a more complex picture of shifting priorities, divisive debates, reduced visibility, and persisting if largely unsuccessful campaigns and organizations after 1920 (Taylor 1989a). Nonetheless, by most measures of movement activity, it is plausible to see 1920 as the end of one movement whose principal issue had become the right to vote, and the beginning of a period of relative decline in women's political mobilization.

The 1960s witnessed a revival in feminist mobilization that sets that decade qualitatively apart from the 1920–1960 period. This analysis therefore treats the contemporary women's movement, which originated in the 1960s and persists to the present day, as a single social movement and unit of analysis. Again, such a periodization is not meant to deny either the historical links between earlier and later activism or the diversity that characterizes the contemporary movement. But such a periodization is meant to suggest that the contemporary movement shares enough of a common core and is sufficiently distinct from earlier women's mobilization and activism to be defined as a separate and distinct movement.

The major units of analysis in this comparative approach are therefore the women's rights/woman suffrage movement (1848–1920) and the contemporary women's movement (1960s–present). This periodization is not offered as the definitive resolution to the debate sketched above, but rather as a productive orienting assumption for the analysis that follows. For those with different research agendas and theoretical concerns, other orienting assumptions may well be more useful than the one adopted here.

This periodization provides a temporal definition of the social movements involved in this study. In substantive terms, social movements consist of diverse elements, including leaders, followers, organizations, ideologies, resources, sentiments, dissatisfactions, and visions. Different definitions emphasize different elements, thereby pointing to diverse configurations of what constitutes "the movement" under study. The emphasis in this study will be on movement organizations for two reasons. First, sociological research into social movements has increasingly recognized that virtually all social movements that persist for any time at all assume some organizational form. Whether this involves bureaucratic, centralized, goal-directed organizations or loosely connected associational patterns and social networks, organizational forms provide a key indicator of what a movement is, where it came from, and where it is going. The second reason is practicality: organizations often leave traces and evidence that more ephemeral elements of social movements do not. Organizations will thus be used as more concrete indicators of the social movements under study, not because movements can be reduced to their organizations but rather because organizations frequently provide the connecting threads for many other elements that comprise social movements.

Using organizations as important indicators of social movements simplifies but does not completely resolve the problem of defining a movement. An additional device for handling definitional problems is a distinction between the core and the periphery of a social movement. The core of a movement consists of explicit movement organizations, widely acknowledged leaders, self-identified followers, clearly articulated ideologies, and readily identifiable resources. The periphery of a movement consists of more passive followers, more diffuse sentiments and attitudes, organizations that share some but not all the goals of the movement, and networks of people sympathetic to movement goals. During periods of movement mobilization and growth, the core grows and the periphery becomes more active; during periods of movement demobilization and decline, the core shrinks and the periphery becomes less active. Beyond the movement stands a portion of the public that is uninformed and disinterested; against the movement stand the institutional structures that the movement challenges, the diffuse and traditional sentiments supportive of those structures, and perhaps a countermovement with its own core and periphery.

Applying this organizational emphasis and this core/periphery distinction to this comparative study yields the following conceptualizations of the movements under study. The core of the women's rights/woman suffrage movement consisted of the women's rights conventions and networks before the Civil War and the major woman suffrage organizations from 1869 up through 1920. The periphery of this movement involved other movements and their organizations, including abolitionism, temperance, social purity, moral reform, social science, domestic science, and Progressive Era reformers. The core of the contemporary women's movement consists of central movement organizations such as NOW on the one hand and looser networks of self-identified feminist groups on the other hand. The periphery of the contemporary movement has consisted of the civil rights, antiwar, and New Left movements, some governmental bureaus and social service agencies, some professional women's organizations, some labor unions with largely female memberships and feminist sympathies, some academic institutions supportive of feminist issues, and the like. Via the connecting thread of movement organization in the core and periphery of both movements, it is also possible to trace other movement elements (leaders, followers, ideologies, resources, strategies, tactics) and assess their role in these movements.

This approach to the study of social movements reflects recent developments within the discipline of sociology. For much of this century, social movements were classified as a form of collective behavior alongside panics, crazes, and crowds. All these behaviors were presumed to be short-lived, spontaneous, unorganized expressions of volatile emotional states. In the 1950s, mass society theory became a leitmotif in U.S. sociology, and modern society was conceptualized as a mass of atomized and anomic individuals cut loose from the anchors of traditional societies. The most isolated were presumed to be vulnerable to the appeals of extremist groups and to be likely recruits for collective behavior. The underlying premise of the irrationality of social movement participants was not systematically challenged until the 1960s, with the rise of relative deprivation theory. For this approach, individuals are presumed capable of making rational judgments about their situation in comparison with others, and then acting on those judgments. This more benevolent assumption about movement participants resonated with the affinities of many sociologists for the civil rights movement and the New Left movement, just as the earlier assumptions about the irrationality of collective behavior complemented most sociologists' distaste of fascism and communism abroad and the radical right and left at home.

During the 1970s, a new approach to the study of social movements appeared under the rubric of resource mobilization theory. According to this perspective, social movements are an extension of politics by other means, and can be analyzed in terms of conflicts of interest just like other forms of political struggle. In sharp contrast to the collective behavior tradition, resource mobilization theory views social movements as normal, rational, institutionally rooted, political responses on the part of aggrieved groups. The border between conventional politics and social movements thus becomes blurred, but does not disappear altogether. Whereas established, special-interest groups have routine, low-cost access to powerful decision-makers, social movements must pay higher costs to gain a comparable degree of influence within the polity. Resource mobilization theory also assumes that potential recruits weigh the relative costs and benefits of movement participation and opt for participation when the potential benefits outweigh the anticipated costs. Although the dilemma of "free-riders" and the role of different incentives remain subjects of debate, those debates assume rational actors on the individual level just as they assume the normality of movements on the collective level.

Whereas earlier theories tended to explain the emergence of movements in terms of grievances (rational or irrational, relative or absolute), resource mobilization theory argues that grievances are necessary but not sufficient in explaining social movements. More important are the actual and potential resources that an aggrieved group can mobilize in pursuit of its goals. Until a certain threshold of resources is attained, movements are not likely to emerge even from groups with substantial grievances. Alongside this stress on resources, the theory has also highlighted the role of organization. Whereas mass society theory viewed the isolated individual as the likely recruit, resource mobilization theory has demonstrated convincingly that preexisting social organization often facilitates the mobilization of social movements in the first place. From this view, it is the most connected people rather than the most isolated ones who are likely recruits for social movements. Once movements emerge, organization continues to be a major variable in the analysis of subsequent activity. Again, there are numerous debates over which organizational forms are most strongly related to successful outcomes and whether organization inevitably tames and moderates movements, but the centrality of organization in the study of social movements is now firmly established.

Unlike earlier approaches, resource mobilization theory also has the potential to weave the study of social movements into the broader fabric of the political economy. The emphasis on resources as both the basis for and the goal of movement mobilization is well suited to studying class-based movements over broad periods of social history. At the same time, this framework applies equally well to the mobilization of non-class constituencies whose collective identity arises from common racial, ethnic, gender, cultural, religious, generational, or national characteristics. Finally resource mobilization theory has recognized the central role of the state in facilitating, obstructing, or otherwise mediating the process of movement mobilization. Mobilization occurs when political opportunity structures become more favorable for a given group, and the state is frequently the major actor shaping these opportunity structures. In addition to its role as a mediator in movement mobilization, the state has become an important target of many social movements due to its growing power over all aspects of modern social life. For all these reasons, resource mobilization theory is useful in relocating social movements at the very center of societal struggles over the distribution of scarce and valued resources.

Beyond resource mobilization theory, there are broader issues of sociological significance that can fruitfully be addressed in a comparative study of women's social movements. One concerns the centrality of gender in social relations and the distinctiveness of women (and men) as a social group. Unlike some social categories, gender cuts across virtually all other groups because both women and men are found in all classes, races, ethnic groups, religions, and the like. This means, on the one hand, that feminist movements have truly revolutionary potential because their constituency is part of virtually all other social groups. It means, on the other hand, that women are also and always members of more than gender groups in ways that may inhibit or preclude their participation in women's movements. A comparative analysis of women's movements promises to illuminate the circumstances in which feminist mobilization on the basis of gender is most likely to occur, as well as the factors influencing which women will identify with and actively participate in women's movements.

A second issue of sociological significance concerns the relation between structure and agency. The dialectical connections between these two can be fruitfully explored by an analysis of social movements since movements have their roots in existing social structures and yet are self-conscious efforts to modify those structures. At all levels of abstraction, structure both facilitates and constricts social action; this seems an especially appropriate orienting assumption in the study of social movements. A comparative study illuminates how social structures at various levels of generality have simultaneously facilitated and constricted collective action, and how that collective action has both modified and sustained those social structures.

A third sociologically significant issue concerns the relation between social change and social movements. Many movements arise in periods of rapid social transformation that upset traditional arrangements, redistribute resources, create opportunities, and raise expectations. Many movements contribute to further social change in the goals they attain, the institutions they modify, and the reactions they provoke. However, long-lived movements provide an opportunity to examine yet another connection: the manner in which changes in social structure over time are mirrored by transformations in movements that survive those changes. This link is less explored because few movements survive long enough to embody it. Those movements that do exhibit "long waves" of high activity alternating with relative dormancy offer especially rich occasions for exploring the connections between social change and social movements.

A fourth issue arises because every social analysis rests on an implicit model of society that makes simplifying assumptions and brackets certain questions in order to pursue a given research agenda. The underlying model of society in this analysis presumes that the United States is an advanced capitalist social formation driven by the dyanmics of capital accumulation and organized by an interventionist state. These dynamics have generated particular social class structures and relations, which in turn have been modified by periodically effective forms of class struggle. Rather than privileging class domination and struggle, however, this model recognizes multiple systems of power relations based on class, race, and gender, which cross-cut, intersect, reinforce, and contradict one another as the dynamics of capitalist development unfold. Instead of debating the primacy of one or another of these systems, it is more important to recognize their historical variability and their interrelatedness as a complex ensemble of social relations. This model of society provides a backdrop for this comparative analysis of women's movements, and will guide the exploration of the distinctiveness of women as a social group, the relation between structure and agency, and the connections between social change and social movements.

The chapters that follow present the comparative analysis of two women's movements in six areas. The first chapter examines the origins of women's movements, attending to both background factors and proximate causes with particular attention to the relation between non-feminist "parent" movements and subsequent women's movements in both periods. The second chapter analyzes the role of social movement organizations in both periods and how different organizational forms and relations have been related to movement goals and patterns of success and failure. The third chapter considers ideologies that have animated women's movements in both periods, and seeks both commonalities and differences in the ideologies that were predominant in the suffrage struggle and those that are evident in the contemporary women's movement. The fourth chapter looks at the nexus of gender, class, and race by documenting how women's movements in both periods have been primarily rooted in white, middle-class groups while occasionally transcending these barriers to include women from other social classes and racial groups. The fifth chapter studies the formation of countermovements and illustrates some quite striking parallels as well as differences between antisuffrage movements and antifeminist groups active in the present or recent past. The final chapter addresses the endings and futures of women's movements and provides an overall assessment of the accomplishments of the suffrage movement and some speculations on the likely future of the contemporary women's movement.

Chapter
one

Roots
and
Origins

Social movements are often described as collective responses to a group's experience of subordination. Although the description may be apt, it does not constitute an explanation of the origins of social movements, because there are many cases of group subordination and few instances of social movements. Explaining the origins of social movements requires a clearer analysis of the multiple factors that must come together before such a collective response to group subordination is possible.

Smelser developed one such analysis of these multiple factors by identifying six conditions that are individually necessary and collectively sufficient to produce a social movement. Structural conduciveness and structural strain are permissive background factors that may be followed by the formation of generalized beliefs and a precipitating event that crystallizes the grievances of a group. If these are followed by mobilization for action and the ineffective operation of social control, then a social movement may be expected to emerge through this "value-added" process (1963). This theory has been criticized because it is an overly ambitious attempt to encompass all forms of collective behavior, because it is difficult to identify clear indicators of these six factors, because generalized beliefs are not as irrational as Smelser claims, and because the theory is typically applied only in an ad hoc, ex post facto manner. The theory is nonetheless useful in two ways. First, it provides a convenient way of categorizing and sorting various preconditions of movement origins. Second, it directs attention to broad enabling conditions or background factors as well as more specific causal sequences or proximate causes, both of which are important in understanding the origins of any particular movement.

A more specific focus on social movements led many theorists to emphasize the role of relative deprivation in understanding the origins of movements. For theorists such as Gurr (1970), the social psychological sense of feeling deprived relative to some reference group is a key element in the origins of collective protest. If such a sense of deprivation becomes politicized, then social movement activity is likely to occur. Like Smelser's theory, Gurr's can serve nicely as a post facto description of the roots of some instances of collective action, but it too encounters difficulties in specifying its concepts clearly and in predicting particular instances of collective action. Since relative deprivation is difficult to measure, particularly in large populations, many relative deprivation theorists have relied upon measures of absolute deprivation, hypothesized its translation into a psychologically sensed relative deprivation, and argued that this is a major causal factor. Given the problems of measurement, it has proven difficult to demonstrate that a sense of relative deprivation is either necessary or sufficient to produce a social movement response. Despite these theoretical shortcomings, the concept of relative deprivation introduces an important social-psychological element to our understanding of the origins of social movements.

Resource mobilization theory redirected the search for movement origins in two basic ways. First, it relegated grievances (expressed in generalized beliefs or relative deprivation) to a secondary role in the analysis of movement origins and accentuated the role of resources in explaining movement origins. For this approach, the best predictor of the origins of a movement is the availability of resources; processes that increase the availability of resources to an aggrieved group increase the likelihood of collective action while those that decrease resource availability decrease this likelihood (McCarthy and Zald 1973, 1977; Tilly 1978). Second, it deemphasized the role of individual actors and emphasized the importance of preexisting forms of social organization among the potential constituents of a given movement. Preexisting social networks and connections within aggrieved groups are thus seen as a major resource that is often critical in the early stages of movement mobilization (Oberschall 1973). Conditions that create such links thereby facilitate the development of social movements; those that prevent or weaken such links pose additional obstacles to the mobilization of social movements.

Women's movements provide a rich and relatively unexplored terrain for investigating movement origins. As a social group, women are structurally isolated in ways that make movement mobilization particularly difficult. First, women are distributed throughout all social classes, racial and ethnic groups, subcultures, and religions. Second, the primary identification of women is often with these other groups rather than with women as a group. Third, many women have their closest social ties with individual men and children in marriages and nuclear families rather than with other women (Chafe 1977). The difficulties these factors pose to movement mobilization may be appreciated by contrasting the situation of women with that of racial minorities. Minorities typically share a common cultural heritage, a sense of community, a heightened sense of racial identity, and geographically concentrated residence patterns. For racial minorities, the very processes that create and maintain their subordination (such as segregation and exclusion) also provide some of the facilitating preconditions for mobilizing against that subordination. Compared to other constituencies for emancipatory social movements, the relative integration of women into other social groups and the relative lack of preexisting ties between women constitutes a major obstacle to mobilization on the basis of gender.

The distribution of women throughout class and race structures also means that they will have divergent interests in and reasons for joining women's movements. Women who are relatively privileged by class and race may see women's movements as vehicles for gaining more equality with the men of their group while maintaining class and race privileges. Women who are subject to oppression on the basis of class and race as well as gender may see women's movements as merely one, and not necessarily the most important, part of a larger struggle to eliminate multiple forms of domination. Differences among women on the basis of class interests and racial identity thereby provide another set of obstacles to the mobilization of a women's movement that seeks to speak to the situation of all women.

These reflections suggest two working hypotheses that will guide this comparative exploration into the origins of women's movements. First, the particular difficulties of mobilizing women's movements suggest that such movements are likely to arise only in exceptional circumstances. Specifically, women's movements are likely to arise only when strong connections between women as a unified group are established and when those connections are subject to politicization. The latter condition is important because there are many cases of strong ties without social movements. Second, the often diverse and sometimes conflicting interests of women on the bases of class and race suggest that women's movements are more likely to arise from some constituencies than others. Women who face multiple sources of oppression — on the basis of class, race, and gender — are less likely to initiate women's movements for several reasons. They may be preoccupied with sheer survival; they are likely to have access to fewer of the resources typically needed to initiate social movements; and they often feel that their energies are better directed to class struggle and racial justice than to feminist mobilization. White, middle-class women are more likely to initiate women's movements because sheer survival is not as major a preoccupation, because they have access to more of the relevant resources, and because their social location and biographical experiences may lead them to identify gender inequality as a major grievance that motivates their social movement participation.

The analysis that follows examines the role of background factors and proximate causes in the origins of women's movements in the nineteenth and twentieth centuries. In both centuries, important background factors included changes in the patterns of women's work, in their fertility, and in their educational attainment. The effect of such background factors was to increase the pool of potential recruits to a women's movement. Before movements emerged, however, a number of proximate causes that heightened collective identity and group consciousness also had to be present. In the case of women's movements, other social movements have been important proximate causes that created the political opportunities, provided some of the needed resources, and sometimes generated the grievances that subsequently fueled the mobilization of an independent women's movement. These are some of the common themes linking the origins of women's activism across two centuries. The specifics of each historical era are best seen as variations on these common themes of movement mobilization.

The Woman Suffrage Movement

The deepest structural roots of women's political mobilization in the nineteenth century may be traced to societal transformations associated with capitalist industrialization. By fundamentally altering the ways in which women worked, the places where they lived, and their relation to the larger social community, these transformations created structural strains for many women in the United States.

Many of the effects of industrialization on women's position were mediated by changes in the family. Throughout the colonial era and into the early nineteenth century, the family functioned as a major unit of economic production. Although this was a thoroughly patriarchal system, women nonetheless played socially recognized, directly productive roles in the various tasks associated with household production and familial survival (Chafe 1977). The process of industrialization gradually undermined the productive role of the family unit by fostering larger, nonfamilial units of production oriented to production for a capitalist market. As productive work was increasingly redefined as activity conducted in exchange for a wage outside the household, many women lost directly productive economic roles (Strasser 1982).

The loss of a directly productive economic role was accompanied by a reduction in women's reproductive role as well. Industrialization promoted declines in fertility by altering the economic value of children, and thus the value placed on large families. From economic assets in the form of additional labor in family units of production before industrialization, children became economic liabilities in the form of additional dependents in households increasingly reliant on wage labor after industrialization (Huber 1976). The loss of a productive role and the diminution of a reproductive role thereby represented a fundamental transformation in the lives of many women.

The impact of industrialization on the position of women was mediated not only by the family but also by social class. For wealthy women from privileged backgrounds, the impact was minimized if they had not played productive economic roles even in colonial times. For black women in the slaveholding South, the patterns of industrialization described above had no substantial impact on their productive roles in a slave economy. For immigrant women, an industrializing society often meant that they retained their economically productive roles in the new form of wage labor in a market economy. Even for white, middle-class women, industrialization often meant a wage-labor role for women before marriage and childbearing, or throughout a never-married lifetime, or after separation, divorce, desertion, or death of a husband.

Despite this diversity, the emergent ideal and increasing reality for white, middle-class women in an industrializing society centered around the lack of productive roles and the reduction of reproductive roles (at least as measured by declining fertility). It was in this context that a new role of domesticity was created and promoted as a distinctively feminized complement to the masculinized role of economic provider. In the form of the "cult of true womanhood," this role prescribed piety, purity, submissiveness, and domesticity as the appropriate norms of respectable middle-class femininity (Welter 1966). This role also prescribed new and specific obligations for women vis-à-vis the family, the maintenance of households, the care and rearing of children, and the providing of emotional support to men. As men were to specialize in the public sphere of productive work and economic support, women were to specialize in the private sphere of domestic work and emotional support.

The elaboration of this historically new domestic role for white, middle-class women, and the new conception of the private, conjugal, domestic, nuclear family that accompanied it, were important background factors in the emergence of a women's political movement in several ways. For one, such a change represented a type of downward mobility in that it removed some women from a direct role in what was socially recognized as productive work within the society. The promotion of a new, romanticized view of women as the benevolent and moral civilizers of society did not necessarily compensate for this change in the eyes of all women. For another, this domestic role introduced new confinements, limitations, and restrictions on women's behavior by posing a narrower and stricter standard of acceptable female behavior. For some women, the role itself was a major grievance, especially when coupled with the sense of relative deprivation that may have been generated by women's gradual removal from socially recognized productive work.

Alongside the dissatisfactions and grievances felt by some women as a result of these changes, the domestic role made another important contribution to the emergence of a women's political movement. The domestic role for women (and the provider role for men) sharpened the contrast between the social worlds, expected behaviors, and felt experiences of white, middle-class women and men. By promoting a distinctive and essentialist conception of femininity, the domestic role facilitated new patterns of exclusively female association, friendship, and sisterhood (Smith-Rosenberg 1975). The development of homosocial worlds of female friendship was an important component in overcoming the structural isolation that might otherwise have accompanied the shift to conjugal, nuclear families in which some women played privatized, domestic roles. Thus, at the same time that the domestic role took some women out of the increasingly public world of economic production, it fostered a female world of friendship that created new associations, networks, connections, and linkages between women. Such networks, themselves the product of gender segregation, fostered some of the collective identity and group solidarity essential in the later mobilization of a women's movement.

Two institutional forces also promoted what Nancy Cott (1978) has termed the bonds of womanhood; that is, the simultaneous bondage of women to a new domestic role alongside new forms of bonding between women. The first such force was organized religion. At a time when some women were losing access to the public sphere through economic or political channels, religion became an increasingly significant link between women and the broader social community. It remained one of the few socially acceptable means for some women to participate in the larger public world because it was one of the few public institutions that could be reconciled with women's domestic role. Even as the norms of submissiveness, purity, and domesticity required by the cult of true womanhood acted to isolate women from the social world, the fourth norm of piety served to connect women to the social world through involvement in religious activity. Organized religion simultaneously promoted the new domestic role for women and provided them with a public forum for coming together and, in a few cases, taking active and visible stands on social issues within religious communities.

A second important institutional force was education. Women's access to formal education beyond the primary level was closely bound up with the domestic role because domesticity came to be seen as the major rationale for such education in the early nineteenth century. Since the domestic role prescribed intense involvement in motherhood and wifely duties, the legitimation of women's education was precisely that it would foster these skills and inculcate in women a devotion to their families and a competence in domestic labor. Given these premises, female academies and schools were established as part of the effort to socialize women into their appropriate domestic roles. This effort produced some unanticipated consequences, however (Cott 1978:125). Even the highly circumscribed forms of female education that were permitted could have a liberatory effect and stimulate curiosity and intellectual excitement about issues far removed from women's domestic duties. In addition, female education fostered patterns of friendship, solidarity, and collective identity among women as they pursued their educations and found opportunities to overcome their structural isolation. The cases of organized religion and formal education are two instances of institutions that were socially conservative in nature and explicitly intended to promote female domesticity in the early nineteenth century. Ironically, they also served to foster solidarity between women and to provide them with access to the social community as well as the skills to utilize that access for purposes other than female domesticity.

Alongside and growing out of these institutional forces were patterns of association among women that also represented a partial exception to their exclusion from the public sphere. The participation of women in religious revivalism, in benevolent societies, and in charitable groups provided some women with a role in social action and reform that was consistent with their domestic and maternal roles at the same time that it expanded those roles to the broader community. The mobilization of some women into these activities was not a challenge to their domestic role as much as it was a logical extension of that role. As a result, such activity was tolerated and even encouraged as long as women's activity remained within the bounds of appropriate femininity. While some women were doubtless satisfied with such roles, others experienced a heightened sense of frustration at the limits placed on female reform activity, particularly given the contrasts between the roles played by women and men in such groups.

Against this backdrop, the involvement of women in the temperance movement was the logical culmination of a number of social forces. The cause of temperance allowed women to engage in reform activity while deploying a rhetoric perfectly consistent with their domestic role. In this rhetoric, the goal of the temperance movement was to defend the home, protect the family, and strengthen those moral and domestic virtues which had become the special province of women. Although couched in the very terms that had helped to confine white, middle-class women in the first place, their involvement in the temperance movement simultaneously represented a nascent feminist response to the growing economic dependence and social vulnerability of middle-class women. The attack on alcohol was doubtless seen by some women as an indirect challenge to male power, but a challenge that was culturally safe and morally grounded by the appeal to domestic values (Bordin 1981; Epstein 1981). For some women, involvement in the temperance movement crystallized the generalized beliefs and constituted the precipitating event that Smelser has identified as central to the emergence of a full-fledged social movement.

By the 1830s, numerous factors were falling into place for the emergence of some sort of women's movement. Background factors like industrialization and urbanization had eliminated many women's productive role and begun to reduce their reproductive role, causing forms of structural strain for particular groups of women. A newly fashioned domestic role had appeared, but was seen by some women as confining and limiting their activity, thus representing a kind of downward mobility and fostering a sense of relative deprivation as women's dependence on men increased. Such strains, grievances, and deprivations do not necessarily translate into social movements unless other factors are present as well. Some of these were provided by the same domestic role that created some of the dissatisfactions, for this role also promoted social relations and networks of association among women in homosocial worlds that reduced their structural isolation and allowed them to act in concert. Organized religion and formal education contributed more impetus to the process, and the participation of women in certain reform activities consistent with their domestic role was a logical result. The nascent feminism of the temperance movement brought its female participants to the outer edges of acceptable female behavior, as women used their domestic role to challenge some of the immediate results of their increasing subordination. In all these ways, background factors became more conducive to the development of some form of social activism by women.

The discussion of background factors to this point conveys what might be called the standard version of women's mobilization during the 1820s and 1830s. This standard version has been challenged by more recent historical research, which questions the centrality of urban, middle-class women in this process precisely because they were most imbued with the ideologies of separate spheres and true womanhood. Such ideologies certainly could prevent the politicization of female discontent altogether; alternatively, they could infuse women's activism with a presumption of moral superiority derived from these dominant ideologies. In contrast to the standard account, this argument highlights the role of agrarian, Quaker women in the emergence of a women's rights movement. With a long history of sexual equality and considerable social distance from the urban, bourgeois world of separate spheres, such women were likely recruits to a women's rights movement. They were also likely to espouse an ideology of equal rights and social justice based on similarities between the sexes rather than an ideology of moral superiority based on sexual difference, which one might expect from women whose worldviews were shaped by the principles of separate spheres and true womanhood. If the emergence of an egalitarian women's rights movement depended importantly on the role of such agrarian, Quaker women, then many of the background factors highlighted in the standard version of women's mobilization need not be seen as necessary preconditions for such activism (Hewitt 1986).

Of all the proximate causes identified in discussions of the origins of the women's rights movement, the abolitionist movement seems to be the most frequently mentioned (see, for example, Flexner 1975; Sinclair 1965; O'Neill 1969; DuBois 1978; Hersh 1978; Melder 1977). Many commentators have observed that while not all abolitionists supported women's rights, many women's rights advocates had prior experience in the abolitionist movement, and they drew on these experiences as they formulated and pursued the goals of the early women's rights movement. Beyond a basic agreement on the fact that the women's movement somehow emerged from the abolitionist movement, however, there is room for competing interpretations of the exact dynamics involved in this process.

The involvement of women in the abolitionist movement was evident almost from its beginnings. Also evident from the beginning was a tension over the appropriate role of women in the antislavery effort. When the American Anti-Slavery Society was formed in Philadelphia in 1833, women were allowed to attend the meeting and to speak, but they were not allowed to join the society or to sign its founding document. In response, women formed the Philadelphia Female Anti-Slavery Society. Four years later, a National Female Anti-Slavery Society met in New York with eighty-one delegates from twelve states (Flexner 1975:42). By 1840, women allied with the Garrisonian wing of the abolitionist movement had won positions within the American Anti-Slavery Society. However, when they traveled to the World Anti-Slavery Convention in London to act as delegates of the American Society, they were not recognized or seated, because they were women (Sinclair 1965: 56–57). These incidents, and others like them, reflect a dialectic of opposition that was a crucial legacy of the abolitionist movement for later feminist mobilization. In this dialectic, women who worked for abolition in ways that overstepped the normative boundaries of feminine behavior were opposed both by some abolitionists and by the larger society for their efforts. This opposition thematized the issue of gender, which became a mobilizing issue for some female abolitionists who went on to organize around the issue of women's rights both within and eventually outside of the abolitionist movement.

In this process, the role of the Garrisonian wing of the abolitionist movement was critical. By stressing individual conscience rather than religious authority as the basis for action, and by criticizing clerical support of slavery, Garrisonian abolitionism created a path from pious activism to political activism that many women in the movement followed (DuBois 1978:33ff). It was at this point that some abolitionist women stepped over the line that defined appropriate feminine behavior and provoked an oppositional response from the more conventional abolitionist movement. For these reasons, the abolitionist movement may be regarded as a more important forerunner of the women's rights movement than the temperance movement, even if the latter attracted larger numbers of women. Despite their numbers, women's temperance activism tended to remain only nascently feminist; it did not openly challenge the boundaries of normative female behavior. Women in the abolitionist movement did increasingly challenge those boundaries, contributing to the dialectic of opposition that helped to generate a women's rights movement.

As this dialectic unfolded, some abolitionist women began to address the issue of women's rights alongside antislavery. Sarah and Angelina Grimke are the best-known figures to move in this direction, but they were followed by a number of others. In one study of "feminist-abolitionists" as a distinct group set off from earlier antislavery advocates and later woman suffragists, Blanche Hersh (1978) traces the careers of over fifty women who worked for the twin causes of abolitionism and women's rights in this important phase in both movements. By arguing that women were enslaved in ways that paralleled the oppression of blacks and required a parallel movement for their emancipation, these women were the first to formulate what William Chafe (1977) has termed the analogy of race and sex. In Hersh's interpretation, most feminist-abolitionists came to their feminism after their struggles within the abolitionist movement; by this logic, women's consciousness of their own oppression was underdeveloped until they became active in seeking the emancipation of another group and saw the parallels between the enslavement of blacks and the oppression of women. (For an informative critique of the "race-sex analogy" as really comparing only black *men* with *white* women and thereby ignoring black women, see Hooks 1984.)

Hersh's interpretation is part of a larger argument that identifies the abolitionist movement as critical to the emergence of the women's movement in a number of ways. In this argument, the abolitionist movement is seen as providing women with the organizational experience, the oratorical skills, the leadership abilities, the ideological rhetoric, the political analysis, and the social consciousness to address their own subordination in their own movement (see Flexner 1975; O'Neill 1969; and Sinclair 1965 as well as Hersh 1978 for versions of this argument). This argument raises a key question in understanding the origins of the women's rights movement: What was the precise role played by the abolitionist movement in the generation of the women's rights movement that followed on its heels?

At least two answers to this question are possible, and they may be framed in terms of sociological theories of social movements. For the older tradition of movement analysis, the origins of movements are to be sought both in background factors like structural strain and in processes that give rise to grievances that then become the basis of mobilization. For this approach, the role of abolitionism would be important primarily because it created the grievances that then stimulated the mobilization of the women's rights movement. The grievances emerged only with the understanding of the dynamics of slavery, which women acquired via abolitionism and then generalized to their own situation through the analogy of race and sex. For the newer tradition of movement analysis, the origins of movements have more to do with the shifting opportunities for mobilizing resources to sustain a movement. In this view, grievances are assumed to have a long-standing history that predates the emergence of the social movement, and to be secondary because grievances themselves are not sufficient to launch a social movement. For this approach, the role of abolitionism would be important primarily for the resources it provided to women who already had a keen sense of their grievances as women but had previously lacked the resources necessary to respond effectively to their situation.

While it is undeniable that the abolitionist movement provided important resources to women for the mobilization of a women's rights movement, it is debatable whether a consciousness of their own oppression was one of these resources. Close analysis of the generation of feminist-abolitionists does not support the idea that this entire group underwent a uniform process of consciousness-raising about women's subordination only after their work in the antislavery cause. This thesis seems especially weak in the cases of prominent leaders such as Lucy Stone, Elizabeth Cady Stanton, and Susan B. Anthony. Each traveled a different route, but none traveled the hypothesized one toward involvement in the early women's rights movement. Stone and Stanton's feminist sympathies predated their involvement in abolitionism, while Anthony's experiences as a teacher and a temperance worker were most important in leading her into the women's rights movement (see Cott 1980:100–101). While some women doubtless came to the women's rights movement because of a raised consciousness derived from the antislavery movement, this thesis seems unable to account for the important leadership cadre of the early women's movement.

These considerations support Ellen DuBois's claim that "women's discontent with their position was as much cause as effect of their involvement with the antislavery movement" (1978:32). In terms of social movement theory, these considerations suggest that feminist grievances were a long-standing reality for many women and not a new revelation as a result of their antislavery work. Consistent with the claims of resource mobilization theory, however, grievances alone do not suffice to generate a social movement, and that is why a women's rights movement did not emerge any earlier despite preexisting discontent. If DuBois is right, that discontent motivated some women to participate in the major emancipatory social movement of the late 1830s and 1840s: the abolitionist movement, and its Garrisonian wing in particular. As a result of participation in the abolitionist movement, some women gained access to other mobilization resources, which were vital to generating a women's movement. In DuBois's perspective, these resources included an escape from clerical authority, an egalitarian ideology, and a theory of social change (1978:32).

As they participated in the abolitionist cause, novice female reformers acquired important skills in speaking, organizing, and agitating for social change at the very same time that they encountered resistance to their participation in the abolitionist cause. As a result of preexisting grievances, new access to resources, and an internal dialectic of opposition, the issue of women's rights was increasingly discussed from abolitionist platforms throughout the 1840s. These dynamics culminated in 1848 with the well-known Seneca Falls women's rights convention, which drafted a Declaration of Sentiments and Principles that formally launched the women's rights movement. While the precise timing of this convention concerns the biographies of the women involved in calling the convention, the year 1848 is a significant reminder that the women's rights movement began in a social climate of agitation and reform at home and a political climate of revolutionary social change in Europe. Both nationally and internationally, such reform and revolutionary movements created important social and political space for other movements, including women's rights, to build a foundation. Such movement space is yet another resource that some movements bequeath to others as part of the dynamics of social reform and change.

The Seneca Falls convention addressed a broad spectrum of issues, including women's economic position, legal status, occupational possibilities, educational opportunities, familial roles, and political disenfranchisement. After 1848, numerous women's rights conventions were held in various locations until the Civil War. The conventions disseminated and popularized ideas about women's rights through the network provided by the abolitionist movement and by female antislavery societies in particular. At the same time that it facilitated the spread of these ideas, however, the abolitionist movement inhibited the development of women's rights organizations by providing an existing organizational network. Hence, the abolitionist movement nurtured an emergent women's rights ideology while constricting women's independent organizational development. As a result, no major women's rights organizations or associations were formed despite a dozen years of agitation leading up to the Civil War.

This organizational time lag revives the dilemma of defining social movements and thereby dating their origins. If movements are defined on the basis of distinct sentiments, then the women's movement may be dated from the early to mid-1840s. If movements are defined on the basis of networks of people acting on distinct sentiments, then the women's movement may be dated from the series of women's rights conventions initiated at Seneca Falls in 1848 and continuing over the next dozen years. If movements are defined on the basis of independent movement organizations, however, then the women's movement must be dated from the formation of the national woman suffrage organizations, which appeared only after the Civil War.

The emergence of an organizationally independent women's rights movement is the final chapter in the long history of the relations between the antislavery and women's rights causes. During the Civil War, women activists put aside their agenda and concentrated on supporting the war effort and the abolitionist cause. When the Thirteenth Amendment to abolish slavery was proposed in 1863, Susan B. Anthony and Elizabeth Cady Stanton formed the National Woman's Loyal League and collected nearly four hundred thousand signatures on petitions urging Congress to pass the amendment (Flexner 1975:110–111). With passage and subsequent ratification of the amendment in December 1865, the legal status of black men and women became more analogous to that of white women: members of each group were recognized as citizens but were still lacking basic civil liberties enjoyed by white male citizens. Many women who had worked for both abolitionism and women's rights thus came to see this moment as the perfect opportunity to broaden democracy and extend justice by enfranchising black men and women as well as white women, and they began to push for a broadly oriented constitutional amendment to implement this goal.

The response of male abolitionists and Radical Republicans, who had won a major victory with the Thirteenth Amendment and sensed another in the offing, was a major disappointment to women's rights advocates. The male reformers argued that it was "the Negro's hour" and that it would be too risky to link the goal of black suffrage and civil rights with that of female suffrage; this strategy called for immediate work on black rights with vague promises of subsesequent effort on behalf of female suffrage. Without female enfranchisement, "the Negro's hour" really meant black *male* suffrage, a principle emobodied in the proposed Fourteenth Amendment, which specified voting as a male right.

Stanton and Anthony resisted this version of the amendment and fought vigorously for one that would extend suffrage to black men, black women, and
white women. Toward this end, they organized the American Equal Rights Association to seek a broad extension of voting rights under the rubric of "universal
suffrage." Despite these efforts, the Fourteenth Amendment passed with its reference to voting as a male right, thereby writing a sexual distinction on voting
rights into the Constitution for the first time.

The incomplete nature of the Fourteenth Amendment necessitated the Fifteenth Amendment to securely guarantee black male voting rights. Once again,
feminists sought to bring the issues of black and female suffrage together as one
universal reform, only to be met with the stubborn refusal of abolitionists and
Republicans to take their call for universal suffrage seriously. As the Republicans prepared to fight the Democrats over black enfranchisement, some women
came to feel that the "hypocrisy of Democrats serves us a better purpose in the
present emergency than does the treachery of Republicans" (cited in DuBois
1978:77), and they joined Democratic resistance to black enfranchisement because Republicans refused to seek female enfranchisement at the same time. In
an increasingly complex political battle structured by race, gender, and partisan
politics, women's rights advocates thus split over the relative priority of black
rights and women's rights, with Lucy Stone and Henry Blackwell reluctantly
acquiescing to the Republican strategy and Susan B. Anthony and Elizabeth
Cady Stanton rejecting Republican "treachery" and seeking a different political
base for pursuing women's rights (see DuBois 1978 for an excellent and highly
detailed account of these dynamics).

The struggles around black rights and women's rights after the Civil War
are a powerful example of how the politics of race and the politics of gender can
be used by dominant groups as a divide-and-conquer strategy. To Republicans
seeking to implement a Reconstruction program, black rights had an instrumental value that women's rights did not have, and that is part of the explanation for
the "Negro's hour" strategy. For women's rights advocates, this was a bitter lesson, and one that provoked racist reactions on the part of some white women
about extending voting rights to black men but not to white women. In the end,
the abolitionist movement, which had contributed to the emergence of a
women's rights ideology through an earlier dialectic of opposition, also contributed to the appearance of women's rights organizations through a later dialectic
of opposition in the context of Reconstruction politics. In 1869, two national
woman suffrage organizations appeared. The National Woman Suffrage Association (NWSA), founded in May by Anthony and Stanton, and the American
Woman Suffrage Association (AWSA), founded in November by Stone and
Blackwell, signify the end of the tumultuous relationship between abolitionism

and women's rights and the beginning of an organizationally independent women's movement in the United States.

The Contemporary Women's Movement

The women's movement that emerged in the 1960s was the result of diverse forces that coalesced during the post–World War II period and culminated in a significant and substantial movement by the end of the 1960s. Once again, it is helpful to distinguish between background factors and proximate causes as a means of understanding how these forces combined to promote a women's movement at this time.

The deepest structural roots of the women's movement that originated in the 1960s may once again be traced to a capitalist economy that continued to industrialize and urbanize U.S. society throughout much of the twentieth century. After World War II, these patterns were evident in specific trends toward a more diverse occupational structure, growth in clerical and service-based occupations, and patterns of suburbanization. These economic changes were closely interrelated with changes in the family and women's roles within the family. For at least some groups of women, these changes, in tandem with more proximate causes and influences, were sufficient to promote the emergence of a new women's movement in the 1960s.

Whereas the loss of an economically productive role helped promote a women's movement in the middle of the nineteenth century, the steady reclaiming of an economically productive role helped promote a women's movement after the middle of the twentieth century. From 1900 to 1920 — the last two decades of the woman suffrage movement — women made up about 20 percent of the labor force. In 1940, they made up about 30 percent of the labor force. In the 1980s, women made up almost 45 percent of the labor force, and the pattern is expected to continue. More important than the numerical increase is the composition of the female work force. In the 1920s, over three-fourths of the women in the labor force were single; today, 60 percent are married. Even more striking, almost half of all mothers with children under age five are now in the labor force and over 40 percent of women with infants under age one are now in the labor force. (Ferree and Hess 1985:2–6; Huber 1976:381).

These figures imply a major shift in the work and family roles of middle-class white women during the twentieth century. In the beginning of the century, paid work was largely the province of young, unmarried women who left the labor force upon marriage and typically never returned. Toward mid-century, women were still likely to leave the labor force upon marriage or during childbearing and child-rearing years, but they frequently reentered the world of paid work as children matured. In the 1980s, marriage is no longer interrupting the work lives of most women, and childbearing and child-rearing is typically posing only brief interruptions or reductions in the labor force participation of many women. Whereas nineteenth-century industrialization gradually displaced most women (and especially middle-class white women) from economically productive roles, twentieth-century economic development has gradually restored a new version of economically productive roles to women, and particularly to middle-class white women.

As labor force participation increased, women were likely to experience "structural strain" from several directions. For one, their increased role in the labor force occurred in a context of sex segregation and discrimination that affected all aspects of their occupational roles. For another, women's domestic obligations were not reduced alongside the increase in their labor force obligations, so that these changes produced a "dual burden" work life for women outside and within the home. Finally, the social climate of opinion was at best ambiguous and at worst virulently hostile to the participation of women in the labor force and in public roles more generally. Thus, while paid work itself may have been an impetus toward a women's movement, paid work in the context of segregation and discrimination, a dual burden, and a hostile climate of opinion was one source of significant structural strain for many women in the post–World War II period (see Rupp and Taylor 1987:12–23).

The twentieth century has also seen increasing educational attainment among women. In 1900, women represented 35 percent of undergraduates and received less than 20 percent of bachelor's (or equivalent) degrees; in 1981, women made up 50 percent of undergraduates and received almost 50 percent of bachelor's (or equivalent) degrees. Significant differences between men and women remain at the level of graduate, doctoral, and professional degrees, but even here, percentage gains have been substantial in the last thirty years. Combined with the fact that many more people are receiving college educations now compared to earlier in the century, the result is a much larger pool of college-educated women who constitute potential recruits for a women's movement. This pool is also subject to structural strains, ranging from educational discrimination to the well-known disparities in earning potential between men and women at comparable educational levels. Finally, these strains include the psychological consequences of heightened expectations due to educational attainment, which may be contradicted by the realities of sex-segregated labor markets and the dual burden of work and family responsibilities.

Long-term declines in fertility rates have been another significant background factor relevant to the emergence of a women's movement (Huber 1976:373–374). As family size has decreased, as the timing and spacing of children have been more reliably controlled, and as women's life expectancy has increased, women's involvement in childbearing and child-rearing has come to occupy a smaller percentage of their overall lifetime (while child-care expectations may have intensified). The exception to this long-term pattern was the baby boom period of 1947–1963, when birth rates and fertility increased. This slight increase in the context of increasing labor force participation and educational attainment may well have accentuated the structural strain of a dual burden for many women, making them potential recruits for movement mobilization. Since the mid-1960s, the reestablishment of declining fertility and projections of continuing low birth rates has yielded a larger and larger group of employed, highly educated women for whom childbearing and child-rearing activities have become one set of responsibilities among several others.

A crucial prerequisite for a social movement is a strong sense of collective identity among the potential constituents for that movement. Of all the background factors discussed here, women's increasing labor force participation was probably the most important in promoting this identity. A competition approach based on population ecology models would suggest that women's labor force participation represented increased competition between men and women for scarce resources. When groups compete for scarce resources within the same domain or niche, a heightened sense of group identity is likely to develop around that competition. This argument may take both a general and a specific form. In general, if the labor market is viewed as a male domain, then an influx of female laborers will prompt competition between women and at least some men for wages and work. Much of this competition may be preempted if women are channeled into sex-segregated occupations, however. The more specific version of the argument is that if and when women seek what are traditionally male occupations, then competition is likely to be greatest and the emergence of group consciousness and collective identity is most likely to occur (Rosenfeld and Ward 1985; Ward and Rosenfeld 1986; see also Chafetz and Dworkin 1986). These background factors do not promote a social movement by themselves, but they do create a larger pool of women who are potential recruits to such a movement.

These background processes provided three key elements for the emergence of a social movement. First, some women gained access to greater resources, which were important in the generation of a social movement. Second, some women also experienced a psychological sense of marginality as a result of their secondary status in employment, education, and other institutions (Ferree and Hess 1985:8). Third, some women also acquired a stronger sense of group consciousness and collective identity. Counterbalancing these factors was the severely hostile climate of antifeminism that pervaded the 1950s and made it very difficult for a politicized and feminist response to these background factors to emerge at this time (Rupp and Taylor 1987:12–23). By the end of the 1950s, an important foundation for a women's movement had been established; the next decade brought that movement to fruition.

The origins of the contemporary women's movement involve several proximate causes and conditions; two of these had no parallel in the women's rights movement of the mid-nineteenth century. First, the woman suffrage movement left an important legacy in the National Woman's Party (NWP), which survived the 1920–1960 period as an "elite-sustained movement" and contributed to the reemergence of a more prominent women's movement in the 1960s (Rupp and Taylor 1987). Second, the federal government played a crucial, if often unwitting role in the origins of a women's movement by altering the structure of political opportunities in ways that facilitated women's mobilization. A third proximate cause is more familiar: the existence of a prior movement for racial equality, which created conditions conducive to feminist gains at key moments. When renewed feminist activism occurred, when governmental actions facilitated movement goals, and when the civil rights movement fostered a climate of reform, the contemporary women's movement began to emerge in the early 1960s.

The National Woman's Party was formed at the height of the woman suffrage struggle in 1917 to mobilize women voters in suffrage states toward the goal of federal enfranchisement of all women. After the suffrage victory and ratification in 1920, the NWP introduced the Equal Rights Amendment (ERA) into Congress in 1923. The amendment precipitated a major struggle between the NWP and most former suffragists, who feared that the ERA would undermine protective labor legislation for women. As the ERA debate faded from public view, the NWP survived as an elite, exclusive, hierarchically organized women's party that never wavered in its support for the ERA. From the 1920s to the 1960s, the NWP was an elite-sustained "movement halfway house" for the cause of women's rights (Rupp and Taylor 1987).

The perception that the ERA and female protective labor legislation were antithetical was still very much alive as John F. Kennedy took office in 1961. For several decades, the Women's Bureau in the Department of Labor had been concerned with the status of women within the labor force, and it had an active constituency of labor union women and middle-class women's groups. While championing equal pay for women, the Bureau was equally committed to maintaining protective labor legislation for women, and thus was firmly opposed to the ERA (Harrison 1980:632). However, continued activism by the NWP around the ERA during the presidential election made it expedient for Kennedy to recognize women as a political constituency in some way. His response was not to support the ERA but rather to appoint a Presidential Commission on the Status of Women headed by Women's Bureau director and longtime ERA opponent Esther Peterson. To no one's surprise, the Commission fulfilled its intended function of blunting the drive for an ERA by reporting that it was an unnecessary reform. However, the unintended and unancticipated consequence of the Commission was to facilitate mobilization, because it became an effective agency in the pursuit of other women's goals, promoted the visibility of women in governmental positions, and institutionalized a forum for heightened discussion of women's issues within the government itself. The commission's 1963 report identified numerous sources of discrimination against women and made twenty-four specific recommendations that prefigured much of the pro-woman legislation that emerged over the next several years. In this way, a governmental effort to blunt the ERA unwittingly contributed to the mobilization of a revived women's movement (Harrison 1980; Rupp and Taylor 1987:166–174; Ferree and Hess 1985:51).

The Presidential Commission quickly gave rise to fifty state commissions that conducted research and issued reports on the status of women throughout the country. These commissions and their activities created a network of knowledgeable, politically active women who were documenting extensive sex discrimination and creating a climate of expectations that remedial steps would be taken (Freeman 1975:52). One of the most immediate results of the Presidential Commission's work was the passage of the Equal Pay Act in 1963. "Although its focus was narrow, the Equal Pay Act marked the entrance of the federal government into the field of safeguarding the right of women to hold employment on the same basis as men" (Harrison 1980:642). Among the act's limitations were exemptions excluding some groups of women and the fact that a stronger version demanding equal pay for comparable work was defeated in favor of the equal work provision. Supporters knew this would allow employers to shift job titles and categories in ways that would perpetuate wage inequality. Nonetheless, the act's passage was a major step in putting the federal government on record in opposition to wage discrimination (McGlen and O'Connor 1983:170).

Another step was taken with the passage of Title VII of the Civil Rights Act, which had a clause prohibiting both race and sex discrimination. According to standard accounts, conservative southern Senator Howard Smith (Virginia) proposed adding sex discrimination to this bill in the belief that this would turn the bill into a joke and allow opponents to defeat it without appearing racist. The strategy backfired when the bill passed. According to Rupp and Taylor, Smith's actions were not simply the instrumental maneuverings of a racist legislator.

Rather, they argue that Smith had supported such ideas before, that NWP members themselves had promoted the strategy, and that Smith "may have acted out of a kind of Southern 'chivalry' toward white women," seeking equal protection for white women if civil rights were to be extended to black men and women (1987:177). The NWP may have used Smith as much as he attempted to use the women's issue in this bizarre episode. While Smith's motives and the NWP's strategy may never be entirely clear, it is clear that Title VII's sex discrimination clause became an important resource in further mobilization. The success of the civil rights movement and the response of the federal government thereby created a more favorable structure of political opportunities to advance the cause of women's rights as well.

This episode has some parallels to the debate after the Civil War over the relative priority of black rights and women's rights which eventuated in the "Negro's hour" strategy of the Radical Republicans. In that case, fear that seeking sex equality would jeopardize race equality led the Republicans to forsake the former and seek the latter. In the Title VII debate, a similar fear apparently was seen as a means for racist opponents to defeat both goals, or failing that, to insure that blacks would not gain rights that women did not. The intertwining of racism and sexism and the complex entanglements of legislative efforts to address these forces are a continuing theme in women's movements. There are multiple ironies in the fact that the abolitionists' actions produced less favorable legislation for women in the nineteenth century than the actions of conservative legislators did in the twentieth century.

In any case, two common threads link the Presidential Commission and the sex discrimination clause of the Civil Rights Act: both involved the NWP and both involved governmental efforts to defeat or forestall a feminist gain. In the case of the Commission, it may have succeeded in blunting the pressure for the ERA, but it set in motion some larger dynamics crucial to movement mobilization. In the case of Title VII, the attempt to use women's goals as a means of defeating other legislation also failed as the Civil Rights Act was passed. If this reading is correct, substantial credit must go to the NWP for its contribution to the revival of a women's movement that ultimately met with its disapproval on a number of grounds (Rupp and Taylor 1987). Nonetheless, the NWP's unflinching support for an Equal Rights Amendment from the 1920s to the 1960s is an important link between the woman suffrage movement and the contemporary women's movement. Substantial "credit" must also go to a government that sought to deflect, moderate, or trivialize these forces but failed, thereby creating more favorable opportunity structures for movement mobilization among women.

The presidential and state commissions, the Equal Pay Act, and Title VII of the Civil Rights Act signified a new recognition of women's issues, implied a proactive government role, and raised expectations for change and improvement. If the government had met these expectations in due course, the mobilization of a new women's movement might have taken longer. The fact that it failed to meet these expectations increased the pace of movement mobilization. Most relevant here was the Equal Employment Opportunity Commission (EEOC), which was the enforcement mechanism for Title VII. The Commission's first director described the sex discrimination clause as a "fluke . . . conceived out of wedlock" (quoted in Freeman 1975:54), and the Commission was notoriously unresponsive to cases of sex discrimination. This combination of rising expectations and stable or declining satisfactions is somewhat reminiscent of Davies's J-curve theory of revolutions. Davies argues that revolutions (and presumably other protest forms) are most likely when "expected need satisfaction" continues to rise while "actual need satisfaction" levels off or declines, creating "an intolerable gap between what people want and what they get" (Davies 1962:6). This particular form of relative deprivation, in the context of growing activity by women on the state commissions, was one factor that promoted the mobilization of some women into a new women's movement.

It is evident again that dating movement origins is largely a function of one's definition of a movement. It is possible to argue, as Rupp and Taylor do (1987), that an organization like the NWP was a "movement" — albeit an "elite-sustained movement" — from its origins in the early twentieth century to the 1960s. Given its lack of interest in recruitment or mass mobilization, it may make more sense to characterize the NWP as a movement organization without a movement (from the 1920s to the 1960s), or an interest group of a particular sort. Other groups of women, such as the Women's Bureau in the Department of Labor or the National Federation of Business and Professional Women's Clubs, also represented somewhat more organized and institutionalized sets of interests than are normally associated with a social movement. By this logic and these definitions, there was no "women's movement" as of the mid-1960s, although virtually all of the elements that would galvanize into such a movement were firmly in place.

In June 1966, the third national conference of state commissions on the status of women was held in Washington, D.C. Representative Martha Griffiths had recently detailed the EEOC's lack of attention to cases of sex discrimination in the House of Representatives, and her remarks were distributed to conference participants. By the final day of the conference, a number of women had begun the process of forming the National Organization for Women (NOW) to pressure for women's rights outside of regular government channels. NOW was explicitly envisioned by some of its founders as a "sort of NAACP for women"

(Freeman 1975:54), as women activists again found the lead of black reformers instructive. In October, NOW was incorporated with three hundred charter members at a press conference in Washington, D.C. The precipitating events that prompted the formation of NOW were EEOC inaction regarding sex discrimination, a stewardesses' suit against airline policies mandating retirement upon marriage or at specified ages, and the practice of sex-segregated help wanted ads in newspapers. Within a year, the organization would grow into a broadly focused, multi-issue women's rights organization.

The organization of NOW was the logical culmination of many of the background factors and proximate causes detailed above. Once organized, NOW was important in the further development of a women's movement. Founded by professional, elite, college-educated women with access to essential movement resources, NOW immediately became embroiled in a series of internal debates about issues, goals, and strategies that has continued throughout much of the organization's history. This dissension should not obscure NOW's historic significance as the first formal women's organization to emerge as part of the contemporary women's movement. As such, it inherited an important legacy from groups like the National Woman's Party and Business and Professional Women, and it contributed to the emergence of many other organizations, like Women's Equity Action League, Federally Employed Women, Human Rights for Women, and the National Women's Political Caucus. Although movement emergence is a process, the formation of NOW in 1966 is as good a date as any for identifying the origins of the contemporary women's movement; at this time, diverse feminist sentiments and beliefs found an organizational center that became instrumental in seeking social change.

The networks of women described previously are often referred to as the older, reformist, bureaucratic, women's rights sector of the contemporary women's movement. As such, the forces that culminated in NOW may be contrasted with the younger, radical, collectivist, women's liberation sector of the contemporary women's movement. Although some of these contrasts can be misleading (particularly the distinction between radical and reformist) and although there was always some overlap between the two groups, the distinction remains a useful one for descriptive purposes. Its historical utility is greatest for the mid- to late sixties and early seventies; after that time, the two sectors blended and intersected to such an extent that the distinction becomes a hindrance rather than a help in analyzing the contemporary women's movement.

This distinction will be more useful in subsequent chapters concerning organization and ideology. For the analysis of movement origins, the distinction is less important than is the overriding fact that both sectors emerged in the same society at roughly the same time. Both sectors shared a common set of background conditions involving economic transformation, urbanization and suburbanization, increasing labor force participation, heightened educational attainment among women, and the like. Without these background conditions, neither sector was likely to have emerged; with them, both were set in motion. It is not background factors that explain the differences between the sectors, but rather proximate causes; these set in motion two rather different orientations within the women's movement.

The proximate causes of the women's rights sector involved the NWP and the unwitting government facilitation of movement mobilization. The origins of the women's liberation sector had little to do with either of these factors, and almost everything to do with the participation of some women in other social movements. Most important here was the involvement of some women in the civil rights movement and in the New Left movement. In both cases, participation simultaneously radicalized and alienated young women. The radicalization occurred as they were exposed to new ways of analyzing and criticizing their society; the alienation occurred as they were subjected to persistent forms of sexism within these movements. The combination produced traces of frustration and dissatisfaction as early as 1965, the beginnings of feminist mobilization by 1967, and the indisputable emergence of a major women's movement by 1969.

According to Sara Evans's authoritative history (1979), southern white women have been the first to articulate the analogy of race and sex in the context of movements for racial equality. It happened with the Grimke sisters in the 1830s as part of the abolitionist struggle; it happened again among southern white women in the 1960s as part of the civil rights movement. Drawing on a supportive religious subculture, these women became publicly involved in civil rights activism and thereby challenged both the racial and sexual order of the South. As northern white students began to go south to join the sit-ins and freedom rides, some white women overcame gender-imposed barriers to participation in high-risk protest (McAdam 1989) and became involved in a struggle that explicitly challenged racial domination and implicitly questioned sexual hierarchy. Throughout much of the movement, black women became role models for white women, and the models they provided conflicted with conventional sex role stereotypes and expectations. An additional impetus to feminist consciousness arose from interracial sexual relations, which sometimes objectified white women as status symbols to black males and sometimes functioned to divide white and black women from each other.

By 1964, black women were raising the issue of female equality within the Student Non-violent Coordinating Committee (SNCC), pointing out that "just as Negroes were the crucial factor in the economy of the cotton South, so too in SNCC, women are the crucial factor that keeps the movement running on a day-to-day basis. Yet they are not given equal say-so when it comes to day-to-day decisionmaking. What can be done?" (cited in Evans 1979:83). As the civil rights struggle continued, as both white and black women invoked the analogy between race and sex, and as black women continued to provide strong role models for white women, the latter continued down the twin path of radicalization and alienation. A definitive, woman-centered analysis never appeared in the civil rights movement, however, in part because of continuing racial and sexual tensions between black and white women and in part because of the hostility or indifference of many men to such an approach. By 1965, whites were being eased out of some of the major civil rights organizations, which were responding to the appeal of black power and black nationalism. The process left white women with an incipient but uprooted feminism that was not yet ready to stand on its own. (For a powerful account of the civil rights movement and the emergence of feminist sensibilities within it, see King 1987.)

By this time, the New Left was making its own unwitting contribution to the emergence of a feminist consciousness and movement. The New Left originally articulated several fundamental feminist motifs, but was unable to see the gender implications of these concepts and unwilling to implement them where relations between the sexes were concerned. This is true for the notion that "the personal is political" as well as the concept of "participatory democracy." In addition, "the New Left affirmed 'feminine' qualities in its assertion of morality and its concern for feelings, community, and process" (Evans 1979:108). Despite these proto-feminist insights, values, and principles, the New Left was quite conventional in its patterns of male domination, in the sexual division of labor within the movement, and in practices of sexual exploitation. The twin pattern of radicalization and alienation thus appeared in the New Left as well by the mid-1960s. It is probable that the alienation was experienced in even sharper form in the New Left than in the civil rights movement, because the New Left was almost exclusively white in composition. Without the complexities of superimposed racial and sexual relations, it was easier to identify the inherent sexism that pervaded most New Left leaders and organizations.

Feminist issues surfaced explicitly at the December 1965 Students for a Democratic Society (SDS) conference, where a women's workshop prefigured feminist consciousness-raising groups by sharing experiences of sexist treatment within the movement (Evans 1979:156–169). For the next three years, feminist issues simmered within both SDS and the New Left more generally, and the mass base for a women's movement began to coalesce on campuses and in communities. Within SDS, resistance to the Vietnam War in general and to the draft in particular had become a leading issue by 1967. Given women's ineligibility for the draft, the issue itself became highly symbolic of sexual inequality because men could directly resist the draft whereas women could only counsel resistance: an accurate replication of traditional sex roles. By 1967, feminist issues were becoming unavoidable within the New Left, but the movement remained unreceptive to any serious consideration of such questions. Given SDS's insistence that groups should organize for their own liberation, and given the powerful model of black power, a separatist solution materialized in response to the increasing radicalization and alienation of many women.

In Evans's account, the dam broke at the National Conference for New Politics held in Chicago in August 1967. The women's caucus drew a lesson from the black caucus by passing a resolution requiring that women receive half of the convention votes and committee representation (1979:198). When their resolution was ridiculed, they drew another lesson from the experience of the black movement: "Women must not make the same mistake the blacks did at first of allowing others (whites in their case, men in ours) to define our issues, methods, and goals. Only we can and must define the terms of our struggle. . . . it is incumbent on us, as women, to organize a movement for women's liberation" (1979:200). After the autumn of 1967, women's groups rapidly emerged in many places, following the social networks and the "radical community" (Freeman 1975:58) created by New Left activism and fueled by a dynamic of radicalization and alienation that could no longer be contained within the New Left. Within a year, a mass movement for women's liberation was well underway.

The simultaneous independent mobilization of the women's liberation movement in different locales surprised everyone, including the participants. There was no center to the movement, no centralized authority orchestrating the process, no leadership cadre consciously fanning the flames of discontent. In many respects, the new women's movement was faithful to its roots in the New Left generally. The sudden emergence of the movement is made somewhat more understandable by seeing the period from 1965 to 1968 as a kind of incubation period for the movement. As women in both the civil rights movement and the New Left movement gained experience, formed connections, organized communities, learned skills, articulated ideologies, and became radicalized, a highly talented pool of movement women was created. As they confronted sexism in myriad forms, as they began to understand how it worked, as their initially timid but increasingly assertive protests met the same indifference and hostility from movement men, many of these women came to see an independent women's movement not just as a possibility but as a necessity. At the time, it was amazing that the women's liberation movement appeared so quickly; in retrospect, it is amazing that the movement took as long as it did to coalesce.

In her analysis of the nineteenth-century women's rights movement, Ellen DuBois has argued that "women's discontent with their position was as much cause as effect of their involvement with the antislavery movement" (1978:32). Hence, abolitionism was important not because it created awareness of female oppression — this already existed — but rather because it provided some important resources for fighting it. The same issue is pertinent in analyzing the women's liberation movement and its relation to the civil rights and New Left movements. It is likely that women's discontent with their position in American society circa 1960–1965 was also as much cause as effect of their involvement in civil rights and the New Left. That is, these movements offered exciting and challenging experiences in contrast to the bland script of traditional gender expectations. But whereas female abolitionists were well aware of their own oppression as women prior to abolitionist involvement, it is less clear whether female activists in the early 1960s had a comparable awareness of their own oppression prior to involvement in these movements.

The crucial factors here are the ages and life experiences of the participants in their respective movements. Most feminist-abolitionists were middle-aged, and many had experience as professionals, wives, and mothers that underscored their unequal treatment. In this respect, the feminist-abolitionists are more analogous to the professional women associated with the women's rights sector of the contemporary women's movement. Most women in the civil rights and New Left movements, by contrast, were college students at the time of their initial involvement. The relative egalitarianism of higher education (compared to work and family roles) in all likelihood did not generate the same awareness of sex inequality for these women. If this analysis is correct, then feminist-abolitionists entered the abolitionist movement with preexisting feminist grievances, whereas women in the civil rights and New Left movements formulated their feminist grievances more directly on the basis of their movement experiences. For the latter group, these movements may have provided their first encounter with explicit, overt, institutionalized sex inequality. Alongside the resources enumerated above, then, was the additional "resource" of emergent feminist grievances created by unequal treatment within these movements.

While the origins of the women's liberation movement can be broadly dated from 1967 to 1969, there continued to be much overlap and interconnection between the women's movement and the broader left in this period. Many women opted to remain within the New Left and work for women's issues within that context, just as others made a definitive break with New Left organizations and devoted all their energy to the emerging feminist cause. As we shall see in subsequent chapters, even those who made complete organizational breaks with prior movements nonetheless carried with them various residues from their earlier political involvements. In both organizational form and ideological belief, the women's liberation movement reflected its heritage in other movements — a heritage that would provide both strengths and weaknesses — while also developing unique organizational and ideological characteristics.

By all accounts, the women's liberation movement emerged with little awareness of and little concern about the women's rights movement that had coalesced into NOW in 1966 (e.g., Freeman 1975; Hole and Levine 1971; Ferree and Hess 1985). The lack of connection was overdetermined. The women's rights movement attracted an older constituency of professional women pursuing a liberal agenda through conventional interest group politics. The women's liberation movement attracted a younger constituency of college students with a more radical orientation to mobilizing a mass movement. By the late 1960s, women in the New Left were predisposed to dismiss the conventional, liberal agenda and tactics associated with the women's rights movement. Despite these differences, the two sectors influenced one another from their inception. The influence of the women's liberation sector on the women's rights branch was particularly significant in two ways. For one, the women's liberation sector helped to radicalize the women's rights sector by broadening the agenda beyond economic and legal issues and by deepening the analysis beyond liberal and legislative solutions. For another, the women's liberation sector helped to create a truly mass movement of women and to popularize feminist issues well beyond the constituency that was attracted to the women's rights sector (Evans 1979:21–23). With the passage of time, the partial convergence of issues, and the emergence of a backlash, the common concerns of both sectors of the contemporary women's movement became increasingly evident and the sharp distinctions between them began to dissolve.

Conclusions

Social movements are relatively rare. For a social movement to arise, a number of factors must combine to provide a group with both the motivation and the capacity to mobilize. This general principle applies with particular relevance to women's movements. As a social group, women are structurally dispersed and distributed throughout all other social groups. This dispersal often means that women do not readily see themselves as a group because their dominant social identities and primary ties are to groups defined by kinship, class, race, ethnicity, or religion. These identifications, along with the multiple effects of male domination, mean that relatively few women will have both the motivation and the capacity to mobilize a women's movement. This dispersal and domination also means that not all women are equally likely to mobilize a movement. For reasons sketched here and explored in depth in a later chapter, white middle-class women have historically been the most likely participants in women's movements.

Explaining the origins of women's movements therefore requires attention to how background factors and proximate causes combine to overcome the structural dispersal of middle-class women and provide them with the motivation and capacity to mobilize a women's movement. This comparative analysis has identified the developmental dynamics of capitalism as the most fundamental background factor in the origins of women's movements, albeit a factor mediated by a multiplicity of other conditions. In the first half of the nineteenth century, these dynamics deprived many middle-class women of economically productive roles; in much of the twentieth century these dynamics drew women into new productive roles in labor markets structured by sex segregation and discrimination. Although these changes appear to be in opposite directions, they both promoted movement mobilization in tandem with other factors. In both centuries, changes in fertility and in women's reproductive roles were also important factors. As smaller families became the norm and the reality in both periods, and as life expectancy for women increased, childbearing and child-rearing occupied a smaller proportion of women's lives. These changes were nonetheless accompanied by even stricter normative expectations about the lives of white, middle-class women. The nineteenth-century ideal of domesticity and the cult of true womanhood found its counterpart in the feminine mystique of the 1950s; both prescribed rigid restrictions on the lives of women, which were otherwise changing in fundamental ways.

These conditions produced proto-feminist responses in both centuries. In the nineteenth century, some women found outlets in religious activity, in formal education, in moral reform societies, in benevolent associations, and in the temperance movement. The strict normative system that emphasized sexual difference also promoted gender consciousness in homosocial worlds of women's activities. In the twentieth century, middle-class women's educational attainment and labor force participation reciprocally reinforced one another and provided life experiences and expectations above and beyond the conventional roles of daughters, wives, and mothers for many women. The juxtaposition of relatively egalitarian educational experiences for college women with highly differentiated and unequal family and work roles undoubtedly sharpened these contradictions for many women (Friedan 1963). In both eras, the real lives of middle-class women increasingly contradicted the narrowed normative expectations of the day.

Background conditions don't produce movements all by themselves, but they do create sources of structural strain for potential movement recruits. The translation of this strain into a movement depends on the establishment of group identity and the growth of group consciousness. In the nineteenth century, such consciousness began to develop in the sharply separate homosocial worlds of female religious, benevolent, and reform activity. Such consciousness did not initially challenge gender arrangements, but it was a prerequisite for later forms of consciousness that did because it promoted a sense of group identity among women. In the twentieth century, initial gender consciousness was promoted by women's increasing labor force participation. Such participation represented competition for scarce resources, particularly when female job-seekers entered traditionally male occupational niches (Rosenfeld and Ward 1985). This conflict and competition fostered a sense of group identity and consciousness that had been lacking previously and was vital to subsequent movement mobilization.

Group identity and consciousness do not lead to movement mobilization unless that identity and consciousness are politicized, however. The role of relative deprivation as an intervening factor is often essential to the politicization of discontent, group identity, and consciousness. Both Freeman (1975:31ff) and Ferree and Hess (1985:24) argue that relative deprivation was critical in the early stages of movement mobilization among middle-class women in the contemporary women's movement; Chafetz and Dworkin (1986:80–82ff) argue that similar factors operated to politicize their nineteenth-century counterparts who launched the women's rights movement. In some cases, a keen sense of relative deprivation may emerge simultaneously with group consciousness and identity; in others, these may be sequential steps. In either case, the end result is the politicization of grievances and group identity; once such politicization occurs, the motivation to mobilize a movement is present. At that point, the most important factor concerns the group's capacity to act on its identity and consciousness. Capacity is a function of access to and control over needed resources, in tandem with appropriate opportunities to utilize those resources in generating a movement. The process of politicization and the emergence of new capacities for movement mobilization may be initiated by background factors, but only come to full fruition in conjunction with proximate causes and conditions that coalesce to produce women's movements.

In the nineteenth-century, the abolitionist movement was the crucial proximate cause of the women's rights movement. Abolitionism provided an outlet for women seeking to escape the most traditional expectations of female behavior, but those same expectations channeled women's role within the movement. Women entered abolitionism with a nascent group identity and consciousness, with an initial set of grievances, and with an emergent sense of relative deprivation. By the time they left, they had acquired skills, gained resources, established networks, refined ideologies, and suffered new insults from male leaders who welcomed their contributions to abolitionism but rejected their bid for serious consideration of women's rights. Two processes working in tandem reinforced the motivation and created the capacity for mobilizing a women's movement: the nurturance of ideological, oratorical, and organizational skills accompanied by the constriction of opportunities for devoting these skills to a sustained women's movement. Like the movements in the 1960s, abolitionism offered a free space (Evans and Boyte 1986) in which women's rights could take root, but it ultimately proved unable to accommodate the tendencies it helped to set in motion. The ultimate result was the emergence of an independent women's movement shortly after the Civil War.

In the twentieth century, several proximate causes combined in the context of conducive background factors to promote another women's movement. Exerting pressure from very different directions, the National Woman's Party and the civil rights movement created a climate in which the federal government became an unwitting facilitator of movement mobilization among women. The participants in this sector of the women's movement already had a well-defined group identity and consciousness, a clearly articulated set of grievances, and a strong sense of relative deprivation. What they previously lacked and now gained was a solid, national network of like-minded activists with access to the kinds of resources necessary for sustained movement mobilization. By the mid-1960s, these resources bore fruit in the form of new and independent women's movement organizations.

The younger sector of the contemporary women's movement emerged from the civil rights and New Left movements. However, because they lacked the age and life experiences of their older women's rights counterparts, these women did not begin their movement careers with a well-defined collective identity and group consciousness as women. This generation's movement experiences were crucial in crystallizing a sense of relative deprivation, politicizing their grievances, and providing the resources, networks, skills, and overall capacity to generate an independent social movement. Like abolitionism's simultaneous nurturance and constriction of the cause of women's rights, the civil rights and New Left movements simultaneously radicalized and alienated an increasing number of female participants, who proceeded to mobilize another sector of the contemporary women's movement by the late 1960s.

In many respects, the origins of women's activism in the nineteenth and twentieth centuries thereby involve relatively minor variations on common themes evident in both historical eras. One such variation involved the extent to which prior movements provided the grievances and consciousness — as well as other resources — that animated women's mobilization. The other important difference between these eras concerns the role of the state. In the mid-nineteenth-century mobilization of the women's rights movement, the state played virtually no role except as the distant target of movement demands for suffrage and some other legal rights. It was only after the Civil War that the state became a major actor in the drama that precipitated the split between abolitionism and women's rights. In the mobilization of the contemporary women's movement, the state has played a more central role from the beginning. The Kennedy administration created an important political opportunity structure for movement mobilization with the establishment of the Presidential Commission on the Status of Women. The civil rights legislation of the early 1960s (and its weak enforcement in the case of women) was also vital in sparking contemporary feminist activism. The state was also a major player (as target and protagonist) in the struggles of the civil rights and New Left movements that gave rise to women's liberation. In all these ways, the contemporary state played a major role in contemporary movement struggles — a role only dimly foreshadowed in women's rights battles a century earlier.

While theorists are in considerable agreement about many of the factors that promote women's movements (for example, Freeman 1983:21–22; McGlen and O'Connor 1983:15; Evans 1979:219–220), there continues to be considerable sociological debate over the relative weight of factors like grievances and consciousness on the one hand and resources and opportunity on the other hand. The more extreme versions of resource mobilization theory dismiss grievances and consciousness as constants that cannot explain the variable appearance of movements (McCarthy and Zald 1973). This emphasis seems appropriate for groups whose conditions of existence readily foster politicized grievances and group consciousness, as exemplified by the position of blacks in South Africa. This emphasis does not apply as well to the case of women's movements (Mueller 1983), because women's conditions of existence do not ensure that politicized grievances and group consciousness will be a constant factor. Indeed, one can turn the logic around by arguing that some women (well-educated, upper-middle-class white women) have always had access to resources and opportunities for political activism, but that grievances and consciousness have been the variables that explain the periodic involvement of such women in feminist movements.

The preceding logic and comparative analysis suggest that women's movements are a function of both motivation (grievances, identity, consciousness, relative deprivation) and capacity (resources, networks, communication, opportunity). Background factors that disrupt traditional social arrangements and create strains and discrepancies initiate the conditions that produce motivation and capacity. However, proximate conditions must also be present if strains are to translate into social movement activity rather than other possible responses.

Certain proximate conditions are especially important in the case of women's movements because they help to overcome the structural dispersal of at least some women to a point where movement mobilization becomes feasible. The cases of the nineteenth-century women's rights movement and the twentieth-century women's liberation sector of the contemporary women's movement suggest that participation in other social movements can be a vital proximate cause of what ultimately become independent women's movements. The case of the twentieth-century women's rights sector of the contemporary women's movement suggests that the legacy of prior feminist mobilization can itself be the proximate cause of renewed women's movement activity. What all these cases have in common is some form of preexisting movement activity that reduces the structural dispersal of some women, who then act as a critical mass in the mobilization of a broader women's movement.

Chapter
two

Organizations
and
Communities

All social movements assume some organizational structure. In some cases, this structure is readily evident in the formal nature of groups with constitutions, bylaws, and leadership structures. In other cases, we may have to look to informal structures and patterns to discern the principles by which the group operates — perhaps unbeknownst to its own members. These variations suggest that the question of organization can always be posed at two levels in the study of social movements. Most abstractly, organization refers to the networks, patterns, structures, and processes among those people who constitute the movement. In this broad sense, all movements are organized. Less abstractly, the question of organization refers to particular, formally structured bodies that pursue some set of movement goals. In this narrower sense, some movements may be unorganized if they lack such bodies. Even when formal organization is present, it will exhibit its own range of variation from highly structured to loosely linked. These variations and distinctions are critical for grasping the complexity of organizational characteristics and their relation to other aspects of social movements.

The resource mobilization perspective associated with McCarthy and Zald offers some useful conceptual distinctions for sorting out the organizational complexity associated with social movement activity. Borrowing from the literature on organizations and economies, they distinguish between social movements, social movement organizations, social movement industries, and the social movement sector. A social movement (SM) consists of preference structures for certain changes within a segment of the population. A social movement organization (SMO) is a complex or formal organization whose goals match the preferences of a social movement. A social movement industry (SMI) consists of all the SMOs whose goals reflect a particular SM. Finally, the social movement sector (SMS) consists of all the SMIs in the society (McCarthy and Zald 1977).

While these distinctions provide an initial orientation to the organizational complexity of social movements, they also rest on some problematic assumptions. For instance, the equation of a social movement with preference structures effectively reduces movements to sets of attitudes. To have effects, such attitudes must be mobilized and organized to produce coordinated action; in McCarthy and Zald's scheme, an SM must become an SMO to be able to act in the world. This "organizational bias" is intended to highlight the centrality of resources and mobilization in movement activity, but it has the effect of denying the efficacy of any mobilization of resources that occurs outside the boundaries of formal SMOs. What is left out is the possibility of SMs mobilizing effectively for particular goals without recourse to the formal, complex structure of SMOs. While it is certainly possible to argue that only formally organized SMs are able to effect change, this should be the conclusion of a sustained and evidentiary analysis rather than an orienting assumption introduced by definitional fiat.

The organizational bias of this schema may be counterbalanced by the addition of a new concept: the social movement community (SMC). This is a parallel to an SMO in that both concepts refer to groups that identify their goals with the preferences of a social movement and attempt to implement those goals. Whereas the SMO does so by recourse to formal, complex organizational structures, however, the SMC does so through informal networks of politicized individuals with fluid boundaries, flexible leadership structures, and malleable divisions of labor. With the addition of this concept, SMIs may now be defined as consisting of all the SMOs and SMCs that are actively seeking to implement the preference structures of a given SM. The addition of the concept of an SMC opens up a number of hypotheses for possible investigation. For one, the level of resources available to an SM may well determine its organization as an SMO or SMC. Groups without the resources needed to sustain an SMO may have to rely on SMCs for seeking their goals. For another, the ideology of a group may determine its relative preferences for SMO or SMC styles of movement activity. Antiauthoritarian beliefs may predispose a group to SMC activity rather than SMO mobilization. Finally, the success of an SM may well depend on whether it can achieve a balance of SMO and SMC activity in pursuit of its goals. While these hypotheses cannot be definitively resolved in this study, they suggest the concept's utility for the analysis of other social movements.

The applicability of the concept of a social movement community for the study of women's movements will become most apparent in analyzing the women's liberation movement. Since this movement had relatively few SMOs, a straightforward application of the original McCarthy and Zald model would prefigure the conclusion that no matter how strong the preference structures of this SM were, they were not translated into any effective action because of the lack of SMOs. In reality, the women's liberation movement deliberately channeled its activism in the direction of creating an SMC to implement movement goals. While considerable disagreement exists about how successful this effort was, the concept of an SMC seems essential even to frame the question of relative success for this sector of the movement. Having argued for the utility of the concept of an SMC, it remains to identify a potential problem: an SMC may gradually fade into a subculture with increasingly tenuous links to SM preference structures. For purposes of conceptual clarity, an SMC cannot refer merely to a distinctive subcultural grouping of people. It must refer only to communities that identify their goals with the preferences of a social movement and attempt to implement those goals. By its very nature, an SMC will have vaguer boundaries than an SMO, but if the relation between SMCs and SMs is kept in mind, these boundaries should remain identifiable.

There are a number of ongoing debates about movement organization that are related to this distinction and can be explored through the study of women's movements. One such debate concerns the relative merits of bureaucratic, centralized structures and less hierarchical, more decentralized forms of movement organization. There is some evidence that bureaucratic, centralized movement organizations may be somewhat more successful because they provide a clear division of labor, an efficient decision-making structure, and a high degree of combat readiness (Gamson 1975). Others have argued that bureaucratic organizations have difficulty sustaining a sense of solidarity and ideological commitment and that decentralized structures may actually be more effective because they accentuate personal friendships and informal networks as a means of reducing alienation and encouraging higher levels of participation (Gerlach and Hine 1970). Rothschild-Whitt (1979) has developed this argument by sketching an ideal-typical model of a collectivist organization oriented to substantive rationality in contrast to the instrumental rationality of bureaucratic organizations, while Wini Breines (1980) has used these insights to argue that the New Left did not fail to achieve bureaucratic efficiency as much as it succeeded in exploring nonauthoritarian alternatives.

A related set of issues concerns recruitment and mobilization of movement participants. The classic argument here is offered by Olson (1968), who claims that movements seeking collective goods will have problems recruiting rationally self-interested individuals who will prefer to "ride free" by sharing in ultimate benefits without contributing to their procurement. The paradox of the free-rider problem is that if everyone acts in line with their self-interest, no one will join the movement and the benefits will not be forthcoming. The solution recommended by Olson is to provide "selective incentives" to those who join movement efforts, providing sufficient rewards to offset costs and induce participation. Critics of Olson (see especially Fireman and Gamson 1979) have argued that he ignores the role of moral, purposive, and collective incentives. The logic of individual self-interest is an inadequate characterization of the motives of those who join movements, many of whom are motivated to do so regardless of a utilitarian calculus of costs and benefits. There is evidence on both sides of this debate (Jenkins 1983), but the free-rider dilemma is best seen as a potential problem that effective movements must resolve.

A third set of issues involves the kinds of transformations organizations undergo. The classic statements by Robert Michels (1961) and Max Weber (1947) claim that over time, all organizations will experience conservative goal transformation, increased concern with organizational maintenance, and a marked tendency toward oligarchy within the organization. Applied to protest organizations, this maxim implies that movement organizations will inevitably become less effective at pursuing movement goals over time. In the most extreme version of this argument, Piven and Cloward claim that formal organization always means the death of effective protest because such organizations only survive by accommodating themselves to existing power structures (1977). Several scholars have challenged the necessity of such transformation in social movements. Zald and Ash argue that there is no "iron law" of conservatization and oligarchization, and that movements may change in different directions depending on the ebb and flow of sentiments in the larger society, relations with other movements, and prospects for success (1966). Jenkins has also argued that greater bureaucratization is not inevitable (1983), and that even trends toward oligarchy can be accompanied by radicalization rather than conservatization. Others have provided case studies of movements that became radicalized over time (Beach 1977; Barnes 1987) and appear to refute the classic expectation of conservatization over time.

The following analysis explores these debates by examining the wide range of organizational forms that women's movements in the United States have adopted. The early women's rights movement illustrates that movements can enjoy some degree of success without formal organizations, while the subsequent history of the woman suffrage movement suggests that sometimes the main function of formal organization is movement maintenance. The history of the later woman suffrage movement reveals multiple and diverse formal movement organizations within a broader, cross-class, multiconstituency alliance that was vital to the success of the suffrage cause. The contemporary women's movement has a shorter history but offers an opportunity to examine the interaction between two movement sectors with diverse organizational styles. The older, bureaucratic sector exemplified by the National Organization for Women emerged first but was quickly overtaken by the younger, collectivist sector known as the women's liberation movement. The relations between these sectors from the relatively progressive late 1960s and early 1970s to the relatively reactionary late 1970s and 1980s offer a fascinating example of the dynamics of social movement organizations. This survey suggests that there is no single ideal organizational form for movements to adopt; that the forms actually chosen will vary with resource levels, ideological preferences, movement goals, and preferred strategies; and that certain forms nonetheless have distinctive strengths and weaknesses that contribute importantly to movement success or failure.

The Woman Suffrage Movement

Organizational issues in the early women's rights movement and the subsequent woman suffrage movement subdivide themselves into three discrete historical periods. The first, from the 1840s to 1869, extends from the origins of the women's rights movement through the Civil War to the establishment of the first independent woman suffrage organizations. The second period, from 1869 to 1890, extends through the organizational life spans of two rival national suffrage organizations to the point of their merger. The third period, from 1890 to 1920, extends from this merger through the growth of a large mainstream organization and the emergence of a rival group to the winning of suffrage. Each period posed distinctive organizational problems for the women's movement, and each witnessed unique organizational responses to these problems.

The first period is noteworthy because for the first two decades of women's rights agitation, there were no formal organizations exclusively or even primarily devoted to the cause of women's rights. In McCarthy and Zald's terms, while there clearly was a social movement during this period (defined as a set of preference structures for social change), there were no social movement organizations to channel and coordinate action around these preferences. The lack of movement organizations may be attributed to at least two causes. For one, the abolitionist movement provided an informal network for women's rights activists and thereby constrained the development of separate and formal women's rights organizations. For another, some women's rights activists, including Ernestine Rose and Lucy Stone, were resistant to formal organization, fearing it would restrict individual activity and prove overly cumbersome (Flexner 1975:83).

Before 1848, most women's rights activity therefore occurred within the organizational framework of the abolitionist movement. The latter was extremely valuable in providing a preexisting network of politically active reformers, opportunities to speak to interested audiences, and an ideology that could accommodate some of the goals of the women's rights movement. However, abolitionism was, at best, unevenly receptive to women's rights activity. It was the Garrisonian wing of abolitionism, with its critique of clerical authority and its insistence on the primacy of individual conscience, that provided the most hospitable niche for the cause of women's rights within the abolitionist movement. The remainder of the abolitionist movement promoted the organization of the women's rights movement in a more negative fashion. By denying women memberships, or voting rights, or access to office-holding, or delegate status, the early abolitionist movement fostered a number of specifically female antislavery societies (for example, in Philadelphia in 1833, in New York in 1837, in Illinois in 1844) where women acquired direct organizational experience in a social movement cause. The famous and infamous refusal of the World Anti-Slavery Convention to seat women delegates from the United States at their London convention in 1840 provided another oft-noted impetus to independent female organization.

While the positive and negative examples of the abolitionist movement provided many women with their earliest organizational experience, this activity built on a prior foundation of less overtly political endeavors. Many women had worked in temperance societies, in moral reform and social purity groups, in relief and aid associations, in philanthropic and benevolent societies, and in church groups. While these activities were consistent with culturally scripted gender expectations that the women's rights movement would subsequently challenge, they nonetheless provided many women with early lessons in organizational processes in relatively unthreatening settings. When the earlier organizational experience provided by benevolent associations was combined with the political lessons of the abolitionist movement, the stage was set for gender-conscious movement organization within the women's rights movement.

The result was not a formal women's rights association, but rather a series of women's rights conventions that met from 1848 up to the eve of the Civil War. The Seneca Falls convention of 1848 has attracted much attention, but its greatest significance may well be that it was the first in that series of conventions. Just two weeks after Seneca Falls, women convened again in Rochester, New York, and within two years women's rights conventions were held as far west as Salem, Ohio. In 1850, the first national convention was held in Worcester, Massachusetts. With the exception of 1857, national conventions were held annually during the 1850s, with many smaller gatherings scattered throughout the New

England and mid-Atlantic states. The conventions were coordinated by a loosely organized central committee of prominent women, which functioned throughout this period but which never mobilized itself into a formal social movement organization (Flexner 1975:83).

Although their organization remained informal, there is strong evidence that these women's rights conventions were the crucial foundation underpinning women's rights activity before the Civil War. In a detailed network analysis of the women's movement over a seventy-year period, these women's rights conventions emerged as the most central hubs in a dense network of social movement actions, groups, and individuals, and they are clearly the dominant organizational feature of the antebellum women's movement. Rosenthal et al. claim that "antislavery agitation and temperance activity fed into the creation of a women's rights movement centered in annual conventions. Leaders from these conventions built the foundation for new (and overlapping) groups that focused on such issues as temperance, dress reform, legislative reform, and, finally, Civil War-related activity. The shape of the network in this period suggests that women's rights was a central, though widely inclusive, ideology that influenced the later activities of its leaders and the character of other organizations in the network" (1985:1043). The results of this network analysis provide another example of how the preference structures of a social movement may be translated into movement mobilization and activism without necessarily giving rise to formal, complex social movement organizations.

The Civil War disrupted the momentum of the women's rights movement while also providing new kinds of organizational experience. Many female reformers worked in the National Women's Loyal League, which collected almost four hundred thousand signatures on a petition seeking passage of the Thirteenth Amendment. An even broader spectrum of women became involved in the Sanitary Commission, which coordinated the movement of medical supplies and personnel to and from the battlefield. As the disruptions of the war created new needs and opportunities for women to perform important public roles, they acquired and demonstrated an organizational competence and confidence that would serve them well in the ensuing struggle for women's rights.

The immediate postwar period was fraught with possibilities for women's rights activists. The increased influence of abolitionists and the pressing importance of voting rights created historically new opportunities for advancing women's rights. However, the postwar coalition of abolitionists and Radical Republicans directed their energy to black emancipation and enfranchisement, assuming that traditional support from female abolitionists would continue. When the Fourteenth Amendment explicitly defined voting as a male right for the first time, women's rights activists tried to recast the issue as one of universal suffrage. Deploying this strategy, they proposed that the American Anti-Slavery Society merge with the women's rights campaign in a national organization to pursue universal suffrage. First proposed at a January 1866 antislavery meeting in Boston, in May of that year the idea became the focus of the first women's rights convention since the Civil War. Held in New York, the convention created the American Equal Rights Association, which fostered local organizations based on the same principles and became a vehicle for numerous campaigns to eliminate racial and sexual barriers to the rights of blacks and women (see Du-Bois 1978:63–65). Thus, the first formal movement organization to be created by the women's rights movement was one devoted to the broad principle of universal rights and motivated by the practical realities of seeking to advance women's rights along with black enfranchisement.

This organization's potential for advancing women's rights was undermined by the ongoing difficulties of advancing black interests, the abolitionist priority of the Negro's hour, the belief that women's rights jeopardized black progress, and the weak bargaining position of women within abolitionist circles. As a result, "antislavery leaders may well have expected the Equal Rights Association eventually to accept black suffrage as its priority" (DuBois 1978:73). The association did not accept such a priority, which only meant that it continued to be plagued by the underlying divisions of interests and priorities that had been present since its founding. These organizational tensions were played out over several years of energetic and political activity around passage of the Thirteenth, Fourteenth, and Fifteenth amendments. Given the lack of attention to women's rights, Susan B. Anthony and Elizabeth Cady Stanton began to question their traditional alliance with the abolitionists and the wisdom of linking women's rights so closely to efforts to advance the rights of black people.

In 1867, Kansas considered separate referenda on black suffrage and woman suffrage, and thereby provided an opportunity for various factions to test their strategies. The Equal Rights Association devoted substantial resources to this effort, only to find local Republicans waging an explicitly anti–woman suffrage campaign in the state. This prompted some suffragists to turn to the Democrats, who were only too happy to cultivate a split in the ranks of progressive forces. Most significant was Anthony's willingness to align herself and the Association with George Francis Train, a Democratic financier well known for his racism. An important schism was thereby created between Stanton and Anthony, who were increasingly willing to leave the Republicans behind in a search for new allies, and Lucy Stone and Henry Blackwell, who continued to insist that woman suffragists owed their allegiance to the Republican party. From this point, "Stanton, Anthony, and the feminists who followed their leadership began to extricate the woman suffrage movement from its deep dependence on abolitionists. . . . The break with abolitionists forced Stanton's and Anthony's wing of the woman suffrage movement to explore new alliances, new constituencies, and new strategies" (DuBois 1978:102, 103).

After two years of seeking common organizational and ideological ground with the Democratic party, the National Labor Union, and the Working Women's Association, Stanton and Anthony concluded that their most likely constituency consisted of other middle-class women. In the interim, pro-Republican suffragists had organized the first woman suffrage organization, the New England Woman Suffrage Association, in November of 1868. However, despite its title and because of the predominance of Republican, abolitionist men in the organization, its main purpose appears to have been promoting black voting rights. Within a short time, most New England states also formed state woman suffrage associations with the same political orientation. When Congress passed a version of the Fifteenth Amendment in early 1869, the differences between suffragists solidified. Pro-Republican suffragists and organizations supported it; Stanton and Anthony opposed it because the amendment would reinforce the disenfranchisement of women while granting the vote to black men.

As opposition to the Fifteenth Amendment became increasingly futile, Stanton and Anthony called for immediate passage of a Sixteenth Amendment extending the vote to women. Having gathered some support for this idea on a western tour in early 1869, they brought this strategy to the Equal Rights Association convention in New York in May of 1869. The already weakened association dissolved at this convention in the course of debate over whether to secure passage and ratification of the Fifteenth Amendment or to proceed immediately to seek passage of a Sixteenth. When Stanton and Anthony could not sway the convention, they organized the National Woman Suffrage Association (NWSA) to pursue a Sixteenth Amendment. As the culmination of years of alienation from Republican, abolitionist, male leadership, the National was explicitly designed to be free of these old entanglements and to remain under the solid control of woman suffragists. The National was willing to support all women's issues, but not to subordinate any women's issues to other political priorities. As such, it "can reasonably be called the first national feminist organization in the United States" (DuBois 1978:190). Within six months, Stone, Blackwell, and other pro-Republican suffragists organized the American Woman Suffrage Association (AWSA), a national version of the New England association already in existence.

After twenty years of informal activism, the woman suffrage movement thereby mobilized two rival organizations within the space of six months. Yet this rivalry was the logical, organizational expression of prior ideological, strategic, and personal differences within the women's movement, particularly given its umbilical connections with abolitionism. The ideological posture of the National Association under Stanton and Anthony was decidedly radical, identifying the connections between women's oppressions and tracing them ultimately to marriage and the sexual division of labor (Buechler 1986). The ideology of the American Association under Stone and Blackwell stopped short of such a holistic critique of women's position, restricting its focus to the right to vote. The strategic differences between the organizations were equally clear. The National was broadly focused, embracing all women's issues and seeking change on a number of fronts through a variety of means while also pursuing a woman suffrage amendment. The American was narrowly focused, concentrating only on women's voting rights to the exclusion of all "side issues," including black suffrage (DuBois 1978:197). These ideological and strategic differences between the leadership of the National and American associations were spiced by differences in personality and temperament, which had surfaced during years of intense struggle with abolitionist men and Republican tactics. Among the members of these organizations, however, the differences were not so sharply drawn, and there may well have been more variation within the ranks of each organization than between them as rival associations.

There are several ironies in the organizational history of the suffrage movement in this period. One is the fact that after twenty years of activism, the movement gave rise not to one but to two rival organizations within a six-month period. A second is the fact that these organizations appeared just as the prospects for actually winning suffrage were beginning to wane. Caught between the hypocrisy of the Democrats, the treachery of the Republicans (DuBois 1978:77), and their own political powerlessness, women's rights activists were unable to take advantage of the new structure of opportunities offered by the postwar period of political reorganization. By the time these suffrage organizations were formed, prospects for progress had all but disappeared with the decline of Reconstruction politics and the postwar reestablishment of institutional stability. Once again, Ellen DuBois (1978) is an excellent guide through this territory when she reminds us that the real significance of these organizational developments was not in their immediate failures or successes, but rather in the fact that woman suffrage had finally become an independent movement. Given its distant origins and ambivalent entanglements with abolitionism, that was a significant accomplishment. From this point on — to paraphrase Marx — the movement made its own history, even if it did not make that history under circumstances of its own choosing.

If the major organizational struggle of the movement in this first period was to establish an independent organizational base from which to pursue women's rights, its major organizational struggle in the second period was to maintain the vitality and political focus of these independent suffrage organizations in an increasingly crowded organizational field. The period from 1870 to 1890 saw the emergence and growth of a large number of diverse women's organizations. While this development eventually contributed to a stronger movement for women's rights, and suffrage in particular, it also deflected and diffused some of the politicized discontent that had animated women's rights activism in the first period. Using McCarthy and Zald's imagery, the social movement industry underwent considerable growth in this period, giving rise to a multiplicity of social movement organizations within this industry and fostering considerable competition for movement followers. It was a competition woman suffrage organizations were not well positioned to win during the closing decades of the nineteenth century.

After 1870, many of the differences between the National and American associations began to fade, although the National under Stanton and Anthony retained a more radical and holistic analysis of women's position. From this point on, however, the major differences between these organizations tended to be tactical rather than strategic. In the early 1870s, one NWSA tactic was to argue that women were in fact already enfranchised by the Fourteenth Amendment, which granted voting rights to citizens. After hundreds of women attempted to vote in the elections of 1872 and carried this defense into ensuing court battles, a string of unfavorable decisions rendered this tactic ineffective. The NWSA then returned to its major tactic of seeking a federal amendment to enfranchise women. Reinforcing its federal orientation, the NWSA held annual conventions in Washington, D.C., to keep the cause before federal legislators. The AWSA opted for a state-by-state approach to enfranchisement, reasoning that it would be simpler to win in smaller political arenas and that an eventual string of state victories would ease the way for eventual federal enfranchisement. Reflecting this orientation, the AWSA convened in a variety of cities around the country to encourage state suffrage battles.

While the dedication of core activists did not lessen in this period, the suffrage movement was notably unsuccessful in advancing the cause of female enfranchisement during the 1870s and 1880s. Incremental progress was reflected in the introduction of the suffrage amendment to newly established select committees in both houses of Congress, but when the amendment was finally debated on the floor of the Senate in 1887 it was resoundingly defeated. The major activity of both suffrage organizations consisted of annual conventions, and the major function of these conventions was organizational maintenance. Given the temper of the times, the lack of opportunities, and the political powerlessness of woman suffragists, organizational maintenance was itself a significant accomplishment. The difficulties these organizations faced encouraged their merger in

1890. The relative lethargy of suffrage activism in this period contrasted sharply with the energy of women in other social causes and movements. The real organizational dilemma confronting the suffrage movement in this period concerned not its own organizations or even their differences, but rather the emergence of other women's organizations and their complicated consequences for the cause of woman suffrage.

These new competitors in the social movement industry reflected an orientation O'Neill has termed "social feminism." In contrast to "hard-core" activists for whom the ballot was essential on the basis of justice and equality, social feminists saw the vote as a tool to achieve other reform goals (O'Neill 1969:52). While social feminism attracted many more followers than hard-core feminism during these decades, their activism was double-edged because their pursuit of other goals prevented them from devoting much energy to advancing the cause of suffrage per se. When they did support this effort, it was because the vote was seen as a tactic for achieving their particular reform agenda rather than a goal worthy of pursuit on more fundamental grounds. Having worked so hard to establish the organizational independence of their cause, suffragists continued to fight the same battle by trying to maintain the primacy of the suffrage issue vis-à-vis competing women's organizations and agendas after 1870.

This pattern was evident in the growth of the temperance movement during the 1870s and 1880s, and particularly in the rise to power of Frances Willard in the Women's Christian Temperance Union (WCTU) in the later 1870s. Until about 1880, women's temperance forces were indifferent or hostile to the notion of woman suffrage. It was only with repeated failures to influence legislatures that temperance women under Willard's leadership began to see the ballot as a potential tool for advancing their cause more effectively. The WCTU thereby came to support woman suffrage, but that support was conditioned by the generally social-feminist perspective that animated the temperance cause. That perspective meant that suffrage would always remain secondary to temperance, that the ballot was important on the basis of expediency rather than justice (Kraditor 1965), and that temperance reformers' support of suffrage was often conditional on suffragists' support of temperance. For temperance reformers, the right to vote was conceived as a means of carrying out women's traditional, culturally scripted duty of protecting the home rather than the symbol and substance of an emancipatory movement to gain women's rights and promote sexual equality (Buechler 1986:117–130). Although the WCTU under Willard may have recruited more women into the suffrage cause in the long run, in the short run its presence as a competitor to suffrage organizations, its appeal to more conservative women, and its instrumental approach to suffrage presented a new challenge to the independence of the suffragist cause.

It is difficult to know with certainty the extent to which suffrage organizations competed with social feminist organizations in this period, but there is some support for the contention that competition existed. The sentiments expressed by suffrage leaders such as Stanton and Anthony suggest that they felt that various social feminist causes were draining potential supporters away from active support of the suffragist cause (see Buechler 1986:106–107, 119–120). In more theoretical terms, Zald and McCarthy have argued that conflict and competition between social movement organizations within a social movement industry are more likely under conditions of declining resources, differing goals, and tactical disputes (1980).

Most telling is the analysis offered by Rosenthal and her associates. They confirm the standard interpretation that women's rights activity in this period was relatively marginal and isolated, and that the movement was characterized by turnover, discontinuity, and quiescence. Despite this, they find that the NWSA was the most central social movement organization in this period, with the strongest ties to other movements and organizations. In analyzing the numerically larger WCTU, they find that this organization was not central to or intensely tied with other women's groups. They conclude that the WCTU was neither a radical catalyst for women's activism nor central in the leadership of the women's rights cause in this period. Since there were few strong links between the WCTU and suffrage organizations, the conventional argument that Willard recruited, radicalized, and mobilized previously apolitical women into the suffrage cause is less convincing. A more plausible reading of the evidence is that the WCTU, and perhaps other social feminist organizations, diverted potential suffragist supporters by offering a more ideologically comfortable avenue for traditional women to become involved in social activism without directly challenging gender restrictions (see Rosenthal et al. 1985).

After the resounding defeat of the suffrage amendment on the Senate floor in 1887, the two suffrage organizations merged to foster a more effective campaign. The merger was facilitated by several factors: the passage of time had softened original differences, Stanton and Stone had retreated from leadership positions, the NWSA had become more moderate, and a new generation of leaders saw no utility in the duplication of effort represented by rival organizations. Against a backdrop of much work and little progress, merger seemed reasonable to all sides, and the National American Woman Suffrage Association (NAWSA) was thereby created at a joint convention in 1890. The merger solved some problems but simply transplanted others, as former interorganizational differences now became intraorganizational disputes. The NWSA faction still retained a broader focus than the AWSA faction, although the new group ultimately arrived at a single-issue focus reminiscent of the AWSA. Differences over the federal versus state strategy for winning suffrage created a more lasting and damaging fault line in the new organization. The NAWSA sought to compromise and use both strategies, producing a muddle that would not be resolved until the last years of the suffrage campaign. Reflecting this strategic compromise, the NAWSA alternated annual conventions in Washington with other sites around the country.

The NAWSA inherited a twenty-year legacy of unsuccessful suffrage work. For some in the new organization, this warranted a search for new strategies. The NWSA and AWSA had been created at a time of tremendous agitation for woman suffrage, but had drifted into a more quiescent strategy of education. The operating belief was that if only enough people could hear the suffragist message, they would be persuaded by its inherent logic and woman suffrage would be forthcoming. By the 1890s, some in the newly formed NAWSA realized that even if "in some states suffrage sentiment was great enough to carry an amendment, that sentiment must be organized to be made effective" (Kraditor 1965:190). These arguments were most often made by Carrie Chapman Catt, chair of the Committee on Plan of Work within the NAWSA. Catt proposed that suffrage groups be organized to mirror political boundaries and legislative districts to concentrate and translate organizational effort into legislative momentum for woman suffrage. In 1896, this strategy succeeded on a small scale in Idaho, where voters granted suffrage to women. Catt would later assume the presidency of the NAWSA and implement the same careful, methodical, highly organized plan of work for winning woman suffrage on the national level.

Between 1890 and 1896, four woman suffrage states appeared in the West: Wyoming, Colorado, Utah, and Idaho. While Colorado and Idaho were the subject of considerable suffragist work (Wyoming and Utah were admitted into the Union with territorial woman suffrage planks intact), western conditions were idiosyncratic enough that these gains could not be regarded as clear feminist victories. No more states would be added to the suffrage column for fourteen years, when the pace of the suffrage campaign began to accelerate toward a final victory. In the interim from 1896 to 1910, a number of important developments laid the groundwork for a more effective suffrage campaign in the second decade of the twentieth century. These developments were largely external to the NAWSA itself, which remained bogged down in old approaches and disputes despite Catt's attempt to infuse the organization with new vigor. What happened instead were the formation and recruitment of new constituencies to the suffrage cause, as the social movement industry concerned with woman suffrage grew and numerous social movement organizations supported the goal of votes for women. In contrast to the competitive relations that diffused and demobilized the drive for the vote from 1870 to 1890, developments in the early 1900s involved a synergistic dynamic that added momentum to the campaign.

At least three new organizational actors became important to the suffrage campaign in this period. First, social reformers active in the settlement house movement began to build important bridges across class and ethnic lines in densely populated immigrant neighborhoods in rapidly growing cities. The conditions faced by these groups added new urgency to the demand for the ballot as a means of exercising much-needed control over the deleterious conditions of rapid urbanization. Second, one offspring of the settlement house movement was the Women's Trade Union League (WTUL), a cross-class feminist organization formed in 1903 to foster progressive improvements by uniting upper- and middle-class "allies" with working-class women. The working conditions of the urban, industrial female labor force provided yet another cogent argument for extending the right to vote to women. Finally, the growing women's club movement reflected a tradition of voluntarist politics (Cott 1987) whose conservative orientation was nonetheless becoming more diversified and more receptive to the movement for woman suffrage. Although these constituencies developed gradually and their support for suffrage was initially tentative, this signified a tremendous broadening of the woman suffrage base from the narrowly middle-class leadership and constituency of earlier years. The limits to this broadening were evident in the NAWSA's capitulation to racism to mollify southern suffragists, but these developments nonetheless represented a marked departure from the insular stance of the earlier suffrage movement.

Ellen DuBois has clarified the extent to which suffrage became a multi-class movement in the twentieth century (1987a; see also Buechler 1986). Elite women became more interested in the right to vote for reasons that reflected their class interests in strengthening the hand of the upper class as well as their gender interests in improving the social conditions of women. Professional women seeking occupational equality added another dimension to the suffrage struggle. As the state became increasingly involved in regulating the conditions of labor, wage-earning women had a growing interest in the ballot. Many of these threads were woven together in organizations like the Women's Trade Union League, which was itself pulled toward the suffrage cause by activists like Harriot Stanton Blatch. "Blatch rewrote feminism in its essentially modern form, around work. . . . Her approach to 'women's work' led Blatch to believe that the interconnection of women's labor fundamentally shaped relations among them" (DuBois 1987a:42). This new feminist ideology, in which the diversity of women's work was central, was organizationally embodied in the Equality League of Self-Supporting Women, organized by Blatch in 1907. The distinctively cross-class character of this organization was mirrored by an equally distinctive tactical militance, which gained new publicity for the move-ment. While all such efforts eventually foundered on the contradictions of class, the timing of the successes fostered by such efforts added vital momentum to the suffrage cause (DuBois 1987a).

Despite the eastern locus of these organizational developments, immedi-ate progress came in western states. In Washington, a quiet, methodical cam-paign led by one of Catt's followers won woman suffrage in 1910; the next year woman suffrage was achieved in California. In 1912, Arizona, Kansas, and Ore-gon were added to the suffrage column. The more ominous news was that east-ern and midwestern states were proving intractable, and elections were being stolen by liquor interests to prevent female enfranchisement in some close con-tests (Flexner 1975: 268–269). Although a well-orchestrated campaign in Illi-nois won a slightly limited form of female suffrage in 1913 (see Buechler 1986), insightful suffragists sensed that this first victory east of the Mississippi was the exception rather than the rule. It is only with the benefit of hindsight that these state victories appear to be a steady march of progress in the suffrage fight. In historical context, these state victories amidst many more frequent defeats deep-ened the strategic dilemma that had always plagued woman suffrage organiza-tions: whether to work on the state or the federal level. State victories made the former strategy appear more plausible than it really was, since there were so many ways to defeat state campaigns and since woman suffrage was now attract-ing formidable enemies. NAWSA would continue to flounder over this issue be-fore it found a workable strategy for winning the vote.

The strongest argument for the federal strategy came from Alice Paul and Lucy Burns. Transplanting strategic lessons from the militant wing of the Brit-ish suffrage movement into an American context, Paul and Burns organized a massive woman suffrage parade that overshadowed President Wilson's inau-gural celebration in April 1913. While working for NAWSA's Congressional Committee, Paul and Burns established the semi-independent Congressional Union that same month. They urged that NAWSA adopt an exclusively federal strategy for winning suffrage. At its 1913 convention, NAWSA rejected this idea and removed Paul from the Congressional Committee. In early 1914, the Con-gressional Union (CU) split from NAWSA and became an independent organi-zation. The CU was not only dedicated to a federal strategy but also to using votes to punish the party in power for not advancing the cause of woman suf-frage. This tactic, also transplanted from the British campaign, clashed directly with NAWSA's nonpartisanship. As the CU campaigned in the 1914 elections against Democratic candidates for not promoting suffrage while in power, the rift between NAWSA and the CU widened.

The organizational differences between these two groups were substantial. NAWSA was a large, heterogeneous, inclusive, membership organization that welcomed any degree of support and tolerated a wide — though not unlimited — range of perspectives. Indeed, it was so large and tolerant and undisciplined that it was as much a follower as a leader in this stage of the movement, functioning as an umbrella for state campaigns, annual conventions, and education and publicity. In 1914, Congress debated the Shafroth-Palmer amendment, a complex measure that would have facilitated state referenda on woman suffrage. The proposal was intended to defend "states' rights" concerning voting privileges, and was of particular interest to southern legislators worried that a federal amendment would jeopardize de jure disenfranchisement of black women and de facto restrictions on black male voting. The CU immediately rejected the idea, but NAWSA waffled for almost a year before finally rejecting the measure.

The CU, by contrast with NAWSA, was a small, homogeneous, exclusive cadre organization that demanded full participation and tolerated no deviation from its carefully chosen course. The focus and intensity of the CU's approach must be credited with reviving interest in the federal woman suffrage amendment. While NAWSA's policies continued to be muddled, the goal, strategy, and tactics of the CU were well defined. For all these reasons, the CU was the more effective organization in the woman suffrage campaign in the years 1914 and 1915. In 1914, it organized in the nine woman suffrage states and urged women voters to reject Democratic candidates for their lack of progress on woman suffrage. In 1915, it began organizing in all forty-eight states. In 1916, CU members founded the Woman's Party in woman suffrage states to solidify the female vote in the Presidential election. The next year, the Woman's Party and the Congressional Union merged to form the National Woman's Party, which would attain an even higher profile in the final years of the campaign for woman suffrage.

NAWSA took a positive step at its 1915 convention when it urged Catt to resume the presidency of the organization. Catt's quiet, methodical, and systematic organizing work had been a connecting thread in NAWSA's few successes, stretching from prior victories in the West to the roots of serious organizing in the East through vehicles like the Woman Suffrage Party in New York State. Catt summarized the situation in December 1915:

> A serious crisis exists in the suffrage movement. A considerable number of women in the various states have turned to the Federal Amendment as the most promising avenue. The victory of the Federal Amendment especially appeals to the women of those states with constitutions which make a successful referendum well-nigh impossible. A considerable number of women in the South are dead

set against the Federal Amendment. The first anti-suffrage organization of importance to be effected in the South has been formed in
Alabama with the slogan: "Home Rule, States Rights, and White
Supremacy." A considerable number of other women wish to work
exclusively for suffrage within their own states. The Congressional
Union is drawing off from the National Association those women
who feel it is possible to work for suffrage by the Federal route only.
Certain workers in the South are being antagonized because the National is continuing to work for the Federal Amendment. The combination has produced a great muddle from which the National can
be freed only by careful action [cited in Flexner 1975: 284].

Under Catt's leadership, the NAWSA increased its membership twentyfold in
two years. In 1916, she proposed a "Winning Plan" that targeted the thirty-six
states most likely to ratify a suffrage amendment and proposed a timetable that
would win the vote by April 1922. Because of the presence of two very different
but equally effective suffrage organizations, that timetable was eclipsed by even
more rapid progress than Catt anticipated.

As of 1915, the social movement industry concerned with winning woman
suffrage was large and diverse. Beyond the two national suffrage organizations
were a plethora of other groups and constituencies who had come to support the
suffrage cause for their own reasons. From differing perspectives, upper-class
women, wage-earning women, professional women, club women, immigrant
women, and some black women and their organizations formed a large periphery of suffrage support around the movement's core of middle-class leadership.
To its credit, NAWSA had consciously cultivated a broader base of support in
the twentieth century by developing arguments that spoke to the specific interests of diverse women as well as their common interests as women. (The major
and glaring exception to this pattern involved black women, who were shunned
for both tactical and racist reasons.) As of 1914, the literature department of
NAWSA offered hundreds of pamphlets on how and why the vote was relevant
to almost every conceivable constituency of women. This ideological commitment to reaching a broader spectrum, vivified in the organizationally diverse,
cross-class, multiconstituency alliance that was taking shape in the 1910s, meant
that the suffrage movement was better positioned to win suffrage than it had
ever been. At precisely this point, the terrain of national politics began to shift
with the 1916 presidential election and the prospect of U.S. involvement in the
First World War.

The CU carried its policy of blaming the party in power into the 1916 election, urging bloc anti-Democratic voting to punish inactivity on the suffrage measure. The tactic won serious consideration of the issue at the Democratic convention, but earned only a compromise plank and no substantial shift in Democratic behavior. It is doubtful whether the tactic had any larger effect. Whereas the CU could claim some role in the defeat of twenty-three out of forty-three western Democrats in the 1914 elections, in the 1916 elections Wilson carried ten of twelve suffrage states, and the WP was even less successful in defeating Democratic candidates for Congress. NAWSA disagreed with this tactic for several reasons: that it would not work, that it antagonized sympathetic Democrats, that the "party in power" logic did not apply to the U.S. electoral system as it did in England, and that it was more prudent to convert individuals on the basis of principle (Kraditor 1965:198–200).

The CU strategy sought to take power rather than ask for it, but its bluff was called when the ballots were counted and bloc anti-Democratic voting failed to materialize. The NAWSA strategy still meant asking for power, but NAWSA was able to ask for it in ways that were increasingly difficult to deny. Wilson and the Democrats were put in a political cross fire: villainized by the CU and lobbied by NAWSA, Wilson moved from indifference to strong support of woman suffrage in a relatively brief time. Wilson's support occurred in the context of a reinvigorated NAWSA acting in accordance with Catt's plan for a coordinated national campaign to win suffrage. Under Catt, NAWSA was converted from a group of amateur reformers to professional organizers who approached their task with unprecedented tactical sophistication (Flexner 1975:283). Catt's plan, couched in military metaphors, distinguished winnable from unwinnable states, brought scarce resources to bear where prospects for success were greatest, converted state victories into congressional pressure, and always kept an eye to the ratification process that would follow any positive congressional action. The unanticipated consequences of the CU's federal strategy and the NAWSA's winning plan were mutually beneficial to the cause.

The next tactical escalation occurred when pickets from the NWP appeared at the White House in January 1917, demanding the right to vote. Questioning Wilson's commitment to making the world safe for democracy when there was none for women at home, and referring to the President as Kaiser Wilson, the pickets earned publicity and polarized attitudes on the suffrage question. The government's response of repressing civil liberties during wartime led to arrests, prison sentences, and hunger strikes, further dramatizing the suffrage cause. NAWSA disavowed the pickets and their tactics, but benefited from the resulting publicity. Even more important, the NWP's tactics led it to be perceived as the radical fringe of a movement whose moderate and increasingly legitimate center was typified by NAWSA. The effect of NWP militance was to move suffrage from an issue that could still be ignored to one that had to be discussed — at least with moderates like NAWSA and Carrie Chapman Catt.

By this point, NAWSA was in a position to take rather than ask for power. In sharp contrast to 1915 defeats in Massachusetts, New York, Pennsylvania, and New Jersey, there were 1917 victories in Ohio, Indiana, Rhode Island, Nebraska, Michigan, North Dakota, and New York. As a combined result of CU militance, NAWSA moderation, state successes, and shifting political opportunity structures, Catt could credibly talk a kind of power politics that had backfired on the Women's Party only a short time ago: "If the Sixty-fifth Congress fails to submit the Federal Amendment before the next congressional election, this association shall select and enter into such a number of senatorial and congressional campaigns as will effect a change in both Houses of Congress sufficient to insure its passage. . . . Our opposition to individual candidates shall not be based on party considerations" (quoted in Flexner 1975:301). Within a month of this declaration at a NAWSA convention, the House passed the woman suffrage amendment by a two-thirds majority on 10 January 1918. Defeat in the Senate delayed full congressional passage until 4 June 1919, with ratification completed on 26 August 1919.

Considerable disagreement remains over whether the CU and NWP tactics of partisan voting and militant protest were beneficial or harmful to the cause. Kraditor (1965) and Flexner (1975) tend to see the results as positive, whereas O'Neill (1969) depicts them as dysfunctional in several respects. While there is no denying that the CU hardened preexisting opposition and antagonized some supporters, on balance the unintended consequences of these very different organizations and their respective tactics served to advance the cause of woman suffrage. Their interaction in the context of wartime political and social upheaval produced a result that neither organization would have been able to bring about on its own. Resting on a solid base of cross-class, multiconstituency support for the vote, the NAWSA and CU accomplished the goal that had eluded the suffrage movement for so long.

Recent research by Rosenthal et al. confirms this interpretation of the suffrage movement as a cross-class, multiconstituency alliance in its last period (1985). Their analysis reveals a cross-class cluster of organizations centered on the WTUL, which was concerned with labor organizing, settlement work, socialism, and progressive politics. More generally, they describe this period as one of "intense activity with ever increasing numbers of organizations, linked by both strong and moderate directional ties. Two clusters (the woman's club movement and the cross-class movement), linked by suffrage organizations, are clearly delineated. . . . The two clusters are both related to the NAWSA, . . . the form of the network in this period confirms that women became involved in suffrage as a single issue" (1985:1044). The social movement for woman suffrage thereby succeeded when multiple social movement organizations representing otherwise diverse constituencies of women mounted an effective campaign for a specific goal. The instrumental nature of the alliance is suggested by how quickly it disintegrated after winning the vote, testifying to the increasing social differentiation of women in the early twentieth century.

The Contemporary Women's Movement

The contemporary women's movement has been a veritable laboratory of experimentation with regard to organizational forms. There has not only been great diversity in organizational structures, but also keen awareness of the dilemmas that inevitably arise in the organization of social movements. The self-reflexive manner in which the women's movement has approached the question of organization reflects its origins, whether in confronting unresponsive government bureaucracies or in resisting the sexism of prior social movements in the 1960s. The self-reflexive approach also results from the central insight that "the personal is political," meaning for many feminists that questions of how a movement is organized and how it operates on a daily basis are as important as the ultimate goals it seeks. This self-reflexive quality of feminist mobilization has not prevented the movement from making strategic and tactical mistakes, but it has meant that those mistakes have been analyzed by movement participants in considerable depth and detail.

In McCarthy and Zald's terms, the social movement industry devoted to changing the position of women and implementing the preference structure of the contemporary women's movement consists of a large number of social movement organizations. This social movement industry cannot be reduced merely to formal movement organizations, however, important as they have been. This movement industry also consists of what I have termed a "social movement community": informal networks of politicized participants who are active in promoting the goals of a social movement outside the boundaries of formal movement organizations. This distinction between SMOs and SMCs is correlated, though not identical, with more familiar distinctions in the literature on the contemporary women's movement. Thus, Freeman distinguishes between an older branch, which has tended to favor top-down, national, formal organizational structures, and a younger branch consisting of "innumerable small groups engaged in a variety of activities" (1975:50). Ferree and Hess contrast the bureaucratic strand of the movement, utilizing formal organizational structures, and the collectivist strand, favoring more communal and egalitarian forms of organization (1985:49–50).

As a sensitizing concept, these variations may be conceptualized as existing on a continuum. At one end are highly formal, fully bureaucratic movement organizations; at the other end are loosely linked, communally connected activists. In between these extremes is a diverse range of movement organizations with varying degrees of formality, hierarchy, and structure. The imagery of a continuum of organizational forms is meant to overcome some of the rigidly dichotomized views of the contemporary women's movement, which describe it as sharply split between two camps. This was most true at the time when much of this literature was published in the early and mid–1970s. Since that time, however, the movement has seen considerable transformation and blending of diverse organizational forms. Although the distinction between bureaucratic and collectivist sectors continues to be useful as a heuristic device for analyzing movement organization, the distinction should not be reified into an ahistorical and unchanging caricature of the diversity of organizational forms in the movement.

Since the following discussion will adopt the bureaucratic-collectivist distinction, it is important to stress at the outset that the development of these organizational forms followed a definite historical dynamic. The National Organization for Women (NOW) was formed in 1966, and several other bureaucratic organizations followed within the next year or two. By 1968, the women's liberation movement was breaking away from other 1960s movements and beginning to form the collectivist sector of the movement. By the early 1970s, the contrasts between these two sectors were drawn most sharply, the movement was at its strongest, and it had many of the features of a mass movement. Through the later 1970s, the contrasts began to break down as women experimented with diverse forms and crossed increasingly vague boundaries from one part of the movement to another. During the 1980s, the distinction persisted in a muted way, as backlash and countermovements helped unify some fragments of the movement and growing strategic sophistication informed movement actions. There were also significant variations within each sector of the movement. NOW vacillated between top-down and grass-roots approaches, while the collectivist sector varied from cadrelike groups to diffuse subcultural communities. If this historical variability and internal diversity are recognized, the distinction between bureaucratic and collectivist sectors can serve a heuristic purpose in analyzing organizational forms in the contemporary movement.

The National Organization for Women, organized in 1966, is the most often cited example of the bureaucratic sector, or the older branch, or the women's rights wing of the contemporary women's movement. NOW emerged from the activities of the presidential and state commissions on the status of women in the face of government unwillingness to seriously enforce recent legislation banning discrimination on the basis of sex. The organization built on a foundation of well-educated, white, middle-class professional women with strong network ties into other organizations and the federal government. In an earlier day, such a constituency might well have joined a more traditional organization like Business and Professional Women, but in the historical context of the civil rights movement and significant federal legislation, NOW was destined to be a rather different organization. Its statement of purpose committed the organization to action "to break through the silken curtain of prejudice and discrimination against women." An organization to undertake such action was required because "there is no civil rights organization to speak for women, as there has been for Negroes and other victims of discrimination. The National Organization for Women must therefore begin to speak" (National Organization for Women Papers 1966).

NOW's broad orientation was evident in its initial structure of task forces to study the position of women with regard to employment, education, religion, the family, mass media, the polity, and poverty. Despite its ambitious agenda, NOW began as a small group of prominent individuals who had professional and organizational experience but were neither skilled nor interested in building a mass movement of women. Hence, the early actions of the group were more modest, focusing on the executive branch of the federal government and the Equal Employment Opportunity Commission, and seeking extensions and full enforcement of policies, executive orders, and laws against sex discrimination in employment. Many of the grievances that NOW addressed in its first year were quite narrow and specific. They included efforts to desegregate want ads and thereby reduce sex discrimination in hiring, and a California legal case that argued that protective labor legislation for women functioned to exclude them from consideration for promotion to senior positions. It was clear to NOW founders, however, that such specific grievances were in fact embedded in a much larger web of discriminatory policies and practices toward women that had to be addressed more globally.

This more global focus was evident in the Bill of Rights for Women, which was proposed at NOW's second national conference in November 1967. Included were support for the Equal Rights Amendment (ERA) and support for reproductive rights, including repeal of abortion laws. These fateful issues had a double significance; in the short term they prompted organizational dissension and schism, and in the long term they became central foci for NOW's organizational activity. NOW's support for the ERA posed a problem for women from the United Auto Workers Union, which stood in opposition to the ERA. Although most union women supported the ERA, they had to keep a lower profile and to stop providing UAW resources to NOW once it decided to support the ERA. NOW's support of abortion reform alienated another segment of professional women, who found the issue unnecessarily divisive and beyond the scope of a woman's rights organization. They proceeded to form the Women's Equity Action League, which limited its focus to legal and economic issues. Yet another group left when NOW was unable to efficiently establish a tax-exempt legal foundation to pursue cases of discrimination. Lawyers who left NOW took some of its best-known cases with them for resolution through the newly formed Human Rights for Women.

The aforementioned divisions were relatively minor differences within the professionally oriented, bureaucratically organized women's rights sector of the contemporary movement. In 1968, a more fundamental split occurred, which prefigured the division between the bureaucratic women's rights orientation and the collectivist women's liberation orientation within the movement. At the 1968 national convention of NOW, the New York chapter, led by Ti-Grace Atkinson, proposed changes in NOW's organizational structure to minimize organizational hierarchy and maximize participatory democracy. The proposal was rejected, and Atkinson left NOW to form the October 17th Movement, later known as The Feminists. This split was overdetermined. In addition to organizational differences there was a fear that the New York branch of NOW would come to dominate the national organization (see Freeman 1975:81–82), and also NOW's eagerness to distance itself from the emerging women's liberation movement and its highly publicized and radical manifestos, ideology, and tactics (see Hole and Levine 1971:90–91). Most recruits to the women's liberation sector did not come from NOW at all, but rather from other social movements. Nonetheless, the 1968 schism between the national organization and much of the New York branch represents the beginning of the sharpest divide between the bureaucratic orientation of NOW and the collectivist orientation of the women's liberation sector of the movement.

There were some successful efforts to unite both wings around specific campaigns. NOW cosponsored Women Strike for Equality on 26 August 1970, which became a focal point for feminists of all persuasions. In general, however, efforts to bring greater unity across the spectrum of burgeoning feminist activism were unsuccessful because there were simply too many points of contention on issues of organization, ideology, strategy, and tactics. Some realized the virtues of diversity from the beginning, recognizing that women's liberation groups often functioned as a radical vanguard that made NOW's progressive agenda seem moderate and almost conventional by comparison — much as militant suffragists had legitimized moderate suffragists fifty years earlier in the struggle to win the vote. The period of the Women's Strike also coincided with and contributed to some of the most rapid growth of the contemporary feminist movement. Although NOW had a firm foundation by this time, it was hardly prepared for the influx of new members or the general growth of feminist sentiment throughout the country. In this period, NOW was a small national leadership group that couldn't keep up with its membership, the momentum of the movement, or the diversity of feminist perspectives taking root in the organization.

As the women's movement became a mass movement, and as some newly mobilized women joined NOW, it inevitably became a more heterogeneous organization. New recruits were often more interested in forming consciousness-raising (C-R) groups than in lobbying for antidiscrimination legislation, and NOW's initial response was to encourage the formation of local chapters and provide considerable autonomy to those chapters. The rapid growth of chapters (fourteen in 1967, seven hundred in 1974) and members (one thousand in 1967, forty thousand in 1974) created a grass-roots foundation where previously there had only been a top-down elite (Freeman 1975:87). This growth also introduced tensions between these levels. In addition to differences over strategy and tactics between the national and local levels, there have also been long-standing disputes over finances, since a substantial portion of dues collected at the local level flow into the national coffers of the organization. More generally, a long-standing fault line in NOW has existed between a national leadership seeking organizational discipline and efficiency and a grass-roots base seeking free rein to pursue local interests. Both levels have looked to the other for degrees of support and types of assistance that have been in chronically short supply.

The growth of local chapters has provided an avenue for the ideology of the women's liberation movement to travel through NOW's grass-roots base. In addition to a preference for consciousness-raising activites, many local chapters have rejected NOW's hierarchical structure for organizing on the local level and have opted for more participatory forms of democracy and consensus modes of decision-making. While these approaches are often successful at empowering movement participants and developing a sense of solidarity, they also clash with the requisite of organizational efficiency at the national level. On specific lobbying issues or electoral campaigns that require coordinated and disciplined organizational responses, the national leadership has often found itself fighting a solitary battle without much support from local memberships. Despite these problems, the blending of approaches and orientations is a testimony to the survivability and adaptability of NOW as a major movement organization. In the estimate of one astute participant and observer of feminist activism, "NOW has moved over time from being the main older branch organization to being the main feminist organization. It has become very much an umbrella group for all kinds of feminists, even those whose primary loyalty lies elsewhere" (Freeman 1975:93).

By the mid-1970s, NOW's umbrella encompassed diverse orientations, which generated considerable conflict over leadership. At NOW's 1974 convention, the organization's first contested presidential election was the focal point for a clash between two factions. The election was won by Karen DeCrow, whose campaign slogan symbolized the increasingly radical orientation of the organization. NOW's original statement of purpose called for bringing women into the mainstream of society; DeCrow campaigned under the slogan "out of the mainstream and into the revolution." DeCrow was reelected in 1975, and her supporters won a substantial share of NOW offices. These events suggest that despite its originally reformist orientation, NOW was a permeable organization that could be significantly influenced and partially redirected by organized challenges from members with a somewhat different agenda. Once in power, this group moved to centralize the organization by establishing a single national office in Washington, creating five new national officers, and establishing state organizations that undercut the autonomy of local chapters (Freeman 1984:548). One example of the shift in NOW's orientation was the adoption of a resolution identifying lesbian rights as a national priority in its October 1975 convention. Although NOW had formally recognized lesbian oppression in 1971 and had established a task force on sexuality and lesbianism in 1973, the 1975 resolution elevated the issue to a major organizational priority and attracted considerable media attention. That same year, the task force on sexuality and lesbianism outlined an ambitious program of action for 1976, including the establishment of support strategies with the National Gay Task Force.

NOW's radical drift and more explicit support of lesbian rights provoked a backlash and led in November 1975 to the formation of a group calling itself WomanSurge. Characterizing itself as the loyal opposition within NOW and seeking a return to the mainstream, WomanSurge argued that "the women's movement must put forth a public image which appeals to the majority of American women. WomanSurge is committed to projecting a style and image that make it possible for mainstream women to identify with the women's movement" (Friedan [Betty] Papers, 1976). The NOW backlash dovetailed with other factors that swung NOW's ideological pendulum back in a more reformist direction. These included the increasing attention the organization was paying to the floundering Equal Rights Amendment as well as the declining impact of the women's liberation sector of the movement on the national organization. In a very few years, NOW was again being criticized for not being radical enough rather than for being too radical. In an article entitled "Out of the Revolution,

Into the Mainstream," Kerry Lobel and Jeanne Cordova argued that "What happened at the 12th Annual NOW Convention is in many respects what is happening to the Women's Movement. NOW moved to the right, and abbreviated feminism in the name of efficiency" (National Organization for Women Papers n.d.[a]).

In point of fact, NOW's organizational resources were stretched to the limit by the late 1970s, and a more specific focus on mainstream issues resulted from several organizational and political forces. Most important among these was the fact that NOW was increasingly entangled in efforts to maintain, sustain, and expand partial victories that dated back to the early 1970s. The Equal Rights Amendment provides one example. Because it had passed Congress in 1972 and won early and easy ratification in a number of states, NOW did not perceive the need for a sustained ratification campaign until quite late. Once organized, the ratification campaign was diverted by two subsidiary struggles to extend the deadline for ratification and to challenge the legality of rescission votes in states which had already ratified the amendment. Reproductive rights provides another example. As the backlash to the 1973 *Roe* v. *Wade* decision grew, NOW became increasingly involved in defending women's access to abortion. In paradoxical fashion, then, some relatively easy gains of the women's movement in the early 1970s prompted sustained counterattack in the later 1970s, and defending those gains consumed a substantial and growing share of scarce organizational resources.

By the late 1970s, NOW was realizing that a substantial commitment to the ERA would be necessary to counter the right-wing backlash, which had begun to mount a very effective "Stop ERA" campaign. The shift is evident in NOW's internal documents. Its 1976–1977 Legislative Program identified ERA passage as one of four "old business" items along with several "new business" items (National Organization for Women Papers n.d.[b]). By late 1977, NOW was hiring political consultants who advised that the situation was not encouraging, that the effort to date had been confused, disorganized, and defensive, and that "this project must be approached for what it is, a political campaign, pure and simple. A political campaign is not a democratic process. One person runs it and has complete control over it" (Friedan [Betty] Papers 1977). By February 1978, NOW was declaring a National ERA Emergency and urging directors and board members at regional, state, and chapter levels to set up meetings to dedicate all organizational resources to winning ratification of the ERA (Friedan [Betty] Papers n.d.). Shortly thereafter, NOW won a three-year extension of the ratification deadline, and its virtually exclusive focus on the ERA continued until the amendment was finally defeated in 1982.

The ERA campaign had an enormous impact on NOW as an organization.

For one, NOW self-consciously changed its image to counter the right-wing ac-cusation that it and the ERA signified the destruction of the family. The ERA focus meant that other feminist issues, including reproductive rights, which were also under attack, received almost no attention from NOW in this period. As NOW actively recruited "paper members" and financial contributions for the ERA campaign, few of these members became involved in local chapters where other issues could be pursued. Finally, and most significantly, NOW became very heavily involved in electoral politics. On relatively short notice, it sought to alter the composition of those state legislatures which had not yet ratified the amendment (Freeman 1984). When the 1980 elections proved disastrous for NOW's ERA campaign on both national and state levels, the organization was left with the very difficult task of lobbying state legislatures to maintain waning ERA support while also trying to win new support from a firmly entrenched opposition.

NOW's return to electoral politics and legislative strategies in the 1980s is consistent with its origins in governmental commissions on the status of women and its early goals of eliminating discrimination in employment. Following this trajectory, NOW (along with other bureaucratic women's organizations) had es-tablished an effective lobbying presence by the early 1970s and had begun en-dorsing political candidates by the mid-1970s. The ratification campaign restored and reinforced the organization's dedication to reformist goals and leg-islative and lobbying strategies. With the waning influence of the collectivist strand within NOW, the organization has essentially become an interest group pursuing pragmatic goals within the framework of electoral politics as part of a women's policy network (Costain 1982; Ferree and Hess 1985). Although the institutionalization of NOW as an interest group is well advanced, periodic chal-lenges continue to arise within the organization. Sonia Johnson's 1982 cam-paign for the NOW presidency testified to the continuing presence of a more radical feminism within NOW, as do continuing calls for the organization to re-turn to a more grass-roots, collectivist, and creative approach to feminist issues (Kauffman 1984).

In the 1985 NOW presidential campaign, there was a return to more mili-tant rhetoric as Eleanor Smeal successfully campaigned against Judy Gold-smith. Smeal had supported Goldsmith's pragmatism in 1982 against Sonia Johnson's more visionary program, but was arguing by 1985 that Goldsmith had lost members, abandoned the ERA, and turned NOW into a wing of the Democratic party. Smeal called for a return to more radical tactics in pursuit of long-standing NOW goals, and the organization returned to the streets for a mass march for abortion rights and birth control in Washington, D.C. in March 1986. Three years later, an even larger march occurred to defend the *Roe* v. *Wade*

decision against an upcoming challenge. The Court's subsequent decision in the
Webster case to return even more control to the states seems destined to elevate
reproductive rights into a major mobilizing issue in the 1990s. One response to
this further restriction on reproductive rights was evident at NOW's 1989 convention. Adopting a strategy reminiscent of Stanton and Anthony's call for a
new political party in the late 1860s as women's rights were abandoned by both
major parties, NOW delegates rejected the two-party system by advocating the
formation of a third party to advance the progressive agenda that has been
largely abandoned by the Democratic party (Rothschild 1989). In the foreseeable future, NOW may be expected to vacillate between two poles that reflect its
position as the major feminist social movement organization and as an institutionalized interest group. As a social movement organization, NOW must be
concerned with maintaining recruitment and mobilization through dramatic tactics and passionate appeals. As an interest group, NOW must be engaged in the
pragmatic coalition-building and lobbying necessary to translate movement energy into legislative gain and public policy. As long as NOW continues to fulfill
both roles, these debates and tensions are likely to be an integral part of the organization.

This brief analysis of NOW illustrates both the utility and the limitation of
the bureaucratic-collectivist distinction in understanding the contemporary
women's movement. While NOW is better described as a bureaucratic SMO, it
has seen considerable variation and transformation in its history. Beginning as
an organization seeking social change, many NOW members (if not leaders) became as interested in personal transformation as in social change. Beginning as
an elite organization, NOW was overwhelmed for a time by the rapid influx of
new members. Beginning as a hierarchical organization seeking efficiency and
discipline, NOW has been pulled toward more egalitarian, participatory modes
of member input. Beginning as a centralized organization, NOW became decentralized and ultimately recentralized over time. Beginning with a national
focus on legislation and lobbying, many local chapters have formulated and pursued their own agendas with relative autonomy. Many of these transformations
must be seen as a function of the historical and sociopolitical context of the organization. When the collectivist sector of the movement was strongest in the
early to mid-1970s, NOW was most likely to depart from the bureaucratic mode
of movement organization with all its correlative characteristics. When the antifeminist backlash was greatest in the later 1970s and early 1980s, the organization returned to a more bureaucratic stance and fought essentially defensive
battles.

The transformations NOW has undergone shed light on social movement
dynamics more generally. The classic literature predicts an inevitable shift to

oligarchy, conservatism, and organizational maintenance, but more recent arguments and evidence have challenged the inevitability of these changes. Consistent with this more recent literature, NOW moved in a notably more radical direction from the late 1960s to the mid-1970s. Freeman cites three reasons: an inherent logic to feminism leads to ever broader concerns; NOW's underlying liberalism predisposed it to move to the left; and the younger branch of the movement operated as an ideological vanguard that radicalized the organization. Of these, the last factor seems most important: "NOW's radicalization . . . is largely due to the ideological pull of the younger branch. Without this influence NOW might not be able to resist conservatization" (1975:100). In a more recent study, Jonasdottir concurs that although administrative centralization has occurred within NOW, this has neither led to conservative goal transformation nor eliminated grass-roots activity. She credits the influence of the overall women's movement, the multilevel organizational structure of NOW, and the progressive value system of feminism, which is resistant to conservatizing tendencies (1988). NOW's history thereby suggests that organizational transformation in social movements is a complex function of ideological, microstructural, and macro-contextual factors, which may combine in diverse ways to produce equally diverse outcomes.

The history of the collectivist sector of the contemporary women's movement provides another lesson in the complexities of organizational transformation in social movements. The women's liberation sector of the contemporary movement emerged out of the civil rights and New Left movements in the later 1960s, rapidly mushroomed into a mass movement during a phase of intensive mobilization and radicalization from 1968 through 1970, and underwent fragmentation, dispersion, and diffusion thereafter. This sector has always been organizationally elusive, in large part because of its conscious eschewal of formal movement organization, but it had a profound transformative influence on large numbers of women (and some men) during its zenith. Since its relative decline in the mid-1970s, this sector has left important movement traces and residues in the form of personal transformation and raised consciousness, feminist counterinstitutions and women's culture, and feminist imprints on mainstream institutions and social practices. Perhaps the most important legacy of this sector is the creation and maintenance of a social movement community of like-minded, informally linked activists who are capable of rapid and intense mobilization around specific issues even in the absence of formal movement organization.

The earliest traces of organizationally independent women's liberationist activities appeared in late 1967 and early 1968. In September 1967, there were the first signs of an irreparable split within the New Left over feminist issues at the National Conference for a New Politics. In January 1968, the New York group Radical Women staged "The Burial of Traditional Womanhood" at an antiwar demonstration in Washington, D.C. In March 1968, the newsletter *Voice of the Women's Liberation Movement* first appeared. In August 1968, a national gathering of radical women occurred in Sandy Springs, Maryland, to discuss goals and priorities. The next month brought a protest of the Miss America contest; massive media coverage created the perception and to some extent the reality of a national movement. In October, the Women's International Terrorist Conspiracy from Hell (WITCH) hexed the New York Stock Exchange. In November 1968, the first truly national women's liberation conference was held in Chicago, as women gathered from thirty-seven states to discuss issues in the emerging movement. In January 1969, counterinaugural activities in Washington sparked new friction between New Left men and women liberationists and provided an additional impetus to the development of an independent women's movement.

As Hole and Levine have illustrated in their well-known work (1971), the emergence of three distinct women's liberation groups in New York provided a good example of the range of organizational forms and ideological issues in the early movement. They credit Redstockings with being the first group to clearly articulate the role of consciousness-raising groups in uncovering the political within the personal and creating a sense of group solidarity among women. Redstockings also initiated the pro-woman line, rejecting the idea that women were brainwashed and defending women's behavior as realistic responses to a position of powerlessness. Another New York group, The Feminists, formed when Ti-Grace Atkinson left NOW; this was a theory and action group that sought a rigorous analysis of the role system that perpetuated female subordination. The Feminists were also dedicated to discovering nonhierarchical forms of group organization and used a lot system to distribute work within the group. A third group, New York Radical Feminists, sought to eliminate the sex-class system by identifying both social and psychological sources and avoiding the rigidities of the other groups. Radical Feminists also developed a complex three-stage process for recruiting new members and building a mass movement.

The fact that none of these groups survived for long was a kind of early warning signal about the centrifugal tendencies of the women's liberation movement. Redstockings' strong dedication to consciousness-raising and the pro-woman line tended to glorify the victim and ultimately led to a posture of inaction. The Feminists' insistence on the lot system and equal work roles fostered harsh criticism of any woman who distinguished herself as an individual, which contributed to the dissolution of the group. The Radical Feminists' attempts to mobilize a mass movement through a three-stage recruitment process nonetheless led to charges of elitism within the group, causing it to break up (Hole and

Levine 1971). The rapid growth, intense mobilization, and creative tactics of these groups were essential elements in the origin and growth of the women's liberation sector of the movement. Because they were new, however, the dysfunctional effects of some of these tactics and organizational forms could not be anticipated soon enough to prevent conflicts from splitting the groups apart. They indicated, in embryonic form, enduring conflicts that would become dominant motifs in the women's liberation movement.

Judging both from these early group experiments and from the perspective of hindsight, the two major distinguishing features of the women's liberation sector of the contemporary women's movement were its commitment to consciousness-raising and its attempts to create relatively structureless groups for accomplishing movement goals. There were precedents for consciousness-raising in both the civil rights and New Left movements (Evans 1979:214), but the women's movement made this technique its own. C-R groups were a direct response to the problem of structural isolation, which precluded many women from becoming active in women's movements. By bringing small groups of women together to share their experiences, rap groups revealed the social patterns in what had previously been seen as individual problems of maladjustment. While women with prior movement experience already had an ideology for developing this consciousness, C-R groups were vital to the growth of the women's liberation sector into a mass movement by recruiting previously uninvolved women. Providing daily illustrations of the claim that "the personal is the political," consciousness-raising created strong bonds of sisterhood, identified immediate changes in personal lives that could be attempted, and sought links between personal change and societal transformation.

Rap groups may be likened to nineteenth-century women's clubs (Freeman 1975:117), which brought women together in a homosocial context and provided the free space (Evans and Boyte 1986) to explore and challenge psychological forms of oppression. By nurturing the expression of feelings and experiences in an all-female setting, women were able to formulate alternatives to male-dominated worldviews and belief systems. Although some criticized rap groups as mere bitch sessions, proponents argued that the links between the personal and the political distinguished the two and made the rap group a precursor to sustained political activism. C-R strategy put experience first, and sought to derive theory and strategy from experience. For many women, consciousness-raising had the irreversible quality of a conversion that fundamentally changed one's way of looking at the world. Having participated in a group, few women could return to their former ways of thinking and living in the social world.

The success of this tactic was so great that by the early 1970s, NOW had become a major instigator of C-R groups because they proved the most effective means of recruiting new members and adding new chapters. The impact of the technique can hardly be overestimated as a recruiting tool for the contemporary women's movement. As powerful as consciousness-raising proved to be, the limits of the technique became evident as groups tried to move from raised consciousness to political activism. Some women weren't interested in the larger project of societal transformation, while others opted for the maintenance and strengthening of homosocial counterinstitutions and women's culture. Even for those who sought to change the dominant social order, the political lessons of C-R groups were obscure; the links between the personal and political did not reveal any unambiguously compelling strategy for social change. Faced with an impasse when it came to identifying effective social change strategies, many rap groups dissolved once their consciousness-raising function had run its course, with some members moving to other groups that sought to bring about broader social change in the dominant society.

The difficulties of moving from consciousness-raising to political activism were inextricably entangled with the movement's second distinguishing characteristic: the preference for small, structureless groups. Notions of participatory democracy had already been a major component of New Left and civil rights activism, but in these movements advocacy of such forms frequently coexisted with systematic male domination. In response to this imperfectly realized ideal, women's liberationists became even more strongly committed to egalitarian, nonhierarchical forms of group organization in an attempt to avoid the problems of oligarchical control and the dynamics of oppression within movements. This insistence led to very creative solutions to the problem of group maintenance, including techniques for rotating group tasks that precluded any one subgroup from formally monopolizing power and resources. It also contributed to the empowerment of women who were rotated into tasks for which they might not have volunteered, and in which they developed important skills and insights into movement dynamics.

However, the movement's dedication to structureless groups also created a number of problems that became increasingly evident as groups wrestled with these issues. One dysfunctional consequence of this ideal was that an antileadership consensus emerged that could be harshly critical of anyone who even attempted to provide guidance and direction for the group. From 1969 through 1971, which has been described as the movement's "McCarthy era" (Hole and Levine 1971:160), these dynamics led to charges of elitism, promoted purges of individuals who were seen as violating the antileadership consensus, and created a group of "feminist refugees" who were banished for violating the ethos of leaderlessness and structurelessness. Because this was also a period of intense media coverage of the movement, another dysfunctional consequence was the emergence of a "star system," which the antileadership ethos was explicitly intended to avoid. If groups refused to select their own leaders, the media often did so for them by seeking out particular "personalities" for their views on movement events. Such "stars" were especially likely to be charged with elitism and to be "trashed" by those defending the antileadership ethos.

As Jo Freeman has noted (1972/3, 1975), the commitment to structurelessness did not produce groups without structure but rather groups with informal structures. This was an ironic result for a movement that had argued against the power of "old boys' networks" in other organizations and yet remained insensitive to how such informal structures could arise within their own ranks. The informal structure of these groups tended to emerge from friendship networks, which created divisions between "ins" and "outs," with no formal recourse for newcomers to gain access to such groups. While friendship networks were useful for some tasks, on balance they were ineffective at achieving goals beyond the maintenance of the group itself. As a result, many groups gravitated away from radical social change and goal attainment toward ameliorative service projects and group maintenance. The preoccupation with internal process promoted personal change over institutional change, reinforcing tendencies already inherent in the consciousness-raising strategy of this sector of the movement. As a result of these dynamics, the radical potential of many of the small groups began to erode at the very time that bureaucratic organizations were moving in a somewhat more radical direction (Freeman 1975:145).

An ideological preference for small, relatively structureless groups has helped the women's liberation movement respond to highly politicized conflict by permitting the formation of a new group whenever differences could not be resolved in a preexisting group. Some of the divisive issues reflect the heritage of the women's liberation movement in other movements, while others have emerged during the mobilization process itself. Some of the earlier schisms were overcome by a massive influx of new members at the turn of the decade who were unfamiliar with the language and history of these divisions. They resurfaced in the mid-1970s, however, when the differing orientations of socialist feminism and radical feminism became increasingly clear within the movement. Socialist feminists sought a synthesis of leftist analyses sensitive to class and race issues, with feminist analyses oriented to gender. Radical feminists asserted the primacy of gender as the root of all hierarchy and domination. Socialist feminists insisted on the need for including working-class women, minority women, Third World women, and an anti-imperialist stance; radical feminists reasserted the primacy of gender and rejected the lingering imprint of Marxism within socialist feminism.

A second major fault line within the movement concerns lesbianism. Many lesbians found the women's liberation movement to be one of the few hospitable places in a heterosexist society, and joined or came out within the movement for this reason. Given its commitment to radicalism, the women's liberation sector was initially more receptive to lesbians than the women's rights sector. Lesbianism became more controversial when some argued that it was the purest form of personal politics one could attain within the movement. The concept of "woman-identified-women" was a logical extension of the strategy of consciousness-raising, insisting that women take other women rather than men as their reference group. Appealing to the notion that the personal is political, this view could privilege lesbian relations over heterosexual or bisexual relations and thereby advocate separatism as the ultimate goal of the women's movement. Although this was powerfully appealing to some, many women found this argument hopelessly utopian and needlessly divisive, pointing out that seeking solutions in personal relationships was a traditional female response that precluded working for social change and ignored other oppressions.

These debates and divisions were strongest within the women's liberation sector during the early 1970s, when positions were articulated in their most radical form. In a highly structured and formally organized movement, these dynamics would have led to major leadership battles and struggles over priorities and directions for the organization — as happened within NOW. In a loosely linked, informally organized, unstructured movement, these dynamics reinforced preexisting tendencies toward diffusion, dispersion, and fragmentation. The results are deceptive, because on the surface it would appear that the women's liberation movement simply burned itself out and that its former members have either gravitated to more organized groups or become inactive. A more appropriate metaphor would be that the late 1960s and early 1970s were indeed the bonfire phase of women's liberation, but rather than burning out, the residual sparks and embers of this white-hot phase have drifted in many directions, where the embers continue to glow and are periodically fanned into flames by the winds of social change. Put differently, the centrifugal tendencies of modern feminism (Cott 1987) have meant that ideas with ideological origins in the women's liberation movement have found their way into numerous institutional and cultural niches, where they continue to modify social organization and inform social practices.

The result of this dispersion is that it is now possible to speak of a "feminist community" that, like the women's liberation movement, is localized and loosely linked but nonetheless can be found in virtually every major city and many smaller ones as well. One center in this multicentered community may be found in women's studies programs and women's centers at colleges and universities, which provide cohesion to these communities and exposure for many thousands of students to feminism as an academic/activist worldview. Other centers include feminist bookstores, restaurants, and coffeehouses, battered women's shelters and rape crisis centers, and self-defense classes. Still others include feminist health clinics, woman-owned businesses, women's caucuses within non-feminist organizations, feminist spirituality groups, and women's peace groups. Women's music and literature serve to connect diverse locales into a national network (see Ferree and Hess 1985:94–103). In some cases, these centers operate as alternative communities or counterinstitutions in quasi-separatist fashion (see Whittier and Taylor [1989] for an analysis of lesbian feminist communities); in other cases these centers have provided a basis for ongoing mobilization and progressive reform of dominant institutions. The role of rape crisis centers and battered women's shelters in transforming both the legal system and the conduct of police and judges in many communities is a case in point.

The survival of a feminist community, particularly through the politically hostile climate of the 1980s, requires an elaboration of social movement theory. The organizational bias of resource mobilization theory is most evident here, for such an approach would conclude that in the absence of formally organized social movement organizations, a social movement is inert. The concept of a "social movement community" — as a parallel to that of a "social movement organization" — is required to conceptually capture the feminist community described here. This community is a direct descendant of the women's liberation sector of the contemporary women's movement, and it continues to play a politically activist role in diverse struggles to improve the position of women. The fact that it is more difficult to identify, measure, and study with traditional theories and concepts about social movements does not mean that it does not exist or is not important, but rather that our theories and concepts must be sensitized to the creative forms that a continually proliferating and dispersing social movement has managed to create in the wake of its most public and dramatic periods of mobilization. One indication that such new theorizing is underway is provided by a recent analysis of the role of primary groups as providing a dialectical blend of spontaneity and democracy, which often leads to effective protest (see Rosenthal and Schwartz forthcoming).

The foregoing analysis of the women's liberation movement may be broadened by considering the history of one particular group that differed in important respects from some of the patterns described previously. The Chicago Women's Liberation Union (CWLU) was organized in 1969 and survived until 1977 as a socialist-feminist action-oriented women's group within Chicago and surrounding communities. It grew out of the Students for a Democratic Society and a Women's Radical Action Project. From its origins, the CWLU saw women's liberation as a revolutionary struggle embedded in a larger struggle for from membership in the group. After the 1975 socialist-feminist conference, an Asian Women's Group (an affiliate of Workers' Viewpoint, a Maoist organization) joined the CWLU and initiated a major debate over the role of Marxism-Leninism as a strategy for progressive movements. Specific struggles over this issue combined with the general decline of the left after 1975 to contribute to the demise of the CWLU in 1977.

The CWLU was also distinctive in its organizational structure. The group proclaimed, "We are dedicated to a democratic organization and understand that a way to ensure democrarcy is through full exchange of information and ideas, full political debate, and through the unity of theory and practice" (Chicago Women's Liberation Union, n.d.[c]). These principles were embodied in a structure that consisted of a steering committee, a planning committee (added in 1974), an annual membership conference, a small paid staff, work groups, chapters, and general membership. As the main policy-making body, the steering committee consisted of one representative from each chapter and work group and it met every two weeks. The planning committee consisted of five people responsible for day-to-day functioning, coordination of staff, and long-term planning. The annual membership meeting provided an opportunity for members to vote directly on organizational policy, as did yearly program meetings. Since all members were required to be active in either a chapter or a work group, individuals had two avenues of input: through their representative on the steering committee and through membership and program meetings.

Compared to most women's liberation groups, the CWLU thus had a well-defined organizational structure that contributed to greater effectiveness in accomplishing specific tasks and goals. The group's response to the danger of oligarchy was not to eschew organization entirely, but rather to create structures and processes that maximized participation and minimized the opportunities for an oligarchical elite to emerge. By demanding a high degree of activity, involvement, and participation from all members, the CWLU sought to insure that all views and constituencies were continually represented in setting policy. In addition, various subgroups presented position papers and working proposals on how to reform organizational structure and process to maximize participation. While addressing an organizational problem, these policies doubtless heightened recruitment problems because the group demanded such a high level of involvement from its membership. On the whole, however, the CWLU struck a healthy balance between achieving external goals and monitoring internal processes. Its structure thus made it an effective agent of social change and a gratifying form of activism for many of its members.

Groups like the CWLU dissolved because of sectarian disputes within the larger context of the decline of the left. While the CWLU lasted longer than

the liberation of all oppressed peoples. The group was committed to fighting ra
ism, imperialism, and capitalism, to self-determination for all people, and to th
liberation of homosexuals, especially lesbians (Chicago Women's Liberatio
Union n.d.[a]). Seeking the eventual development of a mass movement, the or
ganization nevertheless rejected the model of a large, passive paper membership
by insisting that members play active roles within the organization and the community. Every member of the CWLU was required to join a chapter or work
group and thereby become actively involved in some specific activity of the organization.

Stressing action projects over theoretical development or consciousness-
raising, the CWLU maintained more than a dozen chapters and work groups.
Direct Action for Rights in Employment addressed sex discrimination in city
government. The Abortion Task Force made referrals and worked to provide
high-quality, low-cost abortions accompanied by pro-woman counseling. The
Health Project sought decent, affordable women's health care in several
Chicago hospitals and medical centers. The Action Committee for Decent
Childcare focused on funding and licensing problems around child-care issues.
The Rape Crisis Line provided services to victims of sexual assault, while the
Legal Clinic provided free legal counseling to women. The Graphics Collective
designed and displayed artwork depicting women's struggles, while the CWLU
Rock Band performed and recorded music that affirmed women. The Liberation
School for Women offered a variety of courses in diverse locations throughout
the city to educate and empower women in the struggle for their own liberation.
The Gay Women's Group developed analyses and programs relevant to lesbians.
The CWLU's newsletter kept members informed of all these activities, and its
monthly newspaper, *Womankind*, was designed to reach out to women not already involved in the women's liberation movement (Chicago Women's Liberation Union n.d.[b]).

In addition to its activist orientation, the CWLU differed from many other
women's liberation groups in its ideology and structure. During its origins, it
bridged the ideological split between politicos and feminists by its focus on multiple oppressions while also placing women's liberation at the center of its program. In 1972, the organization adopted lengthy position papers on "Socialist
Feminism: A Strategy for the Women's Movement" and "Lesbianism and Socialist Feminism." In 1975, the CWLU was one of the groups instrumental in calling
a nationwide socialist-feminist conference in Ohio. Its New Left roots and
socialist-feminist ideology gave the CWLU a broader and more inclusive focus
than many groups, but also saddled it with sectarian battles that drained its energy. In 1970 and 1971, the efforts of the Young Socialist Alliance to infiltrate the
group were so disruptive that the CWLU debated a policy to bar party women

many of the small, structureless groups of the women's liberation movement, all of these self-professed revolutionary groups had relatively short lifespans. Although some former members of groups like the CWLU have become politically inactive, many others have become part of the feminist social movement community, where they continue to play an activist role around particular issues. Others have found hospitable niches within national organizations. Still others have become involved in local political campaigns, advocacy groups, and coalition politics. The later 1970s and 1980s have seen the demise of many movement organizations, a dearth of media attention, a considerable backlash and countermovement, and a shift to less flamboyant tactics. The contemporary women's movement nonetheless persists between the twin poles of an interest-group organizational presence on the national level and a feminist social movement community in diverse localities across the country.

Conclusions

Women's movements in the United States have used a strikingly diverse array of organizational forms in pursuit of movement goals. At one extreme is the National Women's Party. The NWP was a cadre organization with rigid hierarchy, tight discipline, authoritarian leadership, close coordination, and tactical militance. At the other extreme is the social movement community derived from the women's liberation movement, with informal networks, loose links, flexible goals, rotating leadership, and decentralized structures. Between these extremes are organizations like the National American Woman Suffrage Association and the National Organization for Women: national, bureaucratic, mass membership movement umbrellas under which a number of specific campaigns were and are carried out. The diversity of forms illustrates the importance of seeing the question of organization at both the formal and informal level, and of appreciating the connections between these levels as movements act over time. Each of these forms of organization also have important implications for movement strategies, tactics, and goals.

The history of organizations in women's movements confirms much of the social movement literature on organization in other movements. One of the truisms of this literature is that bureaucratic, centralized movement organizations are often the most effective means of pursuing instrumental goals and achieving social change. The hierarchy, discipline, and top-down control of an organization like the NWP is the clearest illustration of this priniciple. Although its goals were not as broad, this organization had many of the features of a Leninist vanguard party, which resolutely pursues a clearly defined objective. From its origin in the later stages of the suffrage battle to its promotion of the Equal Rights Amendment in the 1920s, the NWP maintained a singleminded focus on the goals it set for itself and marshalled all available resources toward these goals while tolerating little internal dissent or deviation. Given its orientation, the militant tactics of the NWP make sense as a means of gaining publicity and maximizing pressure on those who had the power to make a difference, even if these tactics did alienate some potential support. Although the recent struggle for the ERA had many parallels to the historic battle for woman suffrage, there was no parallel to the NWP in the ERA struggle. It is possible that if such a tightly disciplined and highly coordinated movement organization had been present from the very beginning of the ratification effort, greater success might have resulted.

Organizations like the National American Woman Suffrage Association and the National Organization for Women are also located on the bureaucratic, centralized end of the organizational spectrum, but both differ in important respects from the NWP. While national in scope, NAWSA was and NOW is a federated group seeking a mass membership and incorporating local, state, and regional subgroups. This creates the potential for a great deal of internal organizational conflict over the allocation of movement resources and decision-making power. By their very nature, such organizations must devote considerable energy to managing this conflict, arbitrating group differences, and formulating organizational policy. Such organizations rarely, if ever, achieve the tightly coordinated discipline of smaller, cadrelike organizations. The NAWSA/NOW comparison is instructive in that many of their internal organizational dynamics were similar despite the fact that NAWSA was a single-issue group and NOW has always been a multi-issue organization. The history of NAWSA suggests that even when pursuing a single goal such as female enfranchisement, a national, federated organizational structure will generate internal conflict, as exemplified by the debate over the Shafroth-Palmer resolution, which paralyzed NAWSA at a vital stage in the suffrage struggle.

The strengths of national, federated mass membership organizations derive from the same organizational features that create some of the problems just described. As mass organizations, they can often generate and mobilize substantial movement resources by calling on a large and diverse membership to contribute time, money, expertise, and energy to movement campaigns. If movement goals include passage or ratification of federal legislation, a federated organizational structure is a virtual prerequisite for success because it permits pressure to be applied on all the state or regional representatives who are essential to winning the legislation. Such organizations are also vital in generating and transmitting information about successes and failures in different areas, creating an important learning mechanism allowing movements to act more effectively in future efforts than they may have in past endeavors. Mass federated organizations also create an institutional presence for a movement, and by that presence often gain legitimacy for at least some of the movement's goals and issues. In so doing, such organizations often create and protect vital social space in which diverse goals, campaigns, and issues can be pursued under the broad umbrella of the national organization.

While centralized bureaucratic organizations are most effective for pursuing instrumental goals and achieving social change, they often face recruitment problems because their goals seem remote from the everyday lives of the potential membership. Hence, selective incentives are frequently required to motivate people to join the organization and overcome the free-rider dilemma. In smaller, decentralized, less structured groups of the sort that were typical in the women's liberation movement, motivation and recruitment were not major problems; indeed, many of these groups were overwhelmed by the influx of new members in the late 1960s and early 1970s. Much of the attraction of these groups was their explicit recognition that the personal was political and that all women had much to gain and share in direct and immediate ways from joining the movement. The loosely structured, open-ended, small-scale character of rap groups made it relatively easy for the timid to come forward and find validation of their experience and support in what had previously been lonely, isolated struggles. Hence, the size, structure, and orientation of these groups made them a very effective recruiting device for the women's liberation movement.

Once again, the features of these groups that made them attractive and powerful recruiting tools simultaneously imposed limitations on what these groups were able to accomplish. In Elizabeth Fox-Genovese's (1979) memorable phrase, the personal is not political enough; hence, these groups were often unable to effectively transcend personal experience, expressive goals, and individual transformation. These outcomes were logical extensions of the lack of structure at the heart of these groups. Jo Freeman has argued that there were two major constraints on the utilization of movement resources by the small groups that made up the women's liberation movement (1979). The first was their unrelenting opposition to any structure that smacked of hierarchy; the second was their adoption of radicalism as a major reference point. The fear of cooptation that accompanied the insistence on radicalism often reduced these groups to inactivity and reinforced the tendency to focus on C-R strategies to the exclusion of more activist undertakings. The resulting paradox was that the self-professedly radical groups were often the ones who accomplished the least structural change, while the reformist groups often accomplished more such change despite their "reformism."

The history of the Chicago Women's Liberation Union demonstrates that it is possible for an organization to overcome some of these typical movement patterns. Though a small group, it was nonetheless dedicated to certain structural principles. Though radical in orientation, it was committed to action projects rather than consciousness-raising. Though clearly structured, it sought to maximize participation from its membership through democratic processes within the organization. Because of its radical ideology, the CWLU tended to recruit relatively small numbers of highly committed members. Because of the demands the organization placed on its membership, even highly committed members quickly felt overwhelmed by the group's commitment to activism. The small size and high demands of the CWLU helped make it effective in carrying out a number of action projects, but these features also made it vulnerable to the forces that led to its dissolution. When the left underwent a general decline in the later 1970s and sectarian disputes overwhelmed the organization, it was not able to maintain itself in a more hostile external and internal climate.

As we have seen, the contemporary movement has left a dual legacy in the form of NOW as a quasi-interest group and as a semi-institutionalized social movement organization alongside a more diffuse feminist community with strong roots in various locales. I have termed the latter a social movement community to underscore its significant role in movement activity despite its lack of formal organization. The formulation of this concept invites speculation about the role of other movement communities before, alongside, and after movements have taken formal organizational shape. In the woman suffrage movement, the concept of a social movement community is one way of capturing the pre-organizational elements of feminist networks and sentiment associated with the abolitionist movement before and just after the Civil War. Created and sustained by periodic women's rights conventions in the antebellum period, this community existed for twenty-five years before taking formal organizational shape. The concept of a social movement community may also have some applicability to the social worlds of moral reformers associated with causes like temperance and social purity, which were one type of recruiting ground for the suffrage movement. Finally, it may be possible to speak of a broader social movement community that coalesced in the early twentieth century and made possible the cross-class, multiconstituency alliance that was instrumental in finally winning the suffrage amendment.

In the contemporary women's movement, the notion of a social movement community may have parallel applications. It is one way of describing the growth of feminist sentiment and networks in both the state commissions on the status of women and the New Left and civil rights movements. The concept's most obvious applicability is to the informally organized small groups and social networks that constituted the women's liberation movement from the late 1960s to the mid-1970s. It is also useful, however, for capturing the persisting nature of feminist sentiment, the establishment of feminist counterinstitutions, and the periodic evidence of overt activism that constitute the contemporary feminist community. In the creation and maintenance of this feminist community, the contemporary women's movement has made its most unique contribution both to the cause of feminism and to broadening our conventional understanding of the forms and processes that social movements can take in pursuit of their varied agendas.

The varied organizational forms of the women's movement also inform our understanding of the nature of movement radicalism and questions of oligarchy, organizational maintenance, and the like. The oft-noted distinction between the radical National Woman Suffrage Association and the more conservative American Woman Suffrage Association has some parallel in the distinction between the more radical women's liberation movement and the less radical women's rights movement. In both centuries, radicalism derived from a dual impulse to question the connections between public roles and private lives in a context of sexual inequality. In the case of NWSA, the focus was on both public/institutional roles and marital/domestic roles. In the case of the women's liberation movement, the challenge was to both societal inequality and interpersonal sexism. More conservative approaches in both centuries tended to limit their focus to specific, public, legally grounded forms of inequality and discrimination.

Concerning movement transformation over time, I have argued elsewhere that the woman suffrage movement underwent a major shift from a broadly focused, ideologically radical movement to a more narrowly focused, specialized movement to win the vote (Buechler 1986). The causes of this transformation involved changes in class structure and organizational dynamics. In the contemporary movement, the orientation of an organization like NOW has been influenced by what Zald and Ash call the "ebb and flow of sentiments" in the larger society (1966). In the early to mid-1970s, NOW took its most radical stance in response to the vitality of the women's liberation movement. With the shift to a more conservative climate and the fragmentation of the women's liberation movement, NOW returned to a less radical posture by the late 1970s. The women's liberation movement was clearly more radical in theory, in vision, and in organizational experimentation than was the women's rights movement. However, as Freeman has noted (1979), the very dedication of this sector to radicalism fostered such a strong antiorganizational sentiment that it was frequently reduced to consciousness-raising and personal transformation.

A final lesson to emerge from this comparative analysis concerns the relation between movement goals and organizational form. The later suffrage movement saw two rather different movement organizations, but both reflected what the leadership of each believed was required to win suffrage. NAWSA under Catt and the NWP under Paul were both designed to win passage and ratification of the suffrage amendment, and their organizational structure was dictated by this goal. As we have seen, NOW has some resemblances to NAWSA, but NOW's organizational structure has undergone much variation in its relatively short history. This variation is due not only to the influence of the women's liberation movement, but also to the multiple issues, shifting priorities, and variable goals that have characterized NOW. Hence, there has been a certain fluidity of organizational form as NOW has pursued different movement goals in turn. By contrast, many of the goals of the women's liberation movement have been too broad to be captured in particular legislation or public policy proposals, so this movement has not needed the organizational structures found in other sectors of the movement. At the same time, this sector's self-conscious attempt to prefigure a nonhierarchical society has led it to eschew the formality of a social movement organization and embrace the collectivity of a social movement community. The diverse goals of the women's movement have thereby promoted a wide variety of organizational forms; this diversity and variety is evident not only in organization but also in movement ideology.

Chapter three

Ideologies and Visions

Social movements require organization to provide the capacity for action, but they also require ideology to supply the motivation to mobilize. In the broadest sense, ideology encompasses the ideas, beliefs, values, symbols, and meanings that motivate individual participation and give coherence to the collective activities of the movement. Ideological beliefs typically provide a critical diagnosis of the movement's surrounding society, an idealized sketch of a preferable alternative, and some suggestion as to how the problematic present may be replaced with a preferable future. Ideologies are present in the very origins of movements because they help constitute the groups that become involved in movement activity. They are critical in the early stages of mobilization because they provide a sense of collective identity that is a prerequisite for acting collectively. As movements survive and achieve some success, ideologies may well provide the basis for schism and disputes between "purists" and "realists" over the future course of the movement. Over time, ideologies may themselves be subject to substantial transformations in response to diverse movement processes. Ideology is thus neither static nor peripheral to movement activity; it is, rather, a central component in the life of a social movement.

The centrality of ideology to social movements requires emphasis because several sociological traditions of analysis have proceeded as if this were not the case. For rather different reasons, the older collective behavior tradition and the newer resource mobilization approach both marginalize the role of ideology in the study of social movements. In much of the collective behavior tradition, the role of ideas as motivators was recognized but the ideas themselves were often simply dismissed as nonsensical fantasies or irrational generalized beliefs

(Smelser 1963). This logically follows from the tendency in this tradition to treat all forms of collective behavior as if they existed on the same continuum. From this perspective, the ideologies of movements were only slightly more complex versions of the fundamentally irrational ideas that motivated panics, crazes, fads, and the like. Several unfortunate consequences resulted from this approach: movement participants were assumed to be irrational; their ideas were assumed to be nonsensical; and even when ideas were acknowledged as motivating action they were dismissed as unworthy of further analysis. These assumptions amounted to an a priori negative judgment on the validity of a movement's ideology and the legitimacy of its grievances, and precluded analysis of movement ideology as a logical expression of a group's material interests.

Several strands of resource moblization theory have treated ideology as equally marginal, though for different reasons. Resource mobilization theorists acknowledge that ideology may be rational and that it may motivate individuals to participate in movements; however, they have also argued that ideology in general and grievances in particular are constantly present in dispossessed groups. If this is so, then they have no utility for explaining the variable (indeed, rare) appearance of social movement activity. In their efforts to explain why movements appear in some times and places and not others, some resource mobilization theorists have therefore dismissed ideology as a constant background factor with no real analytical significance for the dynamics of movement activity. They have focused instead on variable factors such as the degree and type of resources available to a group, thereby explaining periodic movement mobilization as the result of a group's changing access to movement resources and opportunities for collective action (McCarthy and Zald 1977).

As part of a larger theoretical effort to redirect attention away from social psychological processes and toward macro-structural factors, this argument had considerable merit. Now that such a redirection has occurred, it becomes appropriate to restore the study of ideology to a central position in the study of social movements. Ideas, beliefs, values, symbols, and meanings are not necessarily irrational fantasies or irrelevant constants in the genesis and dynamics of social movement activity. If ideology is constitutive of group identity, then ideology is an essential prerequisite for groups to be able to identify opportunities to act and resources to utilize in their social environment. A careful look at many social movement constituencies — workers, women, gays and lesbians, ethnic groups — suggests that group identity is highly variable rather than a simple constant of group life. If the degree of group identity is variable, then grievances based on that group identity must also be variable. It is thus possible to reverse the logic of the resource mobilization argument by identifying group identity and ideology as the variable factors against a backdrop of resources and opportunities that determine when a movement will mobilize for action.

These considerations suggest that a more dialectical view of the relation between ideology and other resources is appropriate. If both are seen as related and interacting factors in movement mobilization, a more nuanced view of movement development becomes possible. Thus, the availability of resources and opportunities may promote action that fosters group identity and ideology. Alternately, the presence of a particular ideology may be equally important in creating and fostering the opportunities and resources necessary for action. Ideology and group identity may thus make the difference between an individual or a collectivity viewing its time, money, and skills as simply discretionary assets and viewing them as vitally needed movement resources. In this sense, the presence or absence of a particular ideology symbolically defines what may or may not be movement resources, with obvious consequences for mobilization by movement groups. All these considerations suggest, in contrast to the collective behavior tradition as well as some versions of resource mobilization, that the analysis of ideology warrants a central place in the study of social movements.

Women's movements provide particularly good examples of the centrality of ideology in the generation of social movements. The structural dispersal of women throughout all classes, races, and other social groups constitutes a major barrier to the mobilization of women's movements. This barrier can sometimes be overcome by utilizing preexisting social networks as a nascent form of organization for movement mobilization, but many such networks exist without generating a women's movement. Ideology is a critical factor in politicizing such preexisting networks, generating collective identity, and motivating women to become involved in a women's movement. It is ideology that redefines traditional practices as instances of oppression, discrimination, or segregation, that frames particular issues as movement grievances and provides the required motivation for individuals to become active movement participants. The argument that grievances are a constant background factor fares particularly poorly in the case of women's movements. For most women throughout most history, sexist practices have not been perceived as grievances that could be altered through movement activity. It is only through an ideological reframing (Snow and Benford 1988) on the movement level and consciousness-raising on the individual level that such practices came to be defined as grievances that could be redressed through mobilization of a women's movement.

The role of ideology and group identity may be clarified through Chafe's distinctions between four stages of group behavior among women (1977:7–8). In the first stage women perform similar activities with no sense of doing so because they are women. In the second, women engage in similar behavior from an implicit understanding of women's place or women's work, which mandates such behavior. In the third stage, women consciously articulate a sense of group identity and act on that identity. In the fourth stage, women not only act collectively but also act out of a shared sense of grievance, anger, or oppression. Chafe suggests that the first two stages represent the bulk of human history, during which gender was a basic principle of social organization but was not consiously articulated. The latter stages represent typically modern forms of collective action that are consciously based on gender identity. Whereas the third confirms societal gender norms (women in charitable societies), the fourth challenges those norms in some fashion (women in feminist movements). The fourth stage in this classification is the least common both historically and numerically, and is also the only stage in which grievances are consciously articulated. Far from being constants, the perception and articulation of grievances by women's movements are relatively rare; and when they do occur they are frequently challenged by countermovements of women. Chafe's distinctions help underscore the extent to which the identification and expression of grievances form a complex process of symbolic framing to which ideology — broadly understood — makes a central contribution.

The following analysis of ideology will distinguish between the woman suffrage movement and the contemporary women's movement, but this should not obscure the continuities between these periods. Olive Banks has argued that older and newer women's movements should be seen as a single, continuous historical process (1981). Within this process, she detects three distinct ideological traditions that may be traced back to the women's rights movement of the mid-nineteenth century. One such tradition was evangelical Christianity, which attracted women because it resonated with societal gender norms but nonetheless promoted the development of a more oppositional feminist stance. One persistent theme in this tradition has been an emphasis on women's moral superiority, which found expression in numerous campaigns for social betterment and moral uplift. A second tradition emerged from Enlightenment philosophy, with characteristic stress on natural rights, liberal individualism, and sexual equality. Whereas the evangelical tradition appealed to a distinctive woman's essence, the Enlightenment tradition emphasized an environmentalist approach to understanding and transcending differences between the sexes. The third tradition is socialist feminism, distinguished by its stress on secular and communal values in contradistinction to the religiosity of evangelical Christianity and the individualism of Enlightenment philosophy. The woman suffrage movement succeeded in part because the demand for the suffrage could be embraced by all three "faces of feminism" identified by Banks. Viewing feminism as a continuous historical process, Banks traces how these traditions of moral superiority, equal rights, and communal egalitarianism continue to inform the feminist movement in the latter half of the twentieth century.

Nancy Cott (1986) has identified some important patterns in the ideological history of women's movements as well. Cott's question does not concern typological distinctions, but rather the conditions under which truly mass movements of women have appeared. Cott stresses that such occurrences are relatively rare and typically short-lived because of the difficulties of mobilizing women across class and race lines. When mass movements have emerged (specifically, the suffrage movement from 1912 to 1919 and the contemporary movement from 1967 to 1974), several conditions have been present. For one, movement ideology in such periods has been able to accommodate both sameness and difference in pursuit of movement goals. For another, such movements have emerged when (some) women have had instrumental reasons for advancing gender interests. Finally, such movements emerged during periods of overall political and cultural rebellion that provided the ideological space, movement resources, and political opportunity for such activity. Cott's argument reminds us that mass movements have thrived not when feminist ideology was seen as an "either/or" issue, but rather when it was seen as a "both/and" question. When women's movements have been able to argue for and from sameness and difference, for equal rights and special contributions, and for justice and expediency, mass movements of women have emerged and thrived.

The analysis that follows examines the role of ideology in the woman suffrage movement and in the contemporary women's movement. In the former case, a dominant theme concerns the ideological transformations the suffrage movement underwent during its lengthy history. As we shall see, these transformations had the paradoxical character of weakening the movement's critique of patriarchal society at the same time that they rendered the movement strategically more effective in pursuing the goal of suffrage. The dominant theme of the analysis of ideology in the contemporary movement is that of diversity, as a number of distinct ideological standpoints have developed (and sometimes subsequently disappeared) in a relatively short time. The diversity of standpoints in the contemporary movement poses its own paradoxes. There are important respects in which that diversity is a movement resource that has contributed to a strong and persistent movement. That diversity has also led to a certain degree of unproductive factionalism, however, and it may actually reflect the deradicalization or the dissolution of earlier and more fundamental challenges to the patriarchal status quo. The evidence about the role of ideology in the women's movement is thus multivocal and polyphonic; it thereby supports multiple and conflicting interpretations about the movement's past history and future trajectory.

The Woman Suffrage Movement

The woman suffrage movement offers a complex case of ideological continuities, contradictions, and transformations over a seventy-year period. Throughout its history, the movement tended to argue for the vote from diverse and often conflicting premises about the nature and role of women. For much of this history, the contradictions and inconsistencies in suffragist ideology appeared to be a weakness, preventing activists from mounting a coordinated campaign for the vote. With the benefit of hindsight, such diversity may be seen as the movement's greatest strength, for it meant that the movement ultimately developed a variety of prosuffrage arguments that appealed to virtually every subgroup of women and resonated not just with their general identity as women but with their particular identities as working women, married women, rural women, middle-class women, or mothers.

While the ideology of the suffrage movement became more instrumentally effective in agitating for the right to vote as the movement entered the twentieth century, a more subtle shift occurred in the meaning of this goal. In the 1850s, the ballot was inextricably linked to a range of demands for women's rights in both the public and private spheres. By the 1910s, the same ballot demand had become detached from this larger program, the movement had become a specialized, single-issue effort, and many prosuffrage arguments reinforced rather than challenged societal notions of gender. In instrumental terms, this was a major victory, because suffragists worked tremendously hard to portray votes for women in nonthreatening terms that would allow legislators to support and ratify the suffrage amendment. In substantive terms, this detachment of the vote from a larger feminist program meant that winning the ballot would not in itself accomplish the multiple goals of the original women's rights campaigns. In symbolic terms, the vote remained overburdened with glorious expectations by suffragists and fearful consequences by opponents; in reality, neither side saw its glory or its fears realized. The causes of these changes in movement ideology involved broad patterns of social change as well as specific movement initiatives, which combined to transform a broadly oriented women's rights movement into a narrowly focused woman suffrage movement.

Olive Banks's comparative study of feminism in Britain and the United

States provides a framework for analyzing specific ideological questions in the women's rights and woman suffrage movements (1981). Banks concurs with the general notion of movement transformation sketched above, arguing that the movement changed from a radical minority movement before 1870 to a more conservative mass movement leading to the suffrage victory in 1920. These shifts in the relative radicalism or conservatism of the movement reflect changes in the specific weight of the three feminist traditions she identifies as contributing to the movement. Evangelism was important in the early period because it drew many women into the abolitionist cause, which proved an important training ground for later women's rights activism and may well have converted some evangelically oriented women to an equal rights orientation. The dominant tradition in this period was that of equal rights, with roots in Enlightenment notions of reason, radicalism, and natural rights. The relative radicalism of this orientation was reinforced by the prominence of the third face of feminism rooted in the socialist tradition, which emphasized economic cooperation and communitarian values. This particular ideological constellation produced a radical women's movement that appealed to a rather small minority of followers.

After 1870, changes in this ideological constellation moderated the orientation of the women's movement. The evangelical orientation to reform became more predominant, and increasing numbers of women became involved in moral reform. Specific campaigns for sexual purity and temperance best exemplify this tendency. Such causes appealed to larger numbers of women because they resonated with dominant cultural norms about the role of women as nurturers, caretakers, and moral guardians. As these women became involved in the movement, the premise of female superiority became more pronounced as the legitimation for women's involvement in these specific causes. By the turn of the century, these same impulses became evident in support for protective labor legislation for working women. The consequence, if not the intent, of such reform was to increase discrimination against and segregation of women in the labor force. As the evangelical tradition became the dominant motif in suffragist ideology, the equal rights and socialist traditions became minor themes in the agitation and argumentation for the right to vote for women.

Aileen Kraditor (1965) characterizes transformation in the suffrage movement as involving a shift in the kinds of arguments the movement made for the right to vote. Until about 1900, the movement tended to rely on what Kraditor calls justice arguments for the vote. After that point, the movement was more likely to use expediency arguments for the vote. Earlier justice arguments claimed that women deserved the vote on the simple basis of justice, and that the ballot for women was consistent with basic political principles embedded in the Declaration of Independence and the U.S. Constitution. Later expediency arguments claimed that women needed the vote to accomplish other goals and objectives, including temperance and protective legislation. These two types of argument were based on different assumptions about equality and difference between the sexes. Justice arguments assumed that men and women were the same in important respects, and that they were entitled to equality on the basis of natural rights and a common citizenship. Expediency arguments assumed that men and women were different in important respects, and that women had a unique perspective on the social world and a distinctive role to play in its reform, which necessitated the ballot. Whereas justice arguments promoted a radical individualism, expediency arguments fostered a social feminism rooted in women's presumed distinctive qualities as a group.

The shift Kraditor describes is best seen as a change in emphasis, because the movement in fact made "expediency" arguments from the beginning and used "justice" arguments to the end (Leach 1980; Buechler 1986). The shift in emphasis is nonetheless important, and it is consistent with Banks's notion of a movement that increasingly relied on an evangelical tradition of social reform rather than an equality tradition of individual rights. Another aspect of this change in movement argumentation for the vote is also important. Justice arguments had an inherently oppositional character because they directly challenged societal gender assumptions. Expediency arguments did not challenge these assumptions, and often reinforced them by using stereotypically feminine qualities as a basis for seeking the vote. The shift from justice to expediency as a basis of suffragist ideology thus had several consequences. It allowed the movement to recruit larger numbers, it brought more conservative women into the movement, it presented a more moderate face to the surrounding society, and it increased movement chances for success in winning the vote. At the same time, it helped detach the vote from a larger feminist program of equality and individual rights, it allowed some groups to argue for the vote to promote conservative ends, and it reinforced rather than challenged dominant notions about sex and gender.

William O'Neill identifies the distinctiveness of the early suffrage movement somewhat differently (1969). For O'Neill, the early movement demanded suffrage as part of a broad agenda aimed at securing equal rights in many areas. The best example here is the consideration given to the "marriage question" by the National Woman Suffrage Association and by Elizabeth Cady Stanton in particular. In one formulation by this group, "woman's chief discontent is . . . her social, and . . . marital bondage." Compared to this, the ballot was "not even half the loaf; it is only a crust — a crumb . . . [a] superficial and fragmentary question" (quoted in O'Neill 1969:19–20). In its critique of marriage, of the cult of domesticity, of the sexual division of labor, and of the legal system that reinforced all these practices, the NWSA exemplified the broader feminist program of emancipation that was present in the women's rights movement before and just after the Civil War and included the right to vote as one among a number of social changes sought on the basis of justice and natural rights. In O'Neill's account, substantial transformation occurred in the orientation of the women's movement in the 1870s and 1880s (somewhat earlier than Kraditor's justice-to-expediency shift), when hard-core feminism was gradually displaced by social feminism. This was also a shift from a premise of equality between the sexes to premises of difference and of a distinctive female essence whose disenfranchisement was all the more regrettable precisely because of the differing worldviews of men and women.

Banks, Kraditor, and O'Neill each illuminate aspects of the major ideological divide within the suffrage movement between the premise of equality and the presumption of difference. The earlier movement, closer to the premise of equality, advocated hard-core feminism based on justice arguments toward the Enlightenment goal of equal rights. The later movement, closer to the premise of difference, advocated social feminism based on expediency arguments toward an evangelical program of ameliorative social reform. This backdrop provides a foundation for closer scrutiny of certain ideological trends within the woman suffrage movement.

My own analysis of the ideological transformation of the woman suffrage movement (Buechler 1986) builds on Ellen DuBois's (1978) study of the radicalism of the early suffrage movement. She notes that the ballot was always treated somewhat differently from other women's rights demands, that it generated substantial opposition within and outside the movement, and that the resolution demanding the ballot barely passed at the historic Seneca Falls convention. The distinctiveness of the suffrage demand was a reflection of the link between voting and independence. In much classical political theory, possessing the suffrage implied social independence and political equality and provided a direct link between individuals and the broader community. To demand the ballot was therefore to demand a major change in women's traditionally dependent status and a direct relation to the public sphere of political activity. The ballot was thus a "particularly feminist demand, because it exposed and challenged the assumption of male authority over women. To women fighting to extend their sphere beyond its traditional domestic limitations, political rights involved a radical change in women's status, their emergence into public life. . . .[T]he suffrage demand challenged the idea that women's interests were identical or even compatible with men's. As such, it embodied a vision of female self-determination that placed it at the center of the feminist movement" (DuBois 1978:46).

Because of its centrality to female independence, the ballot thereby symbolized a radical change in the status of women — and one that was recognized as such by both proponents and opponents of the early movement.

However, this movement did not confine itself to the right to vote (Buechler 1986). Until 1869, this movement is best designated as a women's rights movement precisely because it raised multiple demands that challenged an entire spectrum of civil and legal inequality. This spectrum included economic concerns such as the right to inherit property and to own and dispose of one's wages. It included women's access to the public sphere, evidenced in demands for the right to enter into contracts as independent invididuals, the right to serve on juries, and access to professions that were closed to women by law or custom. Finally, this spectrum included women's position within the family and their traditional lack of power in this sphere; these concerns were evident in movement demands for more liberal divorce laws and provisions for joint guardianship of children. The movement thereby challenged the legal superstructure of patriarchal power; by doing so, it called into question the patriarchal foundation of women's legal status as second-class citizens.

While much patriarchal power found expression in legal statutes that could be altered by legislative action, other manifestations of this power were simply woven into the social fabric as unquestioned assumptions of social organization. The more radical or progressive elements of the women's rights movement distinguished themselves precisely by questioning these assumptions. In their objections to the cult of domesticity, to the notion of separate spheres, to women's economic dependence on men, to women's lack of reproductive self-determination, and to how marriage and the family contributed to the subjection of women, some women's rights activists raised fundamental challenges to the sexual division of labor at the foundation of nineteenth-century society. While activists were often vigorous in raising these issues, the targets of such discontent were often difficult to identify. At various points, women indicted men, tradition, religion, custom, history, and society for conspiring to foster and perpetuate a system of sexual inequality. The fact that the targets of such discontent remained elusive or ill defined did not detract from the power of the analysis or the cogency of the critique; it simply meant that it was more difficult to know how to act on them and to develop preferable alternatives for relations between the sexes.

A final distinguishing characteristic of the early women's rights movement was the alliances the movement formed with other groups and constituencies. For all the effort that was directed to uncovering and protesting the specifics of sexual inequality and oppression, the women's rights movement nonetheless envisioned itself as part of a larger movement on behalf of several dispossessed

groups. This was a logical consequence of the movement's roots within the abolitionist cause. The women's rights movement shared with abolitionism a language of emancipation from oppressive conditions that made them logical allies
throughout the antebellum period. When the movement appealed more broadly
to the natural rights tradition and the Declaration of Independence, it spoke a
generalized ideological vocabulary that applied not only to abolitionism but to
other causes as well. The well-publicized rift that occurred between most abolitionists and many women's rights activists after the Civil War did not involve a
rejection of this ideological heritage, but rather a strategic and tactical conflict
over how best to implement this heritage in the historically specific circumstances of the post–Civil War period. Even as it moved away from the abolitionist movement, the ideological heritage of the women's rights movement led it to
seek similar alliances with the nascent labor movement and women workers in
particular (DuBois 1978).

The early women's rights movement was thereby characterized by depth
of critique and breadth of scope. In the inherent radicalism of the demand for the
ballot, in the multiplicity of demands for legal reform, in the movement's critique
of the sexual division of labor in its various manifestations, and in its ideologically motivated alliances with other movements, the movement forcefully articulated its own particular grievances in a generalizable language of natural rights,
justice, equality, and citizenship. This proved an ideologically potent mix: it located the women's rights movement firmly in the U.S. political tradition while
also using that tradition to mount a radical challenge to the position of women.
This radical challenge was most evident before and immediately following the
Civil War, as the movement sought to translate its broad ideological vision into
sweeping social change.

The emphasis of the early women's rights movement began to change in
response to political events of the late 1860s. The Fourteenth Amendment em-
powered black males and made the first explicit reference to voting as a male
right in the Constitution. Far from aiding the women's rights cause, this meant
that an additional constitutional amendment would be required to enfranchise
women. In response to this setback, to the difficulty of securing constitutional
amendments, and to the perception of many activists such as Susan B. Anthony
that the ballot was pivotal to redressing other grievances, the movement began to
focus more explicitly and exclusively on securing the right to vote. This priority
was organizationally reflected in the founding of the National and American
Woman Suffrage associations; the American consciously limited its goals to
female enfranchisement while the National retained a broader focus that nonetheless saw the vote as essential to the accomplishment of the other goals of the
women's movement. Although ongoing ideological and organizational diversity

within the movement must be recognized, the period from 1868 to 1870 marks
the transformation of the women's rights movement into a woman suffrage
movement.

This same period also marked the closing of an era of political reform and
the erosion of political opportunities for further changes. Abolitionism, the Civil
War, passage of three constitutional amendments, and the beginning of Reconstruction had exhausted the tolerance of the system for debating and implementing social and political reform. This change in the political climate made it more
difficult for suffragists to gain a sympathetic hearing from political elites, and the
prospects for female enfranchisement began to evaporate with the ratification of
the Fifteenth Amendment and the realization that no additional amendment was
likely to win support in the near future. While continuing to work very hard for
the vote, the movement suffered declining momentum during the 1870s and
1880s, which set the stage for further transformation in its ideological arguments
for the right to vote. To this point, the dominant ideological strain had emphasized themes of justice, equality, and natural rights. The movement had assumed
an underlying sameness between men and women, it had embraced the political
philosophy of classical liberalism, and it had pursued some of the radical implications of such a philosophy when applied to women in the context of institutionalized patriarchal power. After this point, this ideological strain was
challenged by an alternative ideology premised on underlying differences between women and men and an essentialist notion of a distinctive female nature.
From the argument that women deserved equal treatment because they were no
different from men, the movement turned toward the argument that women deserved a voice precisely because of their differences from men, and the need for
these differences to find political expression.

The temperance movement provides the clearest, though by no means the
only example of this alternative ideological orientation. There was a clear material foundation for this alternative in the reality as well as the ideology of separate spheres for middle-class women and men in an industrializing economy. As
the lives of women and men became more separate and distinct, as women became more exclusively involved in child care as a specialized role, and as the
home and family came to be seen as a distinct sphere for which women were well
suited by nature and training, the premise of overriding differences between the
sexes appeared to many to be a truism. Temperance became a "women's issue"
when alcohol came to be seen as a threat to the stability of the home and the
family; women became defenders of the home and reformers of the world because that world had begun to threaten the distinctive sphere they were best
qualified to protect. Involvement in the temperance movement was one of the
few options available to women as a powerless, disenfranchised group; in this

sense, temperance activity was political because it challenged the powerlessness of women. At the same time, the ideology of the temperance movement reinforced dominant cultural notions of separate spheres, gender-specific traits, and distinct female and male natures; in this sense, the cause represented a very different orientation from that which had prevailed in the earlier women's rights movement. Perhaps most important, the temperance movement implicitly assumed male dominance and explicitly defended the conventional family; in this basic sense, it remained at best a "proto-feminist" movement (Epstein 1981).

While the temperance and suffrage causes had always had overlapping advocates and followers, the Women's Christian Temperance Union (WCTU) initially rejected the ballot as an appropriate goal and preferred to rely on education and moral suasion. It was only under Frances Willard's direction after 1879 that the organization moved toward voting rights as a means of pursuing the temperance cause more effectively. Many women who failed to respond to justice and equality rationales for seeking the franchise responded enthusiastically to the concept of a "home protection ballot," which defined the vote as an expedient and instrumental tool that women required in order to accomplish their major goal of temperance. To the frustration of old-line suffragists like Stanton and Anthony, many women seemed much more willing to work on behalf of others than on behalf of themselves. The popularity of the social-feminist ideology that fueled the temperance movement spilled over into the suffrage movement as well, so that by the end of the 1880s the original justice and equality ideology based on a premise of sameness had largely been displaced by an ideology stressing women's distinctive nature and special role in social reform based on a premise of difference.

In addition to the temperance movement, this new ideological orientation found a home in numerous other women's organizations and social reform groups. The women's club movement acted out of similar assumptions that women's distinctive nature made them especially well suited to reform, improve, and purify a rapidly changing and increasingly corrupt urban industrial society. Social science associations attracted a large female membership based on the same orientation to reform, and they supported the cause of female suffrage because it would empower a group particularly well suited to implementing a program of ameliorative social reform. In contrast to the earlier women's rights movement, which exemplified Chafe's fourth stage of collective behavior because it consciously challenged dominant notions about the position of women, these later reform efforts exemplified his third stage of collective behavior in which women articulate a sense of group identity and solidarity without directly challenging the dominant culture's definition of women's place. The development of an alternative ideology during the 1870s and 1880s was thus a double-edged sword. It allowed the suffrage movement to recruit and mobilize larger numbers of women who were more likely to respond to what they saw as a more congenial ideology; at the same time, it reflected and reinforced trends of depoliticization as the movement's original challenge to female subordination was increasingly displaced by the goal of social betterment.

These new ideological strains were also reflected in the stance of many reformers toward issues of sexuality and reproduction. In the colonial period, there were relatively few incentives to control marital fertility, and contraception and abortion were most closely associated with nonmarital sexuality. Industrialization and modernization created numerous incentives for smaller families, however. Hence, there were signs of declining fertility and family limitation during the eighteenth century, and strong evidence of the extensive use of both contraception and abortion to limit family size throughout the nineteenth century (D'Emilio and Freedman 1988). The widespread use of abortion reflected its traditional acceptability up until the time of "quickening," when the pregnant woman can detect fetal movement. It was only after the middle of the nineteenth century that physicians began to condemn abortion as morally wrong and medically dangerous. As a result of these efforts by male doctors to establish professional control over women's reproduction, antiabortion laws became common by 1900 and doctors established firm regulatory control over therapeutic abortions (Luker 1984).

Although most women reformers in the second half of the nineteenth century did not openly support abortion or contraception, they did endorse women's efforts to control their fertility by advocating a nineteenth-century version of reproductive self-determination called "voluntary motherhood," which would make pregnancy, childbirth, and motherhood matters of conscious choice. The campaign for voluntary motherhood reflected a mixture of traditional and progressive assumptions. Unlike the free-lovers, whose advocacy of voluntary motherhood also sought to separate sexuality and reproduction, most suffragists and moral reformers wanted to reinforce the link between sexuality and reproduction and to strengthen the respect and dignity they felt should be accorded to motherhood. The movement did not challenge the centrality of motherhood as much as it tried to provide somewhat greater control over the timing and duration of that role. Since most advocates of voluntary motherhood also opposed the use of contraception, their major method for making motherhood voluntary was abstinence from sexual relations when pregnancy was not a desired or acceptable consequence (Gordon 1976).

Many of these reformers espoused the basic premises of social feminism, including a conservative view of gender roles and an emphasis on women's moral superiority and maternal instinct. But their advocacy of voluntary motherhood expressed the implicit sexual politics of social feminism in a particularly clear way. For these reformers, women's right to refuse sex was central to the concept of voluntary motherhood and to the prospects for women's independence. On the interpersonal level, this goal challenged the traditional sexual prerogatives of husbands within marriage. On the collective level, this goal expressed the movement's concern with social purity and its antipathy to male sexual power. Voluntary motherhood required men to curb their sexual impulses and implicitly assumed that the expression of such impulses was subject to learning rather than determined by biology. Opposition to contraception was consistent with these sexual politics, since contraception would simply encourage male lust and undermine the connections between sexuality and reproduction that gave women some power in bargaining over sexual activity. Some advocates of these goals also acknowledged the existence of a female sexuality that was not entirely subordinated to maternal instinct but would find its healthiest expression only when women controlled their own fertility. Some of these beliefs may be caricatured as simply "antisex," but it is important to recognize that in the socio-historical context of the nineteenth century they represented a quest for self-determination as well as an affirmation of some traditional notions of gender and sexuality. The dual-edged nature of social feminism is thus particularly evident in the campaign for voluntary motherhood that persisted to the end of the century (Gordon 1976).

By the turn of the century, the woman suffrage movement could point to several concrete accomplishments. The two suffrage organizations had merged in 1890 to form the National American Woman Suffrage Association. The woman suffrage territories of Wyoming and Utah had been granted statehood and woman suffrage campaigns were victorious in Colorado and Idaho. From 1896 to 1910, however, no further progress occurred despite vigorous campaigns in numerous states. The combination of organizational consolidation, several victories, but more defeats encouraged the specialization of the movement as it moved into the twentieth century. This specialization took several forms. For one, the movement focused exclusively on the goal of winning the right to vote. When other objectives were identified, they were always directly linked to the suffrage issue. For another, the movement became more professionalized and bureaucratized, relying more on paid staff and hierarchical authority to distribute scarce movement resources in the most efficient manner. In ideological terms, specialization meant that movement rhetoric was instrumentally streamlined toward the goal of winning the vote, and that excess or peripheral points and issues were set aside so as not to interfere with this goal.

Movement ideology underwent another important change in this final period. Compared to the mid-nineteenth century, the movement's potential constituency of women had become much more socially differentiated and hetero-geneous. The broad, sweeping claims that the early movement had made on behalf of "all women" no longer appeared tenable in a social world in which the divisions of class, race, ethnicity, religion, region, status, and power were in-creasingly prominent. The movement's response to this differentiation reflected a new tactical sophistication; it developed and publicized specialized and differ-entiated arguments for the vote that linked the need for the ballot to the specific situations of these diverse subgroups of women. The classic prosuffrage argu-ments on the basis of justice and equality did not entirely disappear, but they were displaced by arguments grounded in the particular needs and concerns of these newly emerging, differentiated constituencies of women. By the last dec-ade of the campaign, dozens of these different prosuffrage arguments were being distributed in pamphlet form by NAWSA, linking the need for the ballot to the specific concerns of rural women, widows, working women, mothers, ur-ban women, immigrant women, elite women, and the like.

This diversity makes it more difficult to identify a dominant ideological theme in the later suffrage movement. Whereas the early movement invoked jus-tice and equality themes and the middle movement appealed to women's distinc-tive capacity for social reform, the later movement spoke with a plethora of voices. In many respects, this was the key to its success, because this ideological diversity fostered and reflected a mass base of women who came to see the vote as important to their interests. The social differentiation of women, which made it increasingly difficult to find unity on many issues, paradoxically made it easier to find unity on suffrage, because one of the few commonalities that continued to characterize all women was precisely their disenfranchisement. The lack of vot-ing rights that was common to otherwise very different groups of women became the thread stitching together a coalition of movement followers who could agree on a common goal even as they differed on the reasons why that goal was neces-sary or desirable. Ideological diversity and flexibility thereby made it possible to recruit working-class women through the Women's Trade Union League, immi-grant women through the settlement house movement, middle-class women through the various reform organizations, and upper-class women through city clubs and political equality leagues. Whereas the middle movement had empha-sized and built upon the differences between men and women to argue for the vote, the later movement was more attentive to the differences between women, and managed to convert these differences into a movement resource.

To the extent that there were common themes in later movement ideology, they frequently reflected the concerns of the Progressive Era. Like much of the Progressive agenda, the suffrage cause acquired the dual character of modifying and reforming while also rationalizing and legitimizing dominant social institutions and practices. One example is provided by prosuffrage arguments premised on "municipal housekeeping." Such arguments assumed a sexual division of labor and a version of the separate spheres doctrine: that women were distinctively well suited for domestic labor, care-taking, nurturance, and social maintenance. However, these premises were used to argue for the expansion of womanly influence into the public sphere (at least at the level of the city) by establishing municipal female suffrage so that women could carry out their traditional obligations in a new urban setting that suffered from woefully inadequate and vitally needed services. With the vote, women could engage in municipal housekeeping by establishing sanitation codes, mandating garbage collection, regulating meat inspection, and the like.

Another example is provided by the campaign for protective legislation for women workers. This cause provided one of the most frequent rationales for why working-class women needed the ballot. Although few would deny the importance of protective labor legislation in the conflicts between labor and capital, this goal was almost always framed in sex-specific terms; protections were required for women but not men. As a result, protective legislation typically reinforced dominant conceptions of sex differences, gender-specific traits, and a distinctive female nature. Such measures also created and sustained occupational sex segregation and wage disparities between male and female workers. Such consequences may have been unintended, unanticipated, and regretted by female reformers, but they were often the conscious goal of male workers and union leaders, who saw such legislation as a means of enhancing the income and status of men who were not subject to such protective legislation. This issue highlighted one of the major axes of social differentiation between women, for the impact of protective legislation was often class-specific. Many agreed on its benefits for working-class women, but many also pointed to its unduly restrictive impact on middle-class women and their attempted entry into professional occupations. Gender-neutral protective legislation offered a more satisfactory solution, but presumptions of sexual difference and male opposition to diminished earnings prevented this option from receiving serious consideration.

At the most abstract level, the later suffrage movement thereby operated with a double premise of difference. On the one hand, it continued to assume that significant differences between men and women existed and needed to be incorporated in rationales for woman suffrage. Like the middle period, this continued to be a double-edged sword, for it could mobilize larger numbers of women, but it could also reinforce many dominant conceptions that blocked women's emancipation. On the other hand, the movement became much more aware of the differences among women, and it began to recognize this in prosuffrage arguments. New awareness of differences among women helped to modify the older premise of differences between the sexes. The effect was to de-value unqualified, essentialist conceptions of a universal female nature shared by all women, and to promote more nuanced, situational, and environmental ac-counts of both the differences between men and women and the differences among women.

The major exception to these ideological tendencies was to be found in the circle of activists associated with the National Women's Party. In the early twen-tieth century, this group retained the purest version of an equal rights orienta-tion. In its assumption of overriding similarities between the sexes and its straightforward justice and equality arguments for the ballot, this group's ideol-ogy was quite similar to that of the women's rights movement of a half-century earlier. Women in the NWP were extremely wary of assumptions of difference and the way these assumptions could be turned against the goals of women's emancipation. The survival of this ideological orientation within the NWP re-flects its relatively small size, uncompromising dedication to its goal, militant tactics, and a membership consisting of college-educated, upper-middle-class, professionally oriented women. These women had the most to gain from the un-qualified equal rights orientation that provided the rationale not only for woman suffrage but also for the Equal Rights Amendment introduced by the NWP in 1923. The NWP's greater ideological consistency was closely linked to its nar-rower social base; both formed a sharp contrast to the ideological diversity and broad, mass base of the mainstream suffrage movement associated with NAWSA.

The persistence of this ideology in the NWP is but one example of the uni-versal presence of an equal rights orientation within women's movements. A similar ideology had propelled the early women's rights movement, and has played a major role in the contemporary movement as well. This equal rights ideology, with its characteristic emphasis on equality, natural rights, individual-ism, opportunity and the like, has been a major, continuing ideological thread linking the earliest political mobilizations of women with the latest manifesta-tions of feminist activism. However, the political implications of equal rights have varied with the socio-historical context in which the discussion of equal rights has arisen. In the mid-nineteenth-century women's rights movement, this ideology was the basis of a radical challenge to the position of women in the so-ciety. The radicalism of the challenge derived from the fact that women occupied a quasi-feudal status relative to men and to the overall society. In this context, a liberal ideology prompted demands for substantial change in patriarchal social relations. The radicalism also derived from the breadth of the early movement, and the fact that some leaders, like Stanton, went beyond equal rights in their challenges to the sexual division of labor and the division of society into separate spheres. As noted earlier, Stanton provides a good historical example of a thinker who articulated the radical implications of equal rights in the context of women's near total subordination in mid-nineteenth century U.S. society.

The same themes continued to inform the woman suffrage movement, along with several others, until the vote was won. However, the context of the movement changed, and so did the implications of equal rights. As partial gains were accomplished in various areas, as the quasi-feudal status of women was gradually altered, as some opportunities were in fact granted or won, and as new kinds of inequality were created in the labor market, the ideology of equal rights lost some of its power to generate a radical challenge to the subordinate position of women. Because it was such an obvious case of sexual inequality, the ballot continued to be a logical grievance, for which this ideology was well suited. In other cases, formal equality was granted without accomplishing the substantive goals many women sought. Thus, in the later movement, the limits of equal rights for altering women's position became more apparent. The more limited applicability of this ideology in the later movement interacted with the social differentiation of women. In the mid-nineteenth century, the ideology of equal rights articulated a multiplicity of grievances that affected a wide range of women. By the early twentieth century, this ideology still spoke to all women's lack of the ballot, but beyond this it was becoming a specialized ideology most directly representing the interests of college-educated, upper-middle-class, professionally oriented women; hence its continuing popularity within the NWP and its diminished appeal for the more differentitated constituencies of women in NAWSA.

If the potential of equal rights for challenging women's position was socially and historically variable, the same may be said for the alternative of social feminism, which became the dominant ideology of the later woman suffrage movement. When social feminism, with its underlying assumption of difference, was complemented with an emphasis on women's emancipation, it could have profound implications for empowering women and altering their subordinate status (see Black [1989] for a spirited defense of the transformative potential of social-feminist organizations and ideology). When the same ideology was paired with reform programs that marginalized issues of inequality between women and men, however, its ultimate effect was often to reinforce deeply rooted cultural assumptions about sex differences, gender-specific traits, and essentialist male and female natures. The former combination could support a challenge to the sexual division of labor and the organization of society into separate spheres; the latter combination typically did not and thereby implicitly or explicitly reinforced dominant social arrangements and practices. The comingling of all these ideological orientations within the later suffrage movement created numerous contradictions and tensions between various rationales for the vote. But more importantly, these diverse ideological positions allowed the later suffrage movement to recruit a very diverse cross-section of women who came to agree on the need for the vote even as they differed on the underlying rationales for that goal.

Although the ideology of the later suffrage movement contained a number of internally contradictory premises, a coherent worldview was coalescing during the last decade of the suffrage movement and survives to the present day. This period saw the emergence of modern feminism as a historically specific ideology with a distinctive set of premises about relations between women and men in modern society (Cott 1987). Whereas the nineteenth-century women's movement attempted to speak for all women and disallowed men, modern feminism is rooted in specific principles to which both women and men may agree; in this respect, belief rather than gender qualifies one to be a feminist. Cott's working definition of feminism includes three core ideas. The first is a belief in sex equality, or more clearly an opposition to sex hierarchy. The second is a presupposition that women's condition is socially constructed rather than predestined by God or nature. The third is that women have a distinct gender identity that can form the basis for group consciousness and a community of action. At the same time, modern feminism is also characterized by enduring paradoxes. "Feminism asks for sexual equality that includes sexual difference. It aims for individual freedoms by mobilizing sex solidarity. It posits that women recognize their unity while it stands for diversity among women. It requires gender consciousness for its basis yet calls for the elimination of prescribed gender roles" (Cott 1987:5). In the 1910s, modern feminism was politically left and culturally radical; it rejected moralism, religiosity, and conventionality and embraced assertive individualism, ideological heterodoxy, and healthy female sexuality and eroticism. In Cott's view, the paradoxes of modern feminism may be read as an attempt to accommodate, simultaneously, the values of a common humanity, a distinctive femaleness, and individual diversity within a single worldview.

One expression of this modern feminism could be found in a new movement for birth control that reflected a distinctively different view of female sexuality. This "new concept of birth control . . . meant reproductive self-determination along with unlimited sexual indulgence. This new definition — quite different from that of voluntary motherhood — understood sexual activity and reproduction as two separately justified human activities" (Gordon 1976:189–190). These ideas were part of a broader sexual revolution that sought to liberate sexuality from traditional constraints and repressions. As a self-conscious, ideological movement, these beliefs expressed and supported significant changes in women's sexual behavior. However, "women's gains from these changes were by no means clear and unequivocal" (Gordon 1976:194). By

relaxing constraints on nonmarital heterosexual activity and promoting con-
traceptive use, these ideas deprived women of some of the sexual bargaining
power they had retained when sexual activity remained closely tied to reproductive consequences. The new ethic of liberated heterosexuality was also accompanied by intensified taboos on homosexual activity and a general undermining
of women's homosocial relations, which had typified the later nineteenth century. In a context where women remained unequal to men in so many other respects, the consequences of (hetero-)sexual liberation created new possibilities
for female sexual fulfillment as well as new forms of male sexual coercion.

In the first two decades of the twentieth century, this struggle for birth
control had radical ramifications because it was part of a multi-issue reform
movement that included a broader feminist agenda and significant links to
working-class and socialist movements. Under the organizational efforts of
Margaret Sanger and the theoretical inspiration of Emma Goldman, the radical
implications of a feminist birth control movement were much in evidence during
the 1910s. During these years, the movement fought for freer information about
and access to contraception. In 1916, these goals were translated into direct action with the opening of illegal birth control clinics where women could be fitted
with vaginal diaphragms. These efforts were simultaneously feminist and socialist; they sought reproductive self-determination for women at the same time that
they attempted to provide working-class families with safe, effective, and inex-
pensive means of limiting family size without jeopardizing sexual fulfillment. In
addition, this movement represented a progressive response to early twentieth-
century fears of race suicide and attacks on feminism by strongly advocating reproductive choice for women and challenging the centrality of motherhood as
women's only option (Gordon 1976).

The radical potential of this socialist-feminist alliance around the issue of
birth control evaporated after 1920 with the decline of leftist politics and the
subsequent cooptation of reproductive self-determination by Planned Parenthood agencies. The alliance remains important as a historical example of an attempt to combine feminist and working-class concerns in the modern era, as
well as an example of the character of modern feminism as conceptualized by
Cott. The movement is all the more striking given the fact that it occurred at
the same time that the male-dominated medical profession was seeking control
over women's reproductive lives (D'Emilio and Freedman 1988). The birth
control movement successfully challenged this effort and helped move the medical establishment toward an endorsement of contraception even as that establishment sought to control its availability. The explicitly modern, feminist
politics that drove this movement set it apart from the earlier movement for voluntary motherhood as well as the later emphasis on planned parenthood.

These politics would reemerge in the contemporary women's movement as feminists once again undertook an explicit struggle for women's reproductive self-determination.

Several differences between Cott's depiction of modern feminism and the ideology of the later suffrage movement may be identified. Modern feminism was explicitly political in its rejection of women's subordination, whereas some elements of suffrage ideology were more interested in non-feminist social reforms for which the ballot was simply seen as a prerequisite. Modern feminism explicitly rejected essentialist notions of an unchanging female nature, whereas some elements of suffrage ideology were explicitly grounded in essentialist views of sex differences. Modern feminism was intertwined with the movement for sexual freedom, whereas much suffrage ideology was sexually conservative. Modern feminism was unorthodox and sometimes flamboyant, whereas the suffrage movement had become quite conventional and proper. Despite the differences and despite the fact that many suffragists were uncomfortable with much of modern feminism, feminists could and did support the goal of woman suffrage. Once again, the strength of the later suffrage movement was its ability to accommodate a diversity of rationales and constituencies in the struggle for the vote. This included "modern feminists," even though traditional suffragists and modern feminists often took different positions.

Cott's analysis of modern feminism is important as we turn to the question of comparing and contrasting the ideology of the woman suffrage movement with that of the contemporary women's movement. On the one hand, it suggests even greater ideological diversity among women in the 1910s than most previous accounts. On the other hand, it implies greater continuities between the feminists of the 1910s and the 1970s than is often recognized. Despite its grounding in the early part of the century, modern feminism is therefore an important bridge between the ideology of the woman suffrage movement and that of the contemporary women's movement.

The Contemporary Women's Movement

Movement ideology can be seen as a self-reflexive product of social movements as movement members attempt to make sense out of their positions, values, goals, strategies, and tactics. By this logic, the contemporary women's movement may be judged one of the most ideological movements in recent history for the volume of self-reflexive analysis it has generated. Virtually all contemporary feminist theory is directly or indirectly linked to the contemporary women's movement and the diverse issues and struggles in which that movement has engaged. As a result, the study of modern movement ideology quickly threatens to become a survey of contemporary feminist theory. To avoid such a lengthy though interesting detour, the focus here will be on those ideas and concepts which have directly informed movement mobilization and strategy in one fashion or another. Even with this limitation, it is evident that the contemporary women's movement is ideologically rich, and that the theories and concepts it has helped generate have provided one of the movement's most important resources.

Ideology has played a critical role in generating and sustaining — as well as dividing and fragmenting — the contemporary women's movement. This point merits reiteration in light of those strands of resource mobilization theory which have marginalized the role of grievances or relegated them to the category of social psychology (for example, McCarthy and Zald 1977). The structural dispersal of women throughout all other social groups and the norms of romantic love, compulsory heterosexuality, and the nuclear family have always posed substantial obstacles to female solidarity in general and to feminist mobilization in particular. Hence, unlike some other social movement constituencies, the politicized articulation of grievances can hardly be seen as a constant background factor in the case of women as a group. Such grievances could only be formulated and politicized in tandem with a nascent movement ideology that identified women as a coherent constituency with certain interests that were denied by existing social institutions and practices. The concept of "sisterhood" expressed a rudimentary form of such solidarity in the late 1960s and made a vital contribution to the momentum of the movement in that period. Such examples also illustrate that movement ideology cannot be categorized simply as an aspect of the social psychology of movements. While all ideas and beliefs ultimately reside in the minds of individual actors, their greatest significance may be in establishing the group as a collective actor. Hence, the social-psychological process of individuals coming to believe in group solidarity creates emergent structural properties like solidarity, organization, and mobilization, which are vital to movement prospects. In the case of women's movements, it seems especially clear that a necessary threshold of both resources/organization and grievances/ideology must be reached before movements emerge (Jenkins 1983).

The women's rights sector of the contemporary women's movement that emerged out of the presidential and state commissions on the status of women and culminated in the formation of NOW in 1966 exemplifies the universality of an equal rights or liberal feminist orientation within women's movements. The liberal feminism of the women associated with the early NOW was a direct descendant of the equal rights ideology that had animated the suffrage movement in a prior era. This worldview placed a characteristic emphasis on notions of equality and equal treatment, on the symbolism and vocabulary of natural rights, on the centrality of the individual, and on the need for equality of opportunity. The liberal feminism of this sector reflected its constituency of well-educated, politically active, professionally oriented women — a constituency reminiscent of the later suffrage movement and of the NWP circle of activists in particular. In the most immediate sense, their ideology was a response to all of the obstacles and limitations that institutionalized sexism placed in the path of professionally oriented women like themselves. However, the abstract formulations of liberal feminist ideology could readily be adapted to a range of issues including education, health care, marriage, family and child care, sexuality, politics, and the like.

The revival of interest in and activism around the Equal Rights Amendment was a natural outgrowth of liberal feminism. On the one hand, the ERA exemplified the formal, abstract stress on equality, natural rights, and individual opportunity that was central to the worldview of liberal feminism. On the other hand, it also offered a potent instrument for altering a wide range of discriminatory legislation. With both symbolic and practical value, the ERA was the perfect vehicle for pursuing the goals of the women's rights sector of the contemporary women's movement. The ERA also offers the closest parallel to the goal of suffrage in the later woman suffrage movement. Both combined symbolic and practical goals, both addressed the status of all women in abstract terms, both resonated most strongly with the views of middle-class activists, both required constitutional amendments, both enjoyed the support of mass feminist organizations, and both attracted conservative countermovements that challenged each respective goal. The success of woman suffrage and the failure of the ERA underscores the differences in these campaigns. In the suffrage case, a long history of prior failure had promoted a very high degree of coordination and organization in the later campaigns, along with ideological sophistication and the fortuitous benefits of diverse organizational strategies that unintentionally complemented each other in the fight for the vote. In the ERA case, an old issue nonetheless had new and inexperienced proponents in the late 1960s and early 1970s, sophisticated leadership did not develop until it was too late, and the promotion of equality as an abstract goal could not withstand the damage done by a well-organized, conservative countermovement in a time of growing reaction. Despite different outcomes, woman suffrage and the ERA provide good examples of the goals of a liberal feminist ideology.

Because liberal feminism is so deeply imbued with the larger political philosophy of liberalism, there are characteristic limits to the kinds of social change that liberal feminism typically envisions. To the extent that a meaningful distinction can be drawn between reform and revolutionary change, liberalism is typically a reformist orientation that leaves the fundamental structure of existing institutions intact while seeking to improve their operation and to establish more equal access to those institutions for all citizens. Liberalism's stress on individual rights, opportunities, and freedoms gives a privileged place to the atomized individual and her self-interest rather than to any group of individuals with a more collective self-identity. Liberalism's key assumptions about the political economy of society presume an open and competitive marketplace, with modest and measured intervention by a state whose institutions are themselves limited through institutionalized checks and balances. Perhaps most important, liberalism has traditionally assumed the division of society into public and private spheres. The public sphere of polity, economy, and other public activity is seen as the deliberate creation of rational beings, and therefore open to continued intervention and action. The private sphere of family, household, and personal life is more likely to be seen as a natural and immutable world, and therefore beyond the interventions of a liberal political philosophy.

This brief overview is enough to suggest the ways in which "liberal feminism" is a somewhat contradictory hybrid of worldviews. Whereas liberalism focuses on the individual, feminism presumes collective identity among women as a group. Whereas liberalism takes the private sphere for granted, feminism seeks to analyze and transform the personal relations that constitute this sphere. While these contradictions do not render the term meaningless, they do mean that the implications of these assumptions can differ substantially from one historical period or social context to another. Thus, as we have seen, in the mid-nineteenth century, the equal rights ideology, a forerunner of liberal feminism, could be the basis of a radical challenge to the essentially feudal status of married women. The changes in women's legal and civil status since that time have reduced the radical potential of liberal feminism, but have not eliminated it. The contradiction between liberalism's patriarchal and individualist orientation and feminism's egalitarian and collectivist orientation can promote the development of a feminism that goes beyond liberal foundations toward a more radical premise of women's identity as a sex-class (Eisenstein 1981). In a similar vein, liberal feminism may begin as a critique of sexual inequality in the public sphere, but such critiques inevitably reveal the dialectically reinforcing nature of women's inequality in public and private spheres. NOW's 1968 Bill of Rights nicely exemplifies this argument. The provisions for the ERA, elimination of sex discrimination, equal education, and job training epitomize the classic, liberal focus on public sphere institutions, while the clauses concerning maternity leave, child care, and reproductive freedom extend this liberal and legalistic approach (still rooted in notions of individual rights) into the private sphere of family, child-bearing and -rearing, and domestic labor.

The issue of reproductive rights provides an especially powerful illustration of the radical potential of liberal feminism in the contemporary women's movement. This goal was initially framed in classically liberal and individualist terms as the right to abortion, but it nonetheless challenged the traditional division of society into separate spheres, because granting women power over these "private" decisions had momentous implications for their participation in the public sphere and in the labor force in particular. The emergence of reproductive rights as a major goal of the contemporary women's movement signifies the return of an explicitly feminist rationale for reproductive control after an absence of several decades. The campaign for birth control in the 1910s had been infused with radical politics and feminist premises, but it was substantially de-radicalized in the 1920s and converted into a professional, conservative, respectable, non-feminist, single issue typified by Sanger's American Birth Control League. With this change, birth control was transformed "from a popular radical cause to a reform that operated to stabilize, rationalize and centralize corporate social planning" (Gordon 1976:253), and most women were displaced from leadership positions to become amateur staff under the direction of male professionals in birth control organizations. These changes opened the door for population control strategies that made birth control a means of reinforcing the status quo. When it was not part of a larger eugenic campaign on behalf of dominant interests, birth control "was presented as a remedial aid in the case of abnormal personal problems" (Gordon 1976:326), implicitly denying the sexual politics embedded in this issue.

The establishment of the Planned Parenthood Federation of America in 1942 was the culmination of these trends. These agencies advocated an apolitical, profamily approach that synthesized reproductive control and state planning. They deemphasized the feminist politics of birth control and focused on the family as the unit of application; in seeking to strengthen the nuclear family they also effectively reinforced many of the foundations of male dominance (Gordon 1976). The emphasis on planning was at best double-edged. On the familial level as a birth control initiative, it had the potential to grant women more control over their lives; on the societal level as a population control campaign, planning was a tool of social control in the hands of dominant groups. While these agencies supported women's right to sexual fulfillment, they did so under the influence of conservative and psychiatric views of female sexuality and maternity that helped reinforce the syndrome Betty Friedan would subsequently identify as the feminine mystique. While Planned Parenthood increased the legimitacy of and access to birth control, it remained a less radical and less feminist approach to reproductive issues than the birth control movement of the 1910s or even the voluntary motherhood campaigns of the nineteenth century (Gordon 1976:387–388).

As birth control became more available from 1920 to 1960 in the form of a family-planning strategy divorced from feminist politics, access to abortion was becoming more restricted (D'Emilio and Freedman 1988). Since the late 1800s, medical control over abortion had produced a "century of silence" during which professionals successfully defined themselves as the only legitimate, disinterested parties capable of deciding this question (Luker 1984). By the 1950s, however, several forces were promoting rethinking and reform of abortion practices. For one, medical advances had decreased the need for abortions to save the life of the mother, undermining the only rationale for abortion on which there was a widespread consensus. For another, "strict constructionists" who argued that there was no other rationale for abortion began pressing their case more forcefully with the backing of the Catholic church. Finally, the publicity surrounding the 1962 case of Sherri Finkbine, a woman who sought to abort a fetus deformed by maternal use of the sedative thalidomide, brought abortion into the public arena in a dramatic way (Luker 1984).

The debate over abortion reform unfolded in two stages. Initially, it remained largely within the realm of professionals, who were divided between "strict" and "broad" constructionists and conducted their debate in a pragmatic, nonsymbolic, amoral manner. Many professionals supported a new standard that would balance the life of the fetus against the interests of the woman and permit some abortions that were not medically necessary to save the life of the mother. Though opposed by strict constructionists and religious groups, these efforts were successful in fashioning a new legal compromise in several states, which granted physicians somewhat more latitude in making decisions about abortion. The second stage of the abortion debate began when a grass-roots movement of women demanded not the reform but the repeal of abortion laws, thereby legalizing all abortions and removing the decision from the long-standing control of the medical profession. Building on the political opportunities provided by the new publicity and modest reforms of the first stage of abortion reform, this grass-roots movement reclaimed the question of abortion as a women's issue and reintroduced a feminist analysis that emphasized women's need to gain more effective control over their reproductive lives (Luker 1984).

By the late 1960s and early 1970s, women's right to abortion had become a major demand of the contemporary women's movement, which had strong advocates in both movement sectors. For the first time since the birth control campaign of the 1910s, reproductive issues were infused with a radical and feminist perspective centered in the belief that women have a fundamental right to control their bodies. While using the liberal language of individual rights, the campaign for access to abortion revealed the radical potential of liberal feminist rhetoric: the issue transcended societal divisions between the public and private, social and individual, political and personal. It became a radical demand when placed within a broader feminist agenda and ideology that challenged the subordination of women in many different sectors of modern society. The 1973 Supreme Court decisions in *Roe* v. *Wade* and *Doe* v. *Bolton* did not fully embrace the feminist rationale for a woman's right to abortion, but they effectively struck down all state abortion laws and represented a substantial practical victory that greatly improved women's access to safe and legal abortions.

An important factor influencing whether and to what extent the radical potential of liberal feminism is realized concerns supporting and opposing sentiments in the surrounding social context. In the late 1960s and early 1970s, other feminist ideologies in the women's liberation sector of the movement promoted a more holistic analysis of women's position. Whereas the liberal ideology of the women's rights sector was often an implicit, taken-for-granted worldview, the ideologies of the women's liberation sector were explicit, and even somewhat fetishized objects of intense scrutiny, debate, and critique. In part, this reflected this sector's roots in and emergence from the New Left and campus-based political activism. In the process of establishing its ideological independence, the women's liberation movement went through lengthy debates between "politicos and feminists." In broad outline, politicos insisted on the priority of traditional leftist issues and saw feminist concerns as at best secondary and at worst diversionary. In this specific context, "feminists" were those who insisted on the importance of analyzing the position of women anew and apart from the formulaic slogans of leftist traditions. As this debate unfolded in the late 1960s, the politicos had a well-established theory and practice of activism to which they could turn, whereas feminists were groping for a new theory and language that would establish women's perceptions and experience as central to their politics. The process might have taken longer were it not for the continual provocations provided by the institutional and interpersonal sexism embedded in the New Left (see Hole and Levine 1971:114–122).

Although there were many permutations, the basic issues in this debate were quite clear. For politicos, capitalism was the fundamental enemy, and class-based forms of resistance were the dominant strategy. Internationally, imperialism was the basic issue; solidarity between U.S. radicals and Third World peoples was another key element in political struggle. For politicos, the emerging feminist position obscured important issues, ignored class differences, created false alliances, and diverted movement energy. For feminists, men or the system of sex roles were the fundamental enemy, and gender-based forms of resistance were the dominant strategy. The basic principle of mobilization and struggle involved female solidarity across all other groups and identities. For feminists, the dominant politico position misdiagnosed the problem, denied gender commonalities, perpetuated male dominance, and trivialized women's concerns. In the ideologically superheated atmosphere of the late 1960s, there was little chance that these positions would be reconciled in a single group or organization. Indeed, the debate was "reconciled" when an independent feminist movement broke with the New Left and established itself through separate organizations. This development created the ideological space the feminist movement needed to explore, develop, refine, and articulate its own independent ideological stances. As the New Left fell into decline and disarray after the turn of the decade, the women's liberation movement gained strength and momentum. In time, the politico-feminist debate would return in a more sophisticated discussion of the prospects for socialist feminism.

As an independent women's movement emerged, the concept and practice of consciousness-raising developed with it. The centrality of C-R groups in both ideology and practice underscores the need for a special mechanism to overcome the structural isolation of women and to create forms of solidarity on which a movement could be based. Although C-R groups were sometimes mistaken for and occasionally became something else, their originators were clear about the political role of raised consciousness in mobilizing a movement of women for social change. By taking a woman's individual experience and revealing the patterns of institutional and interpersonal sexism woven into that experience, C-R groups, if they worked as intended, provided rich meaning to the slogan that "the personal is political." Women who entered such groups taking full responsibility for what was perceived as an isolated personal problem often left with an enlightened, liberating, and empowering insight into the societal forces that had structured their lives. C-R groups were powerful because the process of consciousness-raising validated individual experience at the same time that it revealed commonalities with other women that provided a collective identity and a collective power. As a result, the technique met individual needs of self-clarification at the same time that it operated as an effective tool for movement recruitment.

In its ideal form, C-R not only strengthened individual women but also drew them into the movement. Some so-called C-R groups often failed to achieve, or even seek this goal, however, and the political was subsumed by rather than revealed in the personal. Redstockings, one of the groups usually credited with first advocating the use of C-R, evolved to a point where the technique became an end in itself rather than a means to social change; this occurred through their advocacy of the pro-woman/antibrainwashing line. According to this logic, women's behavior was not a function of nature or conditioning, but rather of their own rational and realistic appraisal of how to survive in a sexist society. Hence, women should not be blamed in any way for their oppression, nor did they need to change any aspects of their behavior. In the end, this logic could promote uncritical validation of all experience and unrestrained glorification of the victim. If victims tended to be glorified, then non-victims — women who played strong leadership roles — tended to be vilified. As a consequence, such groups were often politically immobilized as they turned inward and directed their anger and hostility against each other. In one of the earliest histories of the women's liberation movement, Hole and Levine criticized this tendency for its apolitical results, labeling it a kind of female cultural nationalism or female chauvinism (1971:142, 161).

By the early 1970s, a coherent ideology was beginning to coalesce under the rubric of radical feminism. Although Firestone's *The Dialectic of Sex* (1970) is usually cited as exemplary of this perspective, her biologistic interpretation of women's oppression and her technological solutions involving artificial reproduction are atypical of radical feminism as a whole. A core assumption of radical feminism is that women must be seen first and foremost as a political group or as a sex class. As a political group or sex class, all women have some common interests that must be realized through raised consciousness and active struggle. Most radical feminists recognized class and race differences between women, but sex was seen as the most fundamental axis of social structure and the most fundamental source of oppression. The cause of sexual inequality and oppression was alternately conceptualized as the sex-role system or the sex-class system, or simply as patriarchy.

Since these systems were embedded within all social institutions and practices, the latter could not merely be reformed but must undergo radical or revolutionary change to eliminate their patriarchal core. This program of change included economic and political institutions, but many radical feminists concentrated on marriage and family as the social institutions that had more influence on more women than any other. It was here that social practices and cultural norms established and reinforced female oppression and dependence. Norms of romantic love, compulsory heterosexuality, and the motherhood mandate comprised the socially rewarded path that perpetuated the sex-role system of patriarchy; hence all these norms needed to be analyzed, criticized, and overthrown in the struggle to liberate women.

Early radical feminism tended to construe oppression in largely psychological terms. In part, this may have been a reaction to the abstract and abstruse

theorizing of the New Left, which focused on structural sources of societal oppression. In part, it reflected the validation of female experience, feelings, and
emotions that was central to the C-R experience. In part, too, it was a response
to the focus of radical feminism on the family and its highly charged interpersonal relations. The emphasis on psychological modes of oppression revealed
the sexual politics embedded in intimate relationships, but it also sowed the
seeds of confusion and self-destructive behavior within the movement. If politics
and personalities were inextricably intertwined, then a critique of someone's
position was sometimes inseparable from an assault on their person. If dominant
personalities were subject to heavy criticism, then strong leaders felt pressure to
renounce positions of influence and authority. If every aspect of behavior was
under scrutiny, then the charge of being "male-identified" could usually find
some applicability. Given these connections, it is not surprising that personal
validation displaced any larger politics in some versions of radical feminism. For
similar reasons, radical feminism's relation to men — even "feminist men" — was
full of tension and contradiction. For some, men simply were the enemy. For
others, it was not men per se but the sex-role system or the sex-class system that
was the real target. In this view, men could at least be potential allies in the fight
against a sexist system, but only if they renounced the privileges their male status automatically conferred on them. Even if and when this occurred, the politicization of personal lives meant these issues were ever present at least in the lives
of heterosexual women. For all these reasons, the psychological focus of much
radical feminism was both the source of some of its greatest insights as well as the
occasion for some of its most convoluted and self-destructive behavior as it
sought to put its politics into practice (see Ryan 1989).

From the early to mid-1970s, another distinct ideological strain took form
within the women's movement. The perspective of socialist feminism sought a
new middle ground between some of the insights of the old and new left on the
one hand and the hard-earned lessons of the independent women's liberation
movement on the other hand. Whereas Marxists relied on a variety of classic
texts, socialist feminists drew heavily on Engels's *Origins of the Family, Private
Property, and the State* (1884). Despite its historical inaccuracies and anthropolog-
ical errors, Engels's basic insights about the intertwining of male dominance,
private property, and the capitalist mode of production had a powerful influence
on this line of theorizing. Building on this tradition, socialist feminists insisted
on the need to keep the dynamics of class exploitation in view alongside the
processes of sex oppression, to theorize their interconnections, and to devise
strategies that would challenge this interrelated system. Compared to liberal
feminism, this tradition offered a more holistic and systemic analysis of
the causes and consequences of women's subordination. Compared to radical

feminism, this tradition returned attention to public institutions — the economy in particular — as the ultimate source of women's oppression. Compared to both liberal and radical feminism, socialist feminism provided a blueprint that linked the public and private realms and probed the interconnections between these spheres and their consequences for sexual inequality.

As socialist feminists formulated their analyses more self-consciously, many moved toward some version of what came to be called dual systems theory. In this view, the two parallel and intertwined systems of capitalism and patriarchy functioned together to promote class exploitation and sexual inequality in the interests of both capitalists as a class and men as a group. Women who performed unpaid domestic labor in the household provided direct benefits for husbands and indirect subsidies to the capitalist economy. Women who worked in the paid labor force for depressed wages created greater profits for employers and provided a target for latent sexism among male workers that could be used to further divide the working class. This holistic analysis became the basis for criticizing reformist feminist demands, which often spoke only to the interests of a limited group of women or only displaced the dynamics of sexism into new and different arenas without eradicating its root sources. The holistic analysis implied a holistic solution: revolutionary change was required to overturn the dual system of capitalist patriarchy because sex oppression and class exploitation could only be eradicated in a society organized around the principles of socialist feminism.

Although socialist feminism may have provided the most sophisticated analysis of the causes, mechanisms, and consequences of sexual inequality, its theoretical power was not matched by any comparable success at recruiting and mobilizing large numbers. There were several reasons for this. Many women remained suspicious of socialist feminism because they feared a return to the politico-feminist debates and attempts by leftists to relegate feminism to the back of the revolutionary bus. Some women were also suspicious of the emphasis on theoretical abstraction, which at times seemed far removed from the realities of everyday life. Traditional hostility to socialism and the left was extended to socialist feminism as well, making it a less popular choice than other strands of feminism — particularly in a time of growing reaction and the more general decline of the left. A further problem concerned the inability of socialist feminism to identify a plausible strategy. Whereas liberal feminists could chip away at various manifestations of sexism with a faith in cumulative progress, and whereas radical feminists could focus on psychological liberation and alternative relationships and communities, socialist feminism had identified the basic underpinnings of U.S. society as requiring fundamental change, and no satisfying strategy for accomplishing that goal could be easily formulated. However, the most concrete obstacle to the growth of socialist feminism involved continuing sectarianism among various left groups who sought to dominate discussions of strategy. Symbolic of this problem was the first national socialist-feminist conference in Yellow Springs, Ohio, in the summer of 1975. By several accounts, the conference failed to achieve the kind of free-flowing discussion and debate that participants hoped for, and many blamed sectarian Maoist groups for undermining the prospects for a more successful conference (Bunch [Charlotte] Papers, n.d.).

By the mid-1970s, it was becoming something of a cliche to characterize the contemporary women's movement as consisting of liberal feminism, radical feminism, and socialist feminism. This trichotomy concealed ongoing debates over lesbianism within the movement, and the ideological implications of what Freeman has called the "gay/straight split" (1975:134). Within mainstream organizations like NOW, there had been a long struggle over the acceptability and visibility of lesbians within the organization. These were less of a problem within the women's liberation sector, but the ideological implications of lesbianism were hotly contested. In these debates, the perspective of lesbian feminism emerged by taking some of the basic insights of radical feminism and logically extending them into explicit analyses of lesbian identity and practice. Radical feminism had developed the concepts "male-identified" and "woman-identified" to help build feminist solidarity by orienting women to other women. Radical feminism had also promoted the slogan that the personal is political, prompting reflexive examination of all aspects of private life as politically relevant. It was a relatively short and eminently logical step for lesbian feminists to extend these concepts to sexual behavior and emotional attachments. The conclusion was that lesbian relations were the logical, desirable, and politically appropriate expression of feminist principles because only in such relations could the concept of "woman-identified" women find full expression. The logic could not help but convey at least an implicit criticism of heterosexual women, whose sexual relations appeared at best to limit their commitment to feminism, and at worst to provide aid and comfort to the enemy.

This analysis culminated in "lesbian vanguardism": the view that lesbians were in the forefront of the struggle against sexism and provided the model for others to follow. To the extent that lesbianism was defined as the practical expression of one's feminist politics, many heterosexually oriented radical feminist women found themselves in a defensive position. Some attempted to change their sexual orientation, some fell away from the movement, and some defended their radical credentials despite their sexual orientation. Although this debate never reached a clear resolution — and continues in various ways to the present day — it had a profound impact on those who took part in it. The identification of

various forms of lesbian oppression added a new dimension to the feminist analysis of women's position by identifying heterosexism as a cultural bias even more
fundamental than, but closely intertwined with, sexism. Despite the heated debates and potential divisiveness surrounding these issues, lesbian oppression
and its relation to feminism became an issue of central concern to those seeking
to articulate radical feminist and socialist feminist ideology, and it gradually acquired increased visibility and legitimacy within liberal feminist circles as well.

The debates over lesbianism and heterosexism contributed to the evolution of yet another ideological position, identified as cultural feminism. In this
variant of radical feminism, women are assumed to possess a distinctive culture
and temperament that sets them sharply apart from men. The goal of cultural
feminism is to preserve this difference by sharply limiting contact with men.
Such contact, at best, would divert women and their energy from exploring, af-
firming, and reinforcing an essential female nature that is denied and devalued
by the dominant culture. Physical, or at least psychic and emotional separatism
from this dominant culture and men as its carrier is thus essential to resisting
patriarchy and creating an alternative world organized around female values.
Cultural feminism is unlike many other strands of feminism and similar to sexist
beliefs in positing such deeply grounded differences between men and women.
Whereas sexism privileges males and male values over females and female
values, however, cultural feminism offers a powerful critique of the destructive-
ness of the dominant values in male culture and strong affirmation of the alternative value system to be found in female culture (H. Eisenstein 1983; Donovan
1985). While lesbian separatism may be the purest expression of cultural feminism (Frye 1988; Spinster 1988), not all lesbian feminists adopt this perspective;
at the same time, many heterosexual or bisexual women in the contemporary
movement have embraced cultural feminism to one degree or another.

Some strains of contemporary cultural feminism are highly reminiscent of
earlier manifestations of social feminism. In a recent study, Black characterizes
social feminism as seeking increased autonomy for women by using values, beliefs, and experiences typically identified with women as a basis of empowerment (1989). Black proposes a "feminist classification of feminisms" that
distinguishes between social feminism and equity feminism. Equity feminism,
whether liberal, Marxist, or socialist, relies on male classifications to demand the
extension of rights enjoyed by other groups to women. As such, it can be interpreted as an assimilationist approach to gender that, if successful, will integrate
women into a male-defined world. Social feminism, whether maternal, cultural,
or radical, appeals to female values to expand women's traditional roles beyond
the private sphere and promote more fundamental societal transformations in
keeping with those values. Social feminism has a strong separatist theme be-

cause exclusion of males is necessary to maintain and cultivate the distinctive female world that is the basis of its transformative potential. At the same time, social feminism bridges public and private spheres by allowing women to engage in political activity without disrupting their self-image or male expectations about women's behavior. While Black acknowledges the danger that social feminism can be wedded to conservative causes, she argues that the organizational and theoretical benefits of social feminism greatly outweigh the risks associated with this approach (1989).

The diverse ideologies of the contemporary women's movement can be described as analytically distinct thought systems, but the movement has most often been powered by a blending and mixing of ideas, values, and goals from each of these ideological worldviews. The women's rights sector of the movement is the most consistent proponent of liberal feminism, and the success of this sector derives in part from the fact that liberal feminism resonates with dominant cultural values of individualism and equal opportunity even as it argues for extending these values to women. However, this sector of the movement has selectively adopted (or coopted) insights, ideas, and goals from other movement ideologies and incorporated them into its agenda for change. Despite its theoretical sophistication, socialist feminism has become all but dormant as a movement ideology due to the generally low profile of the left after the mid-1970s and the consequences of sectarian disputes. At the same time, this worldview infused liberal feminism and the women's rights sector with a more systemic view of the institutions of economy, polity, family, and household, and socialist feminism helped to shape the agenda, goals, and demands of liberal feminist politics even though a coherent socialist vision was never transplanted into mainstream feminism. For a considerable time, socialist feminism was also the ideology that was most receptive to issues of race, ethnicity and nationality. For all these reasons, and despite its apparent demise, socialist feminism broadened the perspective of the feminist movement and many of its major organizations.

If liberal feminism can be characterized as a subcultural ideology because of the common themes it shares with the dominant culture, then radical feminism is best seen as a countercultural ideology for its holistic challenge to the dominant culture. The depth and breadth of radical feminism's critique of patriarchy and the dominant culture has put it outside what Chomsky and Herman (1988), in another context, have called "the bounds of thinkable thought." One result is that the number of women subscribing to radical feminist ideology is relatively small compared to adherents of liberal feminism; another is that those who do espouse radical feminism typically have a total identification with this worldview such that their identities and all aspects of their lives are seen as a reflection of their political ideology. Radical feminism has always been the main orientation of the women's liberation sector of the movement and of the groups, networks, and alternative institutions that grew out of this sector. Despite the degree of its opposition to the dominant culture, radical feminism has been able to survive even through a significant period of reaction for several reasons. One is the dedication of its followers. Another involves the success of radical feminists in building counterinstitutions in the form of women's centers, bookstores, coffeehouses, health clinics, rape crisis centers, battered women's shelters, and women's music, art, and literature. Women's studies programs and organizations in universities and academic professions have provided a relatively safe haven for sustaining radical feminist thought and culture and for creating regional and national networks of like-minded people. Despite the extent of its challenge to the dominant culture, then, these factors have facilitated the survival of radical feminism.

There have been more attempts to describe the ideology of the contemporary women's movement than to analyze, interpret, or explain it. Nonetheless, at least two main lines of interpretation find substantial empirical support despite the divergent conclusions involved in each. One interpretation, focusing on proliferation, sees generally positive results from an ideologically diverse movement. The other intrepretation, focusing on deradicalization, sees a generally negative outcome in the form of a movement that has lost much of its transformative potential. Maren Carden argues that the women's movement has undergone proliferation as a result of an interaction between its abstract ideology and variation in individual members' reasons for participation (Carden 1978). The combination of agreement on a broad ideology with great variability in specific ideological motivation and selective incentives for participation is what creates pressure for movement proliferation. The danger that proliferation would lead to dissipation is counteracted by the ideological value of sisterhood, which creates a counterforce toward unity. Thus, Carden sees proliferation as creating several positive consequences: it allows the movement to attack a complex problem on many fronts; it provides opportunities to experiment; and it allows the movement to be more resistant to opposition.

Ferree and Hess (1985) also depict a movement whose continuing strength resides in its diversity, although they see potential dangers in this diversity as well. They argue that what they call the New Feminist Movement has no dominant ideology and encourages all efforts by women to take control of their lives. Since male dominance is part of all social institutions, feminist groups and efforts will be (and must be) as diverse as the society they challenge. Such diversity contains its own dangers, however. Significant differences in ideology and strategy may divert energy from the larger struggle, create personal estrangement, and deplete scarce resources. The continuing danger is that diversity will spawn conflict that cannot be successfully resolved, leading to factionalism. In their judgment, however, the movement has proven "remarkably resilient to internal dissent" (1985:111) and diversity has been a strength, not a weakness. In ideological terms, in the midst of extraordinary growth in diverse associations and activities they detect a "coming together" around certain shared goals that has made for a stronger movement despite the obvious strains in such a combination. They characterize movement diversity by recognizing differences in both means (personal transformation versus sociopolitical change) and ends (free individuals versus new communities) and by distinguishing four feminist orientations: career feminists use personal transformation toward the goal of free individuals; liberal feminists use sociopolitical transformation toward the goal of free individuals; radical feminists use personal transformation toward the goal of new communities; and socialist feminists use sociopolitical change toward the goal of new communities (1985:42).

This generally positive view of movement proliferation and diversity is offset by a more negative view of movement deradicalization and dissolution. Bouchier (1978) argues that this is precisely what happened to the radical feminist movement that was in evidence as early as 1967. Soon after its initial success, women's rights organizations adopted notions like feminism, sisterhood, and consciousness-raising from this sector, and the process of deradicalization was underway. Bouchier points to the role of both mainstream and alternative media in "a gentle process of cooptation" (1978:390). As radicals lost the attention of mass media and control of alternative media, they were written out of the history of the very movement they had helped to create. Constant underlying pressures toward institutionalization and professionalization then began to take effect as radicals eschewed leadership roles and others more readily took up such positions. With these changes, a liberal theory of sexism (as sex role stereotyping) became entrenched, consciousness-raising was reduced to therapy, and "feminism had been more quickly and thoroughly integrated into the upper middle class institutional status quo than any other protest movement in history" (1978:394). By the mid-1970s, the deradicalization process was complete, and radicals retreated into cultural or lifestyle feminism. While this contributed to the creation of a feminist counterculture, it was a far cry from the societal transformations envisioned by the original movement.

Barbara Ryan has called attention to another aspect of demobilization that occurred in the contemporary women's movement as a result of a divisive insistence on ideological purity (1989). Analyzing the period from 1966 to 1975, Ryan argues that there was a marked tendency for various theories of women's subordination to become translated into rigid ideological positions, which in turn were very closely associated with personal identity claims. In her words, "radical-feminist leaders became ideological purists in order to create distance between themselves and feminist leaders they felt were establishment women" (Ryan 1989:242). As ideological positions and personal identity became increasingly intertwined, "everybody was trashed. Different groups for different reasons at different times. Too radical, too conservative, too liberal, straight, lived with men, had boy children, etc." (interview subject cited in Ryan 1989:248). In Ryan's estimate, such trashing helped to obscure a shared movement vision as ideological correctness became more important than common goals. Hence, as "disputes over theory turned into disputes over who was most feminist or who was the right kind of feminist" (1989:251–252), these dynamics had a demobilizing effect that may have driven out some of the early movement's most ardent advocates.

The theme of deradicalization has also been explored by those who detect a radical potential in liberal feminism because it rests on a contradictory combination of patriarchal, individualist assumptions with egalitarian, collectivist ones. Under the right circumstances, the implicitly radical emphasis on women's identity as a sex class may transcend the explicitly liberal view of women's identity as an independent, autonomous self and thereby promote a more radical feminism (Z. Eisenstein 1981). This radical potential was an ever-present tension in the politics of the 1970s and produced a complex political struggle by the end of the decade, when several forces emerged to resist the radical implications of liberal feminism (Z. Eisenstein 1984). Revisionist liberalism acquiesced in the neoconservative attack on liberal notions of equality and the liberal welfare state, thereby delegitimating the moral vocabulary of traditional liberalism. At the same time, revisionist feminism in both liberal and left guises retreated from the radical promise of women's solidarity as a sex class and unwittingly strengthened the hand of New Right antifeminists. The common thread in these diverse reactions was the promotion of some conception of sexual difference as more important than the feminist goal of sexual equality. Although outright opposition to feminism was obviously important in this process, Eisenstein identifies "revisionist liberal feminism" as most central in the process of deradicalization. This revisionist feminism, epitomized by Betty Friedan's later work, rejects sexual politics and sexual equality in favor of a revalorization of motherhood and the nuclear family, leaving public institutions essentially unchanged. Thus, the radical potential of liberal feminism has been undermined by revisionist feminism in a conservative climate.

Eisenstein's defense of sexual equality in the face of what she calls revisionist feminism represents one side of what became the dominant ideological debate within the women's movement in the 1980s. Her brand of equal rights feminism has a long heritage of insisting that the sexes are much more similar than different, that equal treatment is the only way to eliminate sexism and establish justice for women, and that the identification of differences between the sexes has almost always served as a prelude to unequal treatment of women. The other side of the debate has been more concerned with exploring the concept of sexual difference and identifying its implications for the goals and strategies of the women's movement. From this perspective, there are significant differences between the sexes that feminism has yet to explore adequately, equal treatment tends to legitimate male standards, and the pursuit of sexual difference holds the key to envisioning a radically different world organized along fundamentally new principles. For proponents of equal rights feminism, the fascination with sexual difference is theoretically flawed in its essentialist assumptions about women and strategically dangerous in its tendency to reinforce separate spheres of ideology and practice. For proponents of sexual difference, the equal rights approach is the more limited theory of change because it leads to an assimilationist strategy of women becoming equal in a world created by men rather than creating a different world; it is also strategically dangerous because strict interpretations of equal rights in a context of sexual difference can create additional obstacles for women.

Many of these tendencies toward both ideological proliferation and movement deradicalization are exemplified in what might be called "academic feminism." The ideology of the contemporary women's movement is closely bound up with developments in more formalized feminist theory. Such theory, in turn, has important institutionalized roots in women's studies departments and programs, professional organizations, publishing houses, and academic journals. While feminist theory and movement ideology may now dialectically inform one another, it is important to remember that the movement and its ideology came first, and that more formal feminist theory only emerged as a subsequent response. The growth and proliferation of academic feminism is thus a compelling example of the power of the contemporary movement; at the same time, feminist theory in its more academic guise provides an important tool for recruiting new participants from a vast pool of students. However, the growth of more academic forms of feminist thought poses all the usual dangers of cooptation, institutionalization, professionalization, and deradicalization that plague many movements. As women's studies becomes another area of academic study, the danger is that the topic will be defined in a depoliticized manner that severs the historical connections between the movement and the academy. As long as those ties are maintained, academic feminism will make a vital contribution by bridging the worlds of feminist theory and movement ideology.

Despite the diversity in ideological approaches examined in this chapter, this analysis has treated ideology as a relatively explicit, consciously formulated, rationally consistent collection of assumptions, arguments, and conclusions. While serving the purposes of exposition and analysis, there is a danger that such an approach may distort the actual nature and role of ideology in social movements. Several caveats are thus in order. For one, the relatively clear distinctions we have drawn between different strains of ideological thought have often not been so strictly drawn by movement participants themselves. In the flux of social movement activity, ideological assumptions and strategical implications that may seem contradictory in the abstract often appear together with no felt sense of contradiction. Hence, there is a danger that the schools of thought delineated here will become reified and discrete entities when they are better seen as part of a complex mosaic. Another caveat concerns how and why ideologies motivate people to participate in social movements. Analytical exposition of an ideology may imply that its most important feature is its logical coherence, but it is likely that more people are motivated by the passion of principle than the logic of coherence in responding to ideological appeals. Hence, the analytical component of ideology cannot by itself answer questions about how and why and which people will respond to a given ideology.

The most important question that may have been slighted by this conception of ideology as explicit, conscious, and rational concerns how movement ideology has or has not trickled down into the lived experience of women who do not see themselves as movement members or sympathizers. In the end, this may prove to be the greatest impact of feminist ideology, but little is known about this issue. Two examples of attempts to answer these questions illustrate productive directions for future research. In one ongoing study, Stall has been interviewing women in a small midwestern town to determine their attitudes toward contemporary feminist stances. She argues that neither liberal feminism nor radical feminism fit comfortably with the experiences and worldviews of these women. Liberal feminism requires adherence to an abstract norm of individual interest and opportunity, while radical feminism often translates into a politics of victimization and/or a politics of rage that encourages purism and separatism. Both ideologies fail to resonate with the communal bonds and practical reciprocity that are part of the network of relationships that constitute ongoing communities. The danger is that both ideologies may characterize such women as "apolitical" when a closer look reveals that they are already engaged in ongoing "modest struggles" to implement feminist goals within the context of their communities. Stall's analysis (1988) implies that while a minority of women may consciously identify with the women's movement and an explicit ideology, many more women are already (have always been?) resisting patriarchal power through the ongoing, modest politics of everyday life. (For a useful overview of the kinds of issues and protests that often receive the support of women — though not always as self-identified "feminists" — see West and Blumberg, forthcoming).

A second example is provided by Stacey's study of post-feminist consciousness, a term she uses to describe the "simultaneous incorporation, revision and depoliticization of many of the central goals of second wave feminism" (Stacey 1987:8). Based on in-depth interviews with several women in a variety of family and work situations located in California's Silicon Valley, Stacey explores the ways in which women who eschew the term "feminist" have nonetheless selectively appropriated feminist ideas into their worldview. While rejecting formal movement identification or involvement, these women have adapted both feminist and non-feminist principles to their particular life situation, and they use this blend of ideas to make sense out of the twists and turns their work and family lives have taken. Once again, while a minority of women may be explicit adherents of a well-defined feminist ideology, the majority of women are more likely to subscribe to the kind of post-feminist or proto-feminist stance explored by Stacey. The implications of this post-feminist consciousness for the demobilization or remobilization of the feminist movement certainly warrants further research. These studies of ideology in everyday life serve as a useful reminder that in the women's movement, ideology is located between the two poles of academic feminist theory and everyday lived experience. Future studies of movement ideology would do well to examine connections in both of these directions.

Conclusions

The histories of the woman suffrage movement and the contemporary women's movement suggest that women's movements have always been characterized by ideological transformation and diversity. At no time in either movement is it possible to identify a single ideology as representative of the movement as a whole, and at many points it is difficult to identify a dominant ideology. This ideological differentiation ultimately reflects the social diversity of women as a movement constituency. Differences of class, race, ethnicity, religion, sexual orientation, and worldview virtually necessitate ideological diversity if women's movements are to reach beyond a rather small and insular base. The consequences of such diversity are also variable. It can be the basis for division, schism, and factionalism, as occurred frequently in the women's liberation movement. It can also be the foundation for a truly mass movement of women in pursuit of a major goal, as occurred in the later stages of the woman suffrage

odd - couldn't this be interpreted as most
un diverse period, at least re goal.

movement. If it is true that such ideological diversity is a prerequisite for mass movements of women, then the major strategic task confronting such movements is to turn diversity into an empowering movement asset rather than letting it become a crippling movement liability.

Given this rich history of ideological diversity, it is difficult to define any generic feminist ideology that adequately characterizes these movements as a whole. Like socialist movements, feminist movements may best be defined not by what they are for but rather by what they are against. All feminist movements oppose the way in which gender has been used to structure a socially unequal world between women and men: "belief in what is usually referred to as sex equality . . . might be more clearly expressed in the negative, as opposition to sex hierarchy" (Cott 1987:4). The other components of modern feminism identified by Cott — a social-constructivist view of women's condition and some sense of gender group identity — do not specify positive goals as much as they identify prerequisites for movement activity. When women's movements are ascendant and waging effective battles for their goals, these core components of feminism become a taken-for-granted backdrop against which ideological differences stand out in sharp relief. When the same movements lose momentum or attract opposition, ideological differences often become less important than the underlying core that distinguishes feminists from non-feminists and provides the former with common ground in their opposition to patriarchal elements of the dominant culture and to reactionary forces seeking to maintain or restore such elements.

While it may not be possible to identify a generic feminist ideology, it is possible to identify major ideological strands that typically accompany women's movements. The most obvious such strand is equal rights or liberal feminism. This view appears ubiquitous: wherever women's movements have appeared, an equal rights, liberal feminist orientation has occupied a major position among movement ideologies. There are at least two reasons for the ubiquity of this equal rights, liberal feminist orientation in women's movements. On the one hand, an equal rights, liberal feminist approach partakes of the dominant political philosophy of capitalist societies and thereby resonates with some mainstream cultural worldviews. On the other hand, an equal rights, liberal feminist approach appeals most strongly to women who are middle-class, college-educated, and professionally oriented — in short, to women who are relatively well off in respects other than gender. These factors combine to insure that an equal rights, liberal feminist approach will gain considerable attention when and where women's movements become mobilized both because it is the type of feminism that is most palatable to the dominant culture and because it is the type of feminism that best articulates the interests of a relatively powerful subgroup of movement participants.

Thus, from the earliest days of the women's rights movement to the most recent pronouncements of NOW, this equal rights, liberal feminist approach provides a strong thread of continuity to women's movements in the U.S. Given this thread of continuity, Zillah Eisenstein's arguments about the radical potential of liberal feminism (1981, 1984) remain important for understanding the future trajectory of the contemporary women's movement. At the same time, the fate of socialist feminism is instructive about the limits to radicalism in social movements. Just as the dominant ideology has been receptive to liberal feminism, it has been hostile to socialist feminism as part of a more general aversion to socialism and leftist politics. This hostility has combined with leftist sectarianism and factionalism to insure that socialist feminism has never been a major ideology within U.S. women's movements, despite its theoretical sweep and wider popularity in other nations such as Britain.

The ubiquitous presence of equal rights or liberal feminism has often been complemented by the substantially different ideological perspective of social or cultural feminism. If liberal feminism has been an integrationist ideology of equal rights based on presumed similarities between the sexes, social or cultural feminism has often been more of a separatist ideology of female principles based on presumed differences between the sexes. Where liberal feminism has denied or minimized any distinictive female traits, social or cultural feminism has emphasized and embraced such traits by arguing that women—by nature or cultural learning—are substantially different from men and that women's distinctive traits form the basis for an alternative world. From the homosocial circles of female reformers in the nineteenth century to the cultural and radical feminists of the twentieth, this is another connecting thread in the history of women's movements in the United States (Black 1989). Seen through the lens of social or cultural feminism, even lesbian separatism seems a difference in degree rather than in kind because it is a logical extension from the premises of cultural feminism concerning differences between the sexes.

In other respects, however, contemporary radical feminism in general and lesbian separatism in particular represent something new that was not foreshadowed or anticipated in the women's rights and woman suffrage movement. Contemporary radical feminism differs dramatically from earlier social feminism in the depth and breadth of the gender-based analysis it has developed, and also in the centrality accorded to patriarchy as the root cause of women's subordination. In addition, contemporary radical feminist ideology has maintained a focus on women's subordination as the central issue. Nineteenth-century social feminism, by contrast, frequently abstracted away from the specificity of gender and women's subordination and addressed itself to broader sets of social problems whose relation to feminist ideology was tenuous at best. Contemporary lesbian separatism differs specifically from social feminism by its explicit and extensive politicization of all "personal life" and its advocacy of a sexual politics that extends to all human relationships. In addition, contemporary lesbian separatist ideology has increasingly pursued separatism as an end goal. For nineteenth-century social feminism, by contrast, separatism functioned more as a tactic and a means to further ends; it did not envision continuing separation of the sexes but rather their harmonious rapprochement based on new values and principles.

The longevity of women's movements makes it possible to raise important questions about patterns of ideological transformation over time. In an earlier analysis of the woman suffrage movement (Buechler 1986), I argued that the women's rights/woman suffrage movement underwent a substantial transformation in its ideology, program, and goals over its seventy-year history. This movement began in the 1840s and 1850s as a broadly oriented, multi-issue challenge to patriarchal power. While its dominant equal rights ideology, derived from Enlightenment philosophy, anticipated liberal feminism, the "radical potential" of this perspective was forcefully articulated by movement spokeswomen such as Elizabeth Cady Stanton, for whom marriage, motherhood, and the family were even more important in the feminist reform program than gaining the right to vote. After the Civil War, this orientation underwent a complex transformation that resulted in a narrower and more specialized movement for the right to vote by the turn of the century. In addition to the narrower focus, equal rights gave way to social feminism as the dominant movement ideology. Because of the ways social feminism endorsed many traditional features of gender roles and relations, it did not pose as fundamental a challenge to patriarchal power as the earlier women's rights movement had. In some respects, the later movement actually reinforced traditional gender arrangements by the kinds of arguments it made for the right to vote. However, what the movement lost in the breadth of its challenge to patriarchal power it gained in the sophistication of its strategy toward winning the vote. As a specialized movement for the right to vote, the later movement was able to build a cross-class, multiconstituency alliance for the ballot, which was essential in the success of that campaign in 1920.

In many respects, the contemporary women's movement began where the woman suffrage movement ended: with a rather legalistic version of liberal feminist ideology directed to a limited and specific set of grievances. Within a year of NOW's founding, however, the agenda broadened to include multiple issues. Within two years, the women's liberation movement was developing a more radical version of feminist ideology that challenged the foundations of patriarchy in personal life as well as in public institutions. The women's liberation movement was able to effect two important changes in the women's movement. On the one hand, it radicalized the movement's ideology and broadened its agenda for change far beyond what liberal feminism had envisioned. On the other hand, it popularized the women's movement and contributed to a truly mass movement of women who became mobilized in the organized struggle against sexism.

By the mid-1970s, these accomplishments began to unravel in the context of a more conservative political climate that included growing opposition to the goals of the women's movement on the part of countermovements. NOW returned to a more legalistic version of liberal feminism and concentrated its efforts on the struggle to ratify the ERA. The women's liberation movement shifted its focus from revolutionary societal change to the creation and nurturance of countercultural institutions, work on specific issues, or simply living one's personal life in accord with feminist principles. Since the mid-1970s, the highly differentiated ideologies that animated the movement have blended and intermingled into a diversity of perspectives with a common core of assumptions. The thesis of deradicalization proposed by Zillah Eisenstein (1984) and Bouchier (1978) has some merit if one compares the radical and popular movement of the early 1970s with the movement at later times. All of the earlier movement ideologies can still be found in various movement subcultures, however, along with new variations and permutations informed by developments in feminist theory. Rather than deradicalization, it is perhaps more accurate to describe the current situation as one of movement demobilization. If new mobilizing conditions arise, the ideology of a revived feminist movement would be likely to retain all the diverse strands that have developed in the last two decades.

Throughout all these transformations and permutations, movement ideology has continued to play a vital role in the life of women's movements. While material resources are essential in creating the capacity for action, ideology is vital in providing the motivation for action. It is ideology that translates individual discontent into movement grievances. It is ideology that transforms aggregates of people into unified and cohesive groups. It is ideology that politicizes preexisting networks of people and mobilizes them into movement activity. It is ideology that facilitates personal change and thereby recruits new members into a movement. It is ideology that literally creates certain movement resources by symbolically framing meanings, motivations, people, and objects in ways that facilitate movement mobilization. Women's movements in the United States provide powerful illustrations of all these functions of movement ideology.

Chapter
four

Classes
and
Races

Issues of inclusion and difference have become a major focus of the contemporary women's movement. In part, this reflects a new awareness that a movement that has often claimed to speak for a universal womanhood has actually spoken with a predominantly white, middle-class voice. These issues are inevitable in a women's movement, however, because women are distributed throughout virtually all other social groups. Movements based on class or race typically appeal to socially concentrated constituencies that already share a common socioeconomic position, a similar status, a distinctive subculture, and a preexisting group consciousness. Movements based on gender, on the other hand, can theoretically appeal to a socially diverse constituency of women from differing socioeconomic positions and statuses who do not share a preexisting subculture or group consciousness. In a paradoxical fashion, the very efforts to identify the common threads that presumably link all women have simultaneously revealed the major differences separating women of different class and racial backgrounds.

In preceding chapters, recent sociological work on social movements has been useful for analyzing movement origins, organizational forms, and ideological issues. This literature is largely silent, however, on questions of movement diversity in general and on the particular role of race, class, and gender in the dynamics of social movements. This silence is a theoretical reflection of the practical reality that most movements tend to draw from relatively homogeneous constituencies. Hence movement diversity and heterogeneity have not received the same degree of attention as many other issues in the contemporary sociological literature. The study of women's movements thereby promises to enrich social movement theory by bringing the issues of diversity, heterogeneity, and inclusion onto center stage in the analysis of social movement dynamics.

Understanding these dynamics requires a working model of the forms of social organization that are the cause of movement grievances and the target of change efforts. For our purposes, these forms may be conceptualized as three interlocking systems of domination based on class exploitation, racial oppression, and gender dominance. Each system of domination has generated social movements by subordinate groups seeking to alter their position in the structure, or, more fundamentally, to alter the structure itself. Because of the complex manner in which these systems of domination are interlocked with one another, the movements that have challenged them have also been interrelated in various ways. Whether these relations have been beneficial or harmful has depended on numerous factors, including the strength of each individual movement, the kinds of goals being sought, and the ability of dominant groups to use class, race, or gender differences to undercut the solidarity and shatter the cohesion of any particular movement.

Movements against any system of domination recruit members by creating or appealing to a shared sense of group identity. People are likely to join a movement when they sense that there are others like them who are suffering similar injustices and that a collective effort holds some promise of change. A shared sense of group identity may be seen as a prerequisite or a product of successful movement mobilization, but without it movements are not likely to be effective in pursuing their demands. From the perspective of someone seeking to mobilize a potentially large consituency, two crucial steps must occur. First, potential recruits must claim the requisite identity in an explicit and central way. That is, seeing oneself as a worker or a black or a woman must be a conscious and salient identity for someone before she is a likely recruit to a social movement based on class, race, or gender. Second, potential recruits must see this salient identity not just in individual terms, but in collective terms that view the fate of any one member of a given group as intimately tied to the fate of other members of the same group. Without a sense of collective identity and shared fate, members of subordinate groups may seek individual mobility, but are unlikely to join social movements.

While systems of domination and movements opposing them have some similarities in the abstract, the concrete, historical processes of class exploitation, racial oppression, and gender dominance differ substantially from one another. One difference involves the degree to which individual and collective identity as members of a subordinate group is an inevitable result of social organization or must itself be meticulously cultivated by movement leaders. As a broad generalization, blacks in the U.S. have had the most consistent individual and collective identification as members of a subordinate group, based on a long history of slavery, segregation, discrimination, and racism. Women have had the least consistent individual and collective identification as members of an oppressed group, based on their distribution throughout all other groups, their proximity to men, and their separation from other women, which is structured into the social institutions of heterosexuality, marriage, and the nuclear family. Workers have had an individual and collective identity stronger than that of women but weaker than that of blacks, based on the shifting fortunes of working-class resistance and the heterogeneous composition of the U.S. working class. If this logic is correct, then it follows that women's movements have had to work harder than racial or labor movements to create the sense of individual and collective identity among their constituents that could sustain movement mobilization.

It also follows from this logic that leaders of women's movements may be unable or unwilling to foster the kind of collective identity among diverse women that would sustain mass mobilization. The inability to do so may derive from limited resources or lack of networks with different groups of women, but this unwillingness or inability is best explained by the intersecting statuses of gender, class, and race. That is, all women are also members of a specific social class and a particular racial group. As a result, one's approach to women's movements will inevitably be influenced not just by one's identity as a woman but also by one's class and racial identity and group membership. Even the most simplified model of class and race hierarchies identifies four possible locations for women within social structure. While women are members of a subordinate gender group, they may also be members of a dominant class and racial group, of a dominant class but subordinate racial group, of a subordinate class but dominant racial group, and of a subordinate class and racial group. Each of these social locations is likely to promote a different view of the overall society and a different approach to feminist issues and women's movements.

Analysis of these highly abstract locations in social structure can be helpful in understanding actual patterns of mobilization. Women who are members of dominant class and race groups may be attracted to feminist mobilization because it addresses their one subordinate status. Alternately, they may feel that their class and race privileges outweigh their gender disadvantages, or that feminist activism might jeopardize their dominant class and race position. Women who are members of a dominant class but a subordinate race are logical candidates for recruitment to both racial and gender movements, just as women who are members of a dominant race but subordinate class are logical candidates for recruitment to both class and gender movements. Finally, women who are members of subordinate classes and races are logical candidates for recruitment to race, class, and gender movements. Our earlier discussion of the salience and strength of group identities would predict that when women are members of other subordinate groups as well, their initial attraction will be to movements based on race or class. This highly abstract analysis implies that the most likely recruits to a feminist movement will thus be women from dominant class and race groups.

These reflections shed some light on why women's movements have historically drawn most heavily from white, middle-class constituencies, although the question is obviously more complex than this simplistic model of social location and structural interest implies. Studies in the sociology of knowledge suggest that one's social location affects not only group interests, but also cultural worldviews; this insight is especially promising for understanding the role of class in women's movements. One thesis that will be explored throughout this chapter is that a middle-class location permits and promotes a type of "class unconsciousness" that contrasts sharply with the class awareness of other groups. In effect, this means that although upper-class women and working-class women are both likely to be highly class conscious (though in very different ways), middle-class women are less likely to see the role of class in structuring the social world precisely because of their class location. This "class unconsciousness" is fostered and expressed through ideological beliefs about individualism, opportunity, and mobility that deny the presence of structural barriers to individual effort. Put differently, the weight of class at the top and the bottom of the class structure is too prominent to be denied or minimized; from the middle of the class structure, on the other hand, it is possible to see the social world in a relatively classless way.

A similar logic may operate in the case of racial hierarchies. Here, the sociology of knowledge would suggest that being a member of a dominant racial group will foster a very different view of the world than being a member of a subordinate racial group. More specifically, one of the privileges of membership in a dominant racial group is the perception that one's own group is the norm, the standard, and the reference point against which "others" are defined and categorized. Taking one's own group as the standard may thereby foster a kind of "racial unconsciousness" in which one's own racial privileges are taken for granted and the racial disadvantages of others are not seen as such. In all these ways, then, the worldview of white, middle-class people may promote forms of class "unconsciousness" and race "unconsciousness" that effectively deny or mask the privileges associated with membership in relatively advantaged class and racial groups.

If the structural location and social worldview of white, middle-class women does promote these forms of class and race unconsciousness, then it follows that they comprise the one group that is structurally and perceptually predisposed to see the world as primarily organized around gender. This perception is one basis for middle-class white women's greater participation in organized women's movements when compared with women from other class or racial backgrounds. Gender dominance may thus affect all women, be recognized by all women, and be resisted by all women, but it is middle-class white women whose resistance is most likely to take the form of independent and autonomous feminist movements. The resistance of working-class women or women of color, by contrast, will always be informed by class or race consciousness as well as gender consciousness. In Nancy Cott's formulation, "The woman's rights tradition was historically initiated by, and remains prejudiced toward, those who perceive themselves first and foremost as 'woman,' who can gloss over their class, racial and other status identifications because those are culturally dominant and therefore relatively invisible" (Cott 1987:9). The theme of race and class in women's movements reveals how these prejudices have shaped these movements, as well as the occasions and potentials that have and do exist for overcoming them.

The following analysis examines these abstract, structural realities in the context of historically specific efforts to improve the status of women in the woman suffrage movement and the contemporary women's movement. This history reveals considerable diversity in the actual stances taken by these movements toward the nexus of class, race, and gender. It also suggests the difficulties of confronting multiple and interlocking systems of domination, which provide numerous opportunities for powerful groups to implement divide-and-conquer strategies against movements for progressive change. One of the more significant lessons to emerge from this survey is that in both past and present women's movements, barriers of class difference have proven somewhat more permeable than divisions based on race. From the perspective of mobilizing mass movements of women, race has been the most significant "Achilles heel" crippling efforts to build a diverse and potentially revolutionary movement on behalf of women.

The Woman Suffrage Movement

Virtually all scholars have described the woman suffrage movement as a white, middle-class movement. Although this truism is accurate as far as it goes, it has obscured variations and complexities of class and race relations within the movement. At various points in its history, the woman suffrage movement ignored black women, actively rejected black women, spoke eloquently against slavery, and engaged in explicit and virulent racism. There were also significant changes in the class structure during this period, altering the referent of the term "middle class" as a characterization of the movement (Buechler 1986). As the middle-class nature of the movement changed over time, so did its stance toward class issues. At various points, it recruited working-class women, ignored them, rejected them, and tactically sought alliances with them. The variations and complexities of class and race do not mean that the truism about a white, middle-class movement is wrong, but rather that it is time to move beyond the truism to understand the nuances of these dynamics.

The class and race orientation of the early women's rights movement took shape within the context of the abolitionist movement, which contained its own differences by class and race. For most middle-class activists, abolitionism was first and foremost a moral crusade that required ending slavery but bore no relation to working-class issues being raised by the labor movement. For working-class abolitionists, on the other hand, slave labor degraded both slaves and "free" labor, and antislavery work was seen as part of a larger struggle against the two-faced enemy of labor: "the lord of the loom and the lord of the lash" (Sacks 1976:34). As the leadership of the women's movement formulated its agenda within this larger abolitionist context, it bore the imprint of its middle-class origins. In a time of entrepreneurial, competitive capitalism, "middle class" typically designated small property-owners and their associated interests. Thus, the earliest articulated demands of the middle-class women's movement involved the right of women to inherit property. Such a right had no meaning to working-class women, and reflected the particular class interests of the early women's movement. The movement soon expanded its agenda to include women's control over their own wages and earnings, a demand that had considerably more relevance to the situation of working women. Even so, the activities of working-class women in the labor movement of the time suggest that it was the overall level of wages earned by workers rather than women's control of wages that was the main working-class concern.

The women's movement also inherited a particular view of racial differences from abolitionism. Blending abolitionist goals with varying forms of paternalism, this view sought the eradication of slavery but not full and unlimited equality between the races. This tension was evident when black women tried to join female antislavery societies to work for the abolition of slavery. Discrimination against black women in such female abolitionist societies was a frequent occurrence and often prompted black women to form their own separate antislavery societies — just as white women had been forced to form their own female antislavery societies when male abolitionists rejected any meaningful role for white women in abolitionist work (Terborg-Penn 1978:18–19). In fact, as Terborg-Penn also notes, the best-known black supporters of the early women's rights campaign were men, among whom Frederick Douglass is the most widely known example. The fact that white women mobilizing an equal rights campaign in the context of the abolitionist movement were more likely to accept support from black men than from black women is an interesting testimony to the intersecting hierarchies of race and gender, which provided at least a partial voice for white women and black men while effectively silencing black women.

Perhaps the most well-known link between the women's movement and the issue of race in the antebellum period was the oft-invoked analogy that likened the position of women to that of blacks. Given the roots of the women's movement in abolitionism, it was perhaps inevitable that the language used to decry slavery would be appropriated to dramatically identify sexual oppression. And given the class backgrounds and racial identities of most women's rights advocates, it is not surprising that they tended to push the analogy further than the evidence warranted. As Angela Davis has argued, it was precisely those women who were most well-off who were most likely to invoke the comparison between enslavement and womanhood; while this made the analogy increasingly farfetched, it also meant that white middle-class women within marriage felt a certain affinity with blacks within slavery — an affinity that white, male abolitionists could not have shared (Davis 1983:34).

The greatest validity in the analogy of race and sex concerned not the substantive conditions of blacks and women, but rather the social controls the dominant society employed to maintain the subordinate position of both groups (Chafe 1977). A major flaw in the analogy was the material differences in the life-chances of blacks and women, which tended to be glossed over when the analogy was invoked. The most serious problem with the analogy was its implicit denial and silencing of black women by virtue of the general interpretation that "blacks" in effect meant black men while "women" essentially meant white women. Thus, the equation of being black and being female managed to avoid the issue of being black *and* female, and thereby sidestepped the complex intertwining of race and gender. Sojourner Truth's famous speech confronted this issue directly:

> The man over there says women need to be helped into carriages and lifted over ditches, and to have the best place everywhere. Nobody ever helps me into carriages or over puddles, or gives me the best place — and ain't I a woman? Look at my arm! I have ploughed and planted and gathered into barns, and no man could head me — and ain't I a woman? I could work as much and eat as much as a man —

when I could get it — and bear the lash as well! And ain't I a woman?
I have born thirteen children, and seen most of 'em sold into slavery,
and when I cried out with my mother's grief, none but Jesus heard
me — and ain't I a woman? [Quoted in Flexner 1975:91]

The famous refrain "Ain't I a woman?" gained some of its power from the fact that it was one of the few challenges to the implicit and explicit ways in which the analogy of race and sex obscured many of the complexities of racism and sexism at the same time it illuminated some of their similarities.

The 1848 women's rights convention at Seneca Falls is one indicator of the emergence of a more independent women's movement that sought to identify its own agenda while retaining important ties with the abolitionist movement. The Declaration of Sentiments and Principles drafted at this gathering articulated the agenda of the early woman's rights movement at the same time that it expressed the class and race backgrounds of the women who led the effort. The convention and its documents focused on the limitations experienced by white, middle-class women as a result of the institution of marriage. In the 1840s, these limitations were considerable, given how traditional customs and legal precedents combined to deny married women any meaningful status outside their relationship to their husband. The agenda of the early movement was broad because the discriminations they faced were many, but the common thread in the agenda and the protests was the role of marriage in perpetuating the subordination of women. Demands for control of property and wages, for greater access to education, for increased opportunities in professions, for easier divorce and for joint guardianship of children all challenged the limitations marriage imposed on white, middle-class women in particular. The right to vote was the most direct challenge to this subordinate status, which helps to explain why it was such a controversial issue at the convention. It also underscores the irony that the black abolitionist Frederick Douglass's support of this proposal was probably crucial to its narrow victory among the assembled delegates.

The agenda of the early woman's rights movement was not overtly racist or explicitly antithetical to the interests of working-class women. But it was blind to the rather different interests and needs of black and working-class women. In this sense the agenda was clearly class-bound and race-bound, and when white, middle-class women's rights activists claimed to speak for a universal womanhood their stance became implicitly racist and classist by denying the importance of any status other than gender in shaping the situation of women. Identifying the institution of marriage as the major source of women's oppression made sense to white, middle-class women because it was indeed the major determinant of their position in a world that was relatively privileged by race and class. But such an analysis had limited appeal to black women, whose lives were more profoundly shaped by slavery and institutional racism, and it also had limited appeal to working-class women, whose lives were more importantly influenced by wage labor and the conditions surrounding that labor. These realities meant that the women's rights movement did relatively little to ally itself with either the working-class women's movement or with black women's resistance to slavery and racism, which in turn perpetuated the class-bound and race-bound nature of their program of reform (see Davis 1983:54–59).

Issues of class and race within the antebellum women's rights movement remained implicit because the movement never had a concrete opportunity to implement its agenda in the form of specific proposals and policies. The movement continued a venerable tradition of agitation and education up until the Civil War, then supported the northern war effort, and suddenly found a new array of political opportunities after the Civil War. With the northern victory, the abolitionist movement and the Republican party were finally in a position to implement their reform program. The manner in which they did so was fraught with both opportunities and dangers for the women's rights movement. As debate over postwar reform unfolded, the initial strategy of the women's rights movement was to present black suffrage and woman suffrage as "equal and inseparable demands" (DuBois 1978:55). The abolitionists' newfound political power made them less rather than more likely to support this strategy, however. As abolitionists cautiously sought to extend and protect the civil and legal rights of black men through Reconstruction legislation, many women's rights activists began to feel that abolitionist support for women's rights was largely rhetorical in nature.

The worst fears of some feminist leaders were realized when the proposed Fourteenth Amendment referred to voting as a male right. In this form, that Amendment promised to advance the cause of black suffrage while explicitly repudiating woman suffrage. Stanton and Anthony responded by proposing a universal suffrage campaign and seeking to unite the American Anti-Slavery Society and the women's rights movement. When this proposal failed, they established their own American Equal Rights Association in May 1866 in New York City to pursue the goal of universal suffrage. The very next month, the Fourteenth Amendment passed Congress and was sent to the states for ratification. While advancing the status of black men and retarding that of women, the amendment nonetheless was criticized by abolitionists because it did not go far enough toward insuring voting rights for black men. Feminists had their own more fundamental criticism of how the amendment marginalized woman suffrage. Both criticisms were voiced through the Equal Rights Association, and it became apparent that this newly formed organization embodied many of the tensions it had been intended to resolve between black suffrage and woman suffrage. In a very short time, those tensions led to the demise of the organization as the ratification of the Fourteenth Amendment and introduction of the Fifteenth Amendment split the ranks of the women's rights movement.

In November 1868, the New England Woman Suffrage Association was formed. The title was somewhat ironic, however, in that the organization was dominated by Republicans, abolitionists, and men. As a result, it became a vehicle for the "Negro's hour" strategy that black enfranchisement should take strategic priority over woman suffrage. The New England group supported the Fifteenth Amendment as the next logical step in Reconstruction. Congressional passage of that amendment in February 1869 clarified the differences among woman suffragists. The New England group strongly supported ratification, while Stanton, Anthony, and other suffragists associated with the publication *Revolution* were equally strong in their opposition because the Fifteenth Amendment enfranchised black men and left sex as the only basis on which some people would remain disenfranchised. The New England group placed a greater priority on black suffrage, with some members believing that universal male suffrage would open the door to woman suffrage. The *Revolution* group placed equal priority on black enfranchisement and woman suffrage, and feared that a sequential approach would delay woman suffrage indefinitely. Hence, their opposition to the Fifteenth Amendment was grounded in a perception that enfranchising black males would make it more rather than less difficult to enfranchise women. One group saw universal male suffrage as a step toward full democracy; the other group saw it as a retreat from democracy by empowering more men while perpetuating women's disenfranchisement (DuBois 1978: 162–174).

The objections of Stanton and Anthony to the Fifteenth Amendment were, as DuBois puts it, "simultaneously feminist and racist" (1978: 174). The feminism was reflected in the increasingly strong insistence on sexual equality as part of the postwar reform agenda. The racism was evident in the increasingly frequent appeals to racial prejudice, as women's rights advocates described a world of heightened tyranny and "fearful outrages" if black men could vote and women could not. If the motives of women's rights advocates were tainted, the same may be said for the Republican party, which saw Reconstruction more as a means of insuring its political hegemony over the South than as a step toward racial equality. Republicans seeking political control and blacks seeking empowerment thereby had a basis for an alliance in which women's rights was peripheral to both. The marginalization of women's rights, in turn, activated the latent racism of some suffragists and prompted them to seek alliances with the openly racist financier George Train and the politically reactionary Democratic party. The result was fragmentation among woman suffragists, between abolitionists and woman suffragists, and between blacks and woman suffragists; these were organizationally reflected in the demise of the Equal Rights Association and the formation of two national woman suffrage organizations. The history of this period illustrates how the pursuit of black rights could be used to marginalize women's rights, and how the pursuit of women's rights could become an obstacle to black rights. Such history is rich in examples of how latent sexism and racism can be activated in situations of conflict, but the rich examples should not obscure the larger structural organization of interlocking systems of domination based on race, gender, and class, which readily turned members of one subordinate group against another in their efforts at emancipation (see DuBois 1978; Davis 1983; Allen 1975; and Hooks 1981).

In the midst of these struggles, the Stanton/Anthony wing was exploring another set of alliances with the labor movement and working women. The egalitarian ideology and reform program of the National Labor Union made it a logical ally of the women's movement and prompted Stanton and Anthony to call for a new political party that would embody the principles and pursue the programs of the labor movement and the women's movement with more integrity than the established parties. In this potentially fruitful alliance, the women's movement could offer to the labor movement a richer understanding of how the sexual division of labor divided workers and prevented a more powerful united front within the labor movement. At the same time, the labor movement could offer to the women's movement a more profound understanding of the dynamics of class and class conflict, and how they created a distinct set of interests among working women that must be recognized if a truly cross-class alliance of women was to result. The full potential of this alliance was not realized from either side. Middle-class women, failing to grasp the depth of class conflict, sought amelioration of that conflict in the name of greater harmony. And the National Labor Union refused to formally recognize the goal of woman suffrage at its 1868 convention, fearing the growing power of an independent women's movement (see DuBois 1978:105–125).

The history of the Working Women's Association (WWA), organized by Anthony and a group of wage-earning women in 1868, provides eloquent testimony to the power of class as an obstacle to cross-class alliances among women. As an organization of highly skilled female typesetters with a history of discrimination at the hands of male printers, these working women were a natural constituency for a suffragist alliance. During its brief existence, however, the WWA gravitated toward middle-class working women and away from the unskilled women who were most in need of organization. Reflecting this middle-class perspective, the WWA under Anthony's direction sought to overcome job segregation by sex by facilitating the use of women printers as strikebreakers. Not surprisingly, these actions led to the demise of the WWA and the expulsion of Anthony from the 1869 National Labor Congress. The form that middle-class feminism took thereby prevented it from grasping the legitimacy of working-class grievances and the importance of trade union solidarity. By the same token, the traditional resistance of male trade unions to female workers prevented the former from responding effectively to the needs of working-class women as well (see DuBois 1978 and Balser 1987). Once again, these dynamics illustrate the power of interlocking systems of domination to impose partial perspectives on those who are actively struggling against at least one of those systems. For all the breadth and vitality of the early women's movement's agenda, it remained class- and race-bound in ways that limited its effectiveness at the same time that it promoted a more autonomous movement in the immediate postwar period.

To summarize: until the Civil War, the women's rights movement was closely connected to abolitionism, was infused with an optimistic spirit of progressive reform, and was developing an incisive analysis of women's subordination. Despite the breadth of its sexual politics, however, this agenda was unmistakeably class-bound and race-bound from its inception. This became more evident in the heated political struggles of the later 1860s, when prospects for actual change were greatest and when the women's movement had its first real experience with power politics and the partisanship that Stanton and Anthony condemned as the "hypocrisy of the Democrats and the treachery of the Republicans" (DuBois 1978:77). Under the pressure of these partisan struggles, the women's movement initially sought to tighten its connections with blacks (by linking the two suffrage demands) and workers (by seeking the support of women workers and labor in general). The failure of these efforts was overdetermined. The racism of some woman suffragists, the single-mindedness of most abolitionists, the partisanship of the Republicans, and the fear of a powerful women's movement were each sufficient to strain the alliance between women and blacks; together they insured its rupture. In similar fashion, the class-bound vision of woman suffragists, the sexist history of much of the labor movement, and the competing loyalties of women workers to class and gender combined to rupture the budding alliance between feminists and labor. Assigning primacy to any one of these factors obscures the fundamental points that interlocking systems of domination generate multiple sources of strain and conflict among subordinate groups, and that such groups must mediate and transcend these conflicts if any of them are to be successful.

For all its shortcomings and unrealized potential, the period before 1870 was nonetheless vibrant and open to reform in a way that the period after 1870 was not. With the ratification of the Fifteenth Amendment, the Republican goal of southern hegemony was secure, the abolitionist cause was perceived as fulfilled, and the door began to close on further reform efforts. Although the woman suffrage movement could pride itself on a newfound independence represented by two national suffrage organizations, the period after 1870 presented the movement with its most difficult situation to date for advancing the cause of women's rights. The society was no longer receptive to reform, but sought stability and normalcy instead. Abolitionists and Republicans who had promised to work on the "woman's hour" after the "Negro's hour" were not redeeming their promise. Blacks were working hard to realize meaningful and substantive change within the framework of Reconstruction. Workers — both male and female — were consolidating their struggles around common interests as laborers in an industrializing economy and a capitalist marketplace. Thus, the organizational and ideological independence of the women's movement in this period also meant a high degree of isolation from other reform constituencies and an increasing distance from centers of power.

As a result of these and other social forces, the woman suffrage movement became even more class- and race-bound in the twenty-year period from 1870 to 1890. It simply ignored the role of race and the position of black women throughout this period. It did not entirely ignore the role of class and the position of workers and women workers in particular, but its approach to class issues reflected an increasingly distinct middle-class perspective. This was not a surprising development for the American Woman Suffrage Association, which had always taken a narrow view of women's rights, shunned cross-class alliances, and remained solidly within the abolitionist frame of reference in its approach to social reform. It was a more substantial shift in orientation for the National Woman Suffrage Association, which had espoused a broader view of women's emancipation and had sought alliances with other groups. One reason for this shift was the rapidly increasing popularity of the temperance movement in the 1870s and 1880s. Despite its feminist dimension, temperance remained a class-bound movement promoting nativist social control of new immigrant groups in a rapidly urbanizing society. To the extent that suffrage and temperance became intertwined, and to the extent that the temperance movement sought this type of social control, the suffrage movement lost any prospect of a cross-class alliance with an increasingly heterogeneous working class.

The more fundamental reason for the alienation between the suffrage movement and the working class concerned changes in the middle class, and hence the middle-class consciousness that woman suffragists brought to the movement. In this period the middle class underwent a process of class formation and development that led many middle-class women to see their role as one of mediating, ameliorating, and transcending class conflict between capital and labor in the name of a more harmoniously balanced and organically integrated social system (see Buechler 1986). The development of this historically specific form of middle-class consciousness among leaders of the woman suffrage movement not only limited its chances for alliances with working-class women but also diluted the radical impulse behind the ballot demand. In the hands of leaders like Elizabeth Boynton Harbert, the suffrage struggle came to emphasize women's duties over women's rights, human rights over women's rights, expediency rationales over justice arguments, and the morally superior role of middle-class women in promoting an increasingly class-bound agenda for social reform (Buechler 1987).

The year 1890 marked an important turning point in the suffrage campaign, as the rival suffrage organizations that had existed since 1869 merged to become the National American Woman Suffrage Association. The merger brought into the suffrage campaign a new generation of leaders who were less interested in education and agitation and more concerned with strategies and tactics for advancing the narrowly defined goal of woman suffrage. Seeing suffrage as a practical reform rather than a feminist revolution, this new leadership began to assemble a coalition of forces that culminated in a mass movement for the right to vote. As a result of this new approach as well as the growing prospects of success, the movement took more definitive stances on race and class than it had throughout much of its history. Despite much nativism and xenophobia, the movement became notably more receptive to working-class women and recruited some of them into the prosuffrage coalition. In the case of black women, the movement went in the opposite direction and adopted openly racist arguments and rationales for pursuing what effectively became the goal of white woman's suffrage.

The movement's increasingly racist posture denied black women a place in the final mainstream campaign for woman suffrage. The relative absence of black women in the later movement (as contrasted with a larger role for working-class women) is sometimes taken to mean that black women were uninterested in suffrage and exclusively oriented to combating racism. This interpretation has been widely challenged by a number of writers who argue that black women were vitally interested in fighting against sexism generally and for suffrage specifically, but that the racism of the white woman suffrage movement made black women's participation all but impossible. Terborg-Penn argues that throughout the history of the white women's movement, black women were interested in feminist issues but faced a consistent pattern of discrimination at the hands of white women (1978:17–27). Bell Hooks cites numerous black women who strongly advocated the goal of woman suffrage, only to be excluded from the movement and see woman suffrage become a tool of white supremacy

(1981:166–171). Paula Giddings identifies black women's distinctive rationale for the vote as a means of resisting sexual exploitation and gaining educational opportunities (1984:121–123). Despite the obstacles of racism, black women's support for and participation in the woman suffrage campaign intensified in the 1910s, though that support was typically channeled through all black organizations (Cott 1987:31–32). The suffrage movement's resistance to the participation of black women at a time when it was becoming a mass movement and actively recruiting diverse groups of women is testimony to the power of racism in U.S. society at the turn of the century, and also testimony to the power of regional and sectional interests in influencing social movements and public policy.

As early as 1867, Henry Blackwell had argued that there were more white women in the South than black women and black men combined, and that enfranchising all three groups would strengthen white supremacy in the South. This rationale for woman suffrage lay dormant for several decades until the campaign heated up at the turn of the century. From that point on, the dominant argument for woman suffrage in the South was that it would strengthen white supremacy (especially if black women could effectively be prevented from voting, as black men had been). NAWSA, in turn, found it impossible to resist this argument, since the South was essential to its overall strategy for winning the right to vote. Hence, a movement born out of ferment for the abolition of slavery came to embrace explicitly racist arguments in favor of granting the right to vote to women. In 1893, a NAWSA convention passed a resolution that revived Blackwell's logic by counting potential women voters against black and "foreign" voters and arguing that woman suffrage would strengthen the hand of dominant racial and ethnic groups. Ten years later, NAWSA recognized "states' rights" as the basis on which chapters would participate in the national organization and the suffrage campaign. This meant that state chapters could determine their own membership policies and could use whatever arguments they felt would be most effective in their areas to advance woman suffrage. In effect, this policy meant that southern suffragists were free to develop prosuffrage arguments on the racist premise that strengthening white supremacy was the main goal of the woman suffrage campaign in the South.

The official policy of NAWSA toward race issues was neutrality; its effective strategy toward winning the vote was one of expediency. The combined result of this neutrality and expediency was a capitulation to racism, as woman suffrage and white supremacy remained in a close embrace throughout the remainder of the suffrage campaign (see Kraditor 1965:138–184; Davis 1983:110–126; Giddings 1984:123–131). This campaign provides yet another example of how interlocking systems of domination structure modes of resistance. Given the history of white supremacy and its institutionalization around the turn of the century, there was no other way in which the South could have been recruited to the suffrage campaign. Given the difficulty of amending the Constitution and the necessity of a broadbased ratification campaign, there was no chance of winning and ratifying a suffrage amendment without the South. Faced with these realities and given its commitment to the most expedient suffrage strategy, the alliance between woman suffrage and white supremacy followed logically. Some suffragists found this alliance welcome, others found it distasteful, and many found it irrelevant, but there was no critical mass within the organization to effectively challenge the strategy of expediency. If there had been, the organization might have followed a more principled strategy and acted more honorably. But principle and honor would not have altered the historical and structural realities confronting the movement, and those realities were powerful enough to make capitulation to racism appear as the only viable option to the leadership of the woman suffrage campaign after the turn of the century.

The same rationale that linked woman suffrage and white supremacy in the South linked woman suffrage and nativist, antiimmigrant, antiworker stances in the North. Just as the vote for women was seen as a way of strengthening the white power structure in the South, it was presented as a means of reinforcing the position of dominant groups in the North against foreign-born immigrants. Some northern suffragists also played the numbers game, arguing that woman suffrage would empower more native-born women than immigrant women and would thereby strengthen the power of dominant groups against outsiders. A stronger version of the same argument advocated that an educational or literacy requirement be attached to suffrage rights, which would disqualify a large percentage of black or immigrant men and women, increasing the potential for social control by dominant groups. All these arguments symbolized the transformation of a movement that had begun with the goal of expanding democratic power by enfranchising all women into a movement that often seemed more concerned with consolidating power and manipulating the franchise to achieve more effective social control by white, upper-class and middle-class native-born elements of the population. As such, these new arguments for voting rights were compatible with those aspects of the Progressive movement that tended to centralize power in the hands of dominant social groups and classes.

The same demographic logic that led some privileged women to argue that woman suffrage would augment the power of dominant groups was also turned against them. While native-born white women insisted that they outnumbered all the minority women who might also be enfranchised by a woman suffrage amendment, critics of the movement argued that differential fertility between these groups was leading to "race suicide" because whites would eventually be outnumbered by nonwhites. Panic over this prospect became the basis for a conservative attack on the women's movement for encouraging women to forgo their duties for more selfish concerns. Women activists differed in their response to this attack. Some accepted the race-suicide logic and its implication that privileged women needed to produce more children. Others accepted the logic but called for different solutions. And the most progressive feminists rejected the race-suicide theory altogether and strengthened their demands for increased opportunities for women that would make motherhood one alternative rather than a woman's destiny. In the end, the race-suicide theorists were not very successful, because their attack led many women to respond with an even more explicit defense of birth control. The debate nonetheless demonstrated how the tactic of using racist and elitist arguments for woman suffrage could easily be turned against the movement (Gordon 1976).

As the suffrage movement entered the twentieth century, a notably different attitude began to emerge among some of its sectors. Whereas the hierarchy of race and rigidities of racism were never overcome within the suffrage movement, the hierachy of class and forms of class consciousness proved somewhat more fluid. As a result, the movement built on some cross-class gender commonalities and recruited a significant number of working-class women into the campaign for woman suffrage. In the period just after the turn of the century, the suffrage movement contained two rather different class orientations. The more conservative wing of the movement remained strongly class-bound in its orientation to reform, and continued to voice nativist and xenophobic arguments about the need to bolster social control by instituting more restrictive forms of suffrage while enfranchising white, middle-class women. The more liberal wing of the movement was able to see across the divides of class and ethnicity to find common ground with working-class and immigrant women, at least regarding the value of the ballot. A key factor in cultivating this more enlightened view was the involvement of many middle-class women in the settlement house movement. Attempting to respond to the varied dislocations of a rapidly urbanizing and industrializing society with high rates of migration, women in the settlement house movement built a bridge across class and ethnic divides, creating opportunities for working-class women to participate in the mainstream suffrage movement in a manner and to an extent that was never true for black women.

One of the best examples of a cross-class bridge was the Women's Trade Union League (WTUL). The League consisted of upper- and middle-class "allies" who worked with working-class women around issues of wages, working conditions, organizing efforts, and legislation. This organization came as close as any did (and perhaps could) in building solidarity and sisterhood across class lines. The attraction of the WTUL for upper- and middle-class women was that it provided a concrete means of working on social problems all but ignored by the traditionally more conservative women's club movement. The WTUL's attraction for working women was that it was one of the few organizations that responded to their situation both as women and as workers. If the labor movement had done a better job of overcoming the sexism within its own ranks, the appeal of the WTUL to working women would not have been as great. Hence, the WTUL flourished because it responded to the multiple needs of women from diverse class backgrounds. The cross-class character that made it special also made it fragile, and suffrage proved to be one of the few common interests that linked women across class lines. As a result, the winning of suffrage brought an end to the kind of cross-class coalition represented by the WTUL (see Dye 1973, 1975; Jacoby 1975).

The common ground the WTUL was able to cultivate around woman suffrage remained limited in important ways. For the middle-class suffrage leadership, the vote had become the most important women's issue and the campaign to which they were willing to devote all available resources. For working-class women, the vote ranked behind wages, working conditions, unionization, and labor legislation. Working-class women supported woman suffrage for class-specific reasons, including the ballot's potential for making working women more effective in their diverse struggles as workers. These class differences in the priority of and rationale for woman suffrage created understandable tensions within the suffrage movement but did not prevent a cross-class, multi-constituency alliance from emerging and waging an effective fight for the ballot. But these class differences often did mean that working-class women were more comfortable working for the ballot through their own organizations. As a result, wage-earner suffrage leagues became increasingly popular as a means for working-class women to support the woman suffrage campaign while retaining a clear, dual identity as workers and as women (see Buechler 1986; Tax 1980; Kraditor 1965).

In the later days of the suffrage struggle, even the conservative wing of the movement welcomed the support of working-class women for the suffrage cause. For most middle-class suffragists, however, receptivity to working-class women in the movement was based on the same principle of expediency that made the movement unreceptive to black women. The participation of working-class women promised to strengthen the suffrage campaign and hasten the suffrage victory in several ways. For one, the situation of working-class women provided a powerful rationale for the vote, which the mainstream movement was quick to recognize and promote. For another, working-class women were seen as important in overcoming the traditional resistance of some working-class men to woman suffrage. Finally, it was clear by the last decade of the movement that some working-class women were willing to work very hard for the ballot among populations where the traditional suffrage movement had little if any influence. All these factors made it expedient to move toward working-class women, just as other factors made it expedient to move away from black women. For many women in the movement, concern with working women was limited to gaining their support for the suffrage campaign and did not extend to any sustained activity on behalf of working-class women.

The class profile of the suffrage movement also came to include truly upper-class women in the last decade of the campaign for the vote. The role of Mrs. O. H. P. Belmont in the suffrage movement is well known, but typically treated as an exceptional case. More recent research has suggested that it was the norm and not the exception for some upper-class women to become involved in the suffrage effort and to play important roles in the final days of the campaign. In Chicago, the biographies of Bertha Palmer, Ellen Henrotin, and Louise deKoven Bowen exemplify this trend (Buechler 1986). The involvement of upper-class women in the movement was telling in several ways. It illustrated and furthered the movement's specialization as a single-issue campaign for the vote that no longer offered a broad challenge to the society as a whole; thus upper-class women could participate in a feminist movement without jeopardizing their class position. But it also signified the ways in which all women had been adversely affected by industrialization. As a cross-class movement, the suffrage campaign brought together upper-class women whose labor had been rendered superfluous with working-class women who were working overtime, and it allowed them to mobilize around at least one commonality of gender — the lack of the ballot — that affected women of all class backgrounds.

This overview of the woman suffrage movement has not challenged the truism that it was a white, middle-class movement, but it has suggested that the issues of race and class were much more complex than the truism implies. Race and class had a different impact on the movement in almost every decade of its existence, depending on other reform constituencies, the prospects for success, the dominant mobilizing strategy, the vision of the leadership, and the structural obstacles the movement confronted in its efforts to enfranchise women. What is needed is a nuanced view that recognizes these variations yet retains sight of the larger patterns. As a white movement, the suffrage campaign was never warmly receptive to black women, although it varied significantly in its support for black rights from an early abolitionist stance to a posture of indifference to a conscious rejection of those rights and a capitulation to racism. As a middle-class movement, the suffrage campaign was always class-bound, but a receptivity to women from other class backgrounds was present in the beginning, absent in the middle, and actively cultivated in the latter days of the movement. In the end, these shifts toward a cross-class alliance and away from a cross-race coalition were, in all likelihood, strategically necessary to win woman suffrage. As such, they provide a powerful example of how interlocking systems of domination can readily pit the interests of some subordinate groups against the interests of others as a means of maintaining and strengthening those systems.

The Contemporary Women's Movement

Issues of class and race have also had a profound effect on the contemporary women's movement from its inception to the present. In the suffrage movement, however, these issues were inscribed in major events and turning points, such as NWSA's opposition to the Fifteenth Amendment or NAWSA's capitulation to a racist suffrage strategy. In the contemporary movement, there have not been the same overt, explicit positions crystallized in major events and turning points. Race and class issues have rather taken the form of a subterranean undercurrent influencing the direction and priorities of the movement without always being clearly identified and recognized as such. It was not until the mid-1970s that this undercurrent came to be broadly recognized and discussed throughout various sectors of the contemporary movement. Since then, there have been substantial criticism and considerable reflection over the role of race and class in the movement. This section sketches this history and discusses these debates.

One expression of class and race bias is the perception that women were not a political force until the emergence of an explicitly feminist movement in the mid-1960s. While this observation may be true for most white, middle-class women, it obscures the prior activism of black women within the civil rights movement and working women within the labor movement. Such activism may not have had gender as its primary focus, but there was a kind of incipient feminism in these race- and class-based movements that predated the emergence of an explicit feminist movement under the direction of mainstream women. The work of women in such groups as the Women's Bureau of the Department of Labor or the Women's Committee of the United Auto Workers reflected the specific concerns of working women in their dual status as women and as workers. This work received little attention through most of the 1950s, but eventually led to more widely recognized accomplishments reflected in the work of the presidential and state commissions on the status of women in the early 1960s and the campaign for passage of the Equal Pay Act of 1963. Through these events, the incipient feminism of women in the labor movement helped lay the groundwork for the emergence of an explicitly feminist movement led largely by middle-class women in the mid-1960s.

The incipient feminism of black women within the civil rights movement was even more fundamental in paving the way for a mainstream feminist movement in the later 1960s. The civil rights movement was an important training ground for many white women who joined it in the early 1960s and would later help to create an independent women's movement. One of the most important lessons was the role model black women provided for white women while they worked together in the civil rights movement. Whereas many white women came from a world defined by what Betty Friedan described as the feminine mystique, they found in black women a powerful alternative role model. Working with strong, assertive, self-directed black women in the civil rights movement helped undermine conventional notions of feminine gender roles and provided a powerful lesson in what the movement would later call "consciousness-raising." The power of these alternative role models was enhanced by the fact that black families virtually adopted northern white women during their stay in the South, creating a degree of intimacy that reinforced the lessons white women were learning through the example of black women (Evans 1979).

Black women in the civil rights movement provided another lesson to white women when they began to articulate their grievances as women within a male-dominated black movement. Paula Giddings (1984) and Bell Hooks (1981) have both documented the existence of male chauvinism and sexist patterns within the civil rights movement. In 1964 in the meetings of the Student Non-violent Coordinating Committee (SNCC), black women explicitly raised the issue of sexism within the movement when they protested patterns of sex segregation and the sexual division of labor, which relegated women to a secondary role within the organization. The histories of this period make it clear that black women were deeply committed to the civil rights agenda, but that they were also becoming critical of how male dominance distorted the potential of the civil rights movement to improve the lives of black women as well as black men. For a short time, there were explicit efforts to create greater solidarity between black and white women, though these efforts eventually foundered on the tensions that arose over interracial sex within the movement and the growing tendency toward a separatist strategy within SNCC (Evans 1979; Chafe 1977).

The emergence of an independent women's movement in the mid-1960s was thus deeply implicated in the complex relations of race, class, and gender both as forms of domination and as bases of resistance. Even a cursory glance at the historical record reveals that black women and working-class women were already mobilizing, albeit in ways that were circumscribed by their other identities as blacks and workers, around issues that would subsequently be defined as feminist. These efforts contributed to the emergence of a mainstream women's movement by establishing important institutional footholds in the Women's Bureau and the presidential and state commissions, and by providing a training ground rich in role models and resistance strategies within the civil rights struggle. In a somewhat paradoxical fashion, the lives of working-class women and black women underscored the peculiar limitations of privilege that characterized white, middle-class women trapped in the feminine mystique. In seeking economic self-reliance and assertive identities as an antidote to the feminine mystique, the mainstream movement was as much following as leading working women and black women.

When the contemporary women's movement assumed an independent organizational form, first in NOW and later in the various small groups associated with the women's liberation sector, it understandably reflected the class and race backgrounds of its leadership. The truism about a white, middle-class movement was apt in the broadest sense because the aspirations of the earliest movement participants were a response to the specific situation of women who were relatively privileged by class and race but were unmistakably restricted on the basis of gender. Friedan's oft-cited work on the feminine mystique (1963) was a powerful statement of how these restrictions were played out in the lives of suburban homemakers in the 1950s and early 1960s, and served as a rallying cry for a generation of women who came to see paid labor as a means of transcending the limitations of gender that were especially apparent in a context of relative privilege by race and class. The movement also attracted professional women who were already working outside the home but whose career mobility was sharply limited by gender discrimination. The notion that unrestricted career mobility could provide an avenue of liberation for such women appeared plausible as an antidote to the mind-numbing routines of domestic labor, the economically vulnerable position of homemakers, and the sexist obstacles confronting women in the labor force. The notion that work necessarily provided an avenue of liberation was not nearly as compelling to black women and working-class women, whose labor market experience suggested that paid labor was as likely to create a double burden for women as it was to provide a means of liberation from gender-based inequality.

The early priorities of the National Organization for Women reflected this belief in the centrality of paid work to the goals of the contemporary women's movement. Founded in large part by an elite group of professionally oriented women, NOW focused from the beginning on enhancing the employment opportunities of women in the labor force. Early lawsuits targeted the Equal Employment Opportunity Commission, sex discrimination in airlines' policy regarding stewardesses, and the common practice of sex-segregated want ads. Although NOW's efforts improved employment opportunities for women, it is also clear that NOW's main goal was fostering access, entry, and mobility in career-type occupations. In short, the focus of NOW was the kind of work that was most likely to be pursued by those with class, race, and educational advantages in the labor market; there is much less evidence in the early NOW of any comparable concern with the kinds of work which most women, and especially working-class and black women, were actually doing in the labor force. In some respects, NOW's early orientation was reminiscent of Susan B. Anthony's Workingwomen's Association in the late 1860s, which also focused on relatively skilled women in the labor force who faced obstacles more on the basis of gender than on the basis of class or race. Also like the WWA, this meant that NOW was somewhat blind to how the dynamics of class and race shaped women's working lives alongside the dynamics of gender.

The kinds of class and race biases evident in the early women's rights sector were also evident in the women's liberation sector of the movement. Like the women's rights sector, most leaders and participants in the women's liberation sector were college-educated; beyond this, however, much of their organizing and activity took place on college campuses and their surrounding communities. Thus, to the extent that college education was a white, middle-class privilege that excluded or minimized the participation of minority and working-class women, there was a substantial mobilization bias in the origins and early orientation of the women's liberation movement. Indeed, as Ferree and Hess point out, the women's liberation sector was even more homogeneous in membership than the women's rights sector, in part because the value agreement and normative consensus that are vital to the survival of collectively oriented groups are more easily achieved with a homogeneous membership (1985:85). As the ideology, goals, and program of the women's liberation sector developed in the late 1960s and early 1970s into a radical challenge to the roots of male domination, this was nonetheless a challenge that implicitly rested on the worldview of white, middle-class women. Identifying the class and race biases of the early women's liberation agenda does not invalidate that agenda, but it helps explain the powerful appeal of this agenda for white, middle-class women and its limited appeal for other groups of women.

This powerful appeal was instrumental in building a mass-based women's movement in the early 1970s as the ERA was introduced, as the *Roe* v. *Wade* abortion decision was handed down by the Supreme Court, and as the two sectors of the movement came together around some common issues. However, this mass-based movement still rested on mobilization biases that made it much easier for some groups of women to participate than others. It was also during this period that internal criticisms about the direction of the movement received a wider hearing. The most familiar of these criticisms came from the women's liberation sector, which faulted the liberal feminism of the women's rights sector for pursuing a limited agenda of legal rights, equal opportunity, and individual mobility. In its place, the women's liberation movement advocated a more radical feminism, which challenged underlying structures of patriarchy and sought more systemic social transformation. While the radical analysis of this sector did indeed offer a more profound challenge to male dominance, its tendency to see gender as the primary oppression limited its appeal to women who faced multiple, interlocking disadvantages of class and race as well as gender. To a considerable extent, the disputes between the liberal feminism of the women's rights sector and the radical feminism of the women's liberation sector reflected differences within a common worldview shaped by particular class and racial locations; hence both sides of the debate had limited appeal for women from different class and racial backgrounds with correspondingly different worldviews.

The fact that the women's movement in the early 1970s had limited appeal for nonwhite, non-middle-class women does not mean that it had no relevance or impact for these women, but rather that its relevance and impact were refracted through a different class and race lens for them. For many working-class women, feminist ideology crystallized long-standing grievances over sexual discrimination, segregation, and harassment, and provided a powerful new language for expressing those grievances and challenging institutionalized sexism within the workplace. Feminism thereby spoke to needs of working women that had rarely been taken seriously in the traditional labor movement. For many women of color, feminist ideology served a similar function of providing a language for naming historic patterns of male domination and machismo that were deeply embedded in traditional cultures and communities. These patterns often persisted even in movements of racial liberation that sought to improve the status of racial minorities but remained blind to internal sources and consequences of sexual inequality within those movements.

By the early 1970s, the tendency for working-class women and women of color to selectively appropriate and refashion feminist insights and ideology to fit their particular situation was taking organizational form. One of the earliest such groups was the Union Women's Alliance to Gain Equality (Union WAGE), formed in 1971 in response to a NOW conference in Berkeley. The immediate impetus for organization was the perception of many working-class women that NOW was neglecting their concerns and that a separate organization was necessary if these issues were to be addressed within the women's movement. Union

WAGE leaders distrusted what they perceived as an antimale bias in the middle-class women's movement, which they saw as related to the movement's anti-working class stance. For WAGE members, class, not gender, defined the most important enemy. WAGE leaders were equally critical of the traditionally male-dominated trade unions, however. They acted on these perceptions by advocating a labor ERA that would be qualified by a provision retaining protective labor legislation for women and extending it to men. WAGE subsequently experienced external conflict with NOW and internal conflict between their members' identities as women and workers, and these led the organization to disband in 1982. It was nonetheless an important attempt by working-class women to appropriate the goals and ideology of a middle-class women's movement for their own purposes; as such, they helped to bring a feminist perspective to working-class issues and a class perspective to feminist mobilization (Balser 1987).

Although Union WAGE was relatively short-lived, it helped pave the way for the Coalition of Labor Union Women (CLUW), which was organized in 1974 and continues to the present. CLUW was formed with representation from fifty-eight different unions. CLUW's goals include organizing unorganized workers, with particular attention to sex-segregated, female-dominated jobs in the service sector. Beyond organizing women workers, CLUW also seeks to alter the priorities of the traditional, male-dominated trade union movement, which has historically dismissed both women workers and service-sector jobs as unworthy of sustained organizing efforts. Given dominant economic trends such as women's increasing labor force participation, the shift to a service-based economy, and the decline of a traditional industrial proletariat, CLUW's receptivity to the needs of working-class women in sex-segregated jobs holds the promise of not only meeting the immediate needs of female workers but also of helping to maintain the vitality of the labor movement in a substantially altered economic climate. While CLUW is clearly anchored in the trade union tradition, its focus on working-class women is a good example of the refracted impact of a middle-class women's movement on the situations of women from rather different class backgrounds (Balser 1987; Ferree and Hess 1985:89, 145).

The founding of the National Black Feminist Organization (NBFO) in 1973 was roughly analogous to the creation of WAGE and CLUW in that it was an attempt to appropriate the insights of a class- and race-bound feminist movement and adapt them to the specific condition of a different group of women. The NBFO grew out of a series of meetings in New York in 1972 and 1973 at which "we talked of our individual and collective experience as Black women . . . [the] possibilities for unity among women . . . honestly dealing with ALL issues that confront us as women, lest we be divided . . . [and the] implications to society of our entrance as Black feminists into the women's movement" (Friedan [Betty] Papers 1973, emphasis in original). Eleanor Holmes Norton commented on the founding of the organization that "it took us some time to realize that we had nothing to fear from feminism, but we could not have emerged amidst the confusions of five or six years ago" (cited in Giddings 1984: 344). The NBFO was the most visible of a number of groups that emerged at this time and were oriented to the specific concerns of black women and the interlocking forces of racism and sexism in shaping their lives. Although the NBFO has been criticized by some for its inability to support women effectively in the black community, its emergence in the early 1970s made it an important vehicle for addressing the multiple sources of oppression confronting black women (Joseph and Lewis 1981:33–34). As with CLUW, it is difficult to envision the emergence of an organization like the NBFO without the presence of a strong women's movement developing an incisive feminist ideology for analyzing women's condition. As this ideology developed in its class-bound and race-bound fashion, CLUW and the NBFO reformulated it to fit the specific situations of working-class women and black women.

Since the mid-1970s, the class-bound and race-bound character of the women's movement has been increasingly recognized within the movement, and efforts have been made to enhance movement diversity and power by overcoming these limitations. Considerable debate continues over how successful these efforts have been. There is clearly more rhetorical attention paid to issues of race and class than before the mid-1970s. As Joseph and Lewis wrote in 1981, "A general unease and anxiety about racism now prevails *consciously* in the Women's Liberation Movement, whereas five years ago anti-racist consciousness bore little relation to the practices and emphasis of the movement" (1981:276, emphasis in original). However, the new rhetorical concern has often been belied by a purely instrumental orientation to minority and working-class women, suggesting that deeper levels of racism and insensitivity persist despite the adoption of new rhetoric more conscious of class and race issues. In her powerful poem "And When You Leave, Take Your Pictures With You," Jo Carrillo describes how white feminists "love to own pictures of us," pictures that convey colorful images of strength and happiness, but are less able and willing to relate to women of color "in the flesh" (Moraga and Anzaldua 1981:63–64). In the same collection of writings, Doris Davenport describes how "we experience white feminists and their organizations as elitist, crudely insensitive, and condescending" (Moraga and Anzaldua 1981:86). Analyzing the racism of white women in the movement as a defense mechanism, she argues that "feminism either addresses itself to all wimmin, or it becomes even more so just another elitist, prurient white organization, defeating its own purposes" (Moraga and Anzaldua 1981:89).

NOW provides one example of the growing awareness of these issues within a movement organization, but also of the deeper levels of racism or misunderstanding that persist. As early as 1971, NOW had established a task force to seek coalitions with organizations of minority women and provide support around common issues. In 1973, NOW passed a resolution to enhance the participation of minority women in the organization by removing structures, policies, and practices that inhibited that participation. In 1977, it established a National Minority Women's Committee to ensure that the needs of minority women were fully represented in NOW's program. Since then, the organization has passed numerous resolutions in support of specific issues affecting diverse groups of women (National Organization for Women Papers 1988). These resolutions exemplify a growing awareness of the needs of minority women in organizational rhetoric, but this awareness has not readily translated into sustained and effective action in these areas. In 1979 when the organization was seeking ratification of the ERA, NOW sought to establish chapters in minority communities to build support for the ERA campaign. Many women of color found it a "totally inappropriate approach [to] indoctrinate minority women" on the ERA rather than attracting them to common issues (Giddings 1984:346). To many, NOW's actions demonstrated that its only interest in minority women was to recruit them in support of NOW's goal, with little recognition that the priorities of other groups of women might be substantially different from NOW's.

The same year, NOW elected an all-white group of officers for the second year in a row, in part because NOW's president Eleanor Smeal failed to endorse Sharon Parker, the only black woman running for a national NOW office. Smeal's defense that it would have been tokenism to support Parker because of race was taken by many minority women as a further insult in the context of NOW's all-white leadership. In response, Aileen Hernandez, a past president of the organization, accused NOW of being "too White and middle-class" and sponsored a resolution urging blacks to quit NOW or refrain from joining until the organization seriously confronted racism within the organization and the society (Giddings 1985:346–347; National Organization for Women Papers 1979). Beyond the specific provocations of the election and the ERA campaign was a larger disillusionment: NOW's agenda at the turn of the decade did not reflect any organizational commitment to issues of greatest concern to minority women. The lesson for many minority women was that increasing rhetorical attention to race did not mean sustained organizational commitment to such issues. NOW's instrumental appeal to minority women during the ERA campaign bore some resemblance to the suffrage movement's appeal to working-class women during the suffrage campaign. However, in the latter movement, there was a clearly articulated working-class rationale for the vote and there were working-class suffrage organizations that led to a productive coalition with middle-class suffrage organizations. In the ERA campaign, NOW's approach appeared to many to be a hastily arranged, last-minute tactic that glossed over all the vital issues of difference and diversity its rhetoric had begun to acknowledge.

NOW's uneven success at building bridges across the divides of race and class also reflects its ideological leaning toward liberal feminism, whose goal of individual opportunity is more meaningful for white, middle-class women than for working-class women or minority women. Those individuals and groups associated with the women's liberation network of the contemporary feminist movement have become more ideologically receptive to the problems and potentials of a diverse women's movement. Socialist feminists have always wrestled with the complexities of class and gender, and have now recognized the need to develop a theoretical model acknowledging race as well as class and gender. Radical feminists have also been theoretically receptive to issues of difference, and like socialist feminists have been more likely to see the systemic character of systems of domination based on class and race as well as gender. However, the theoretical receptivity of these traditions to the concerns of minority women and working-class women has not readily translated into effective practice either. Socialist feminism has suffered with the overall decline of the left and the development of a more conservative climate, which has rendered these groups relatively powerless. Radical feminism has established a tenacious foothold in scattered and decentralized community organizations as well as in academic institutions, and this has allowed continued theoretical development. At the same time, separatist strains within radical feminism have severely limited its appeal to minority women and, perhaps to a lesser extent, to working-class women, for whom collective bonds with men from their racial or class backgrounds remain an important priority.

Since the mid-1970s, the contemporary women's movement has thus displayed greater rhetorical attention to race and class in the women's rights sector and greater theoretical development concerning race and class in the women's liberation sector. For a variety of reasons, this rhetorical attention and theoretical development has not readily translated into effective action, but it nonetheless reflects a significant change from the origins of the movement. At a minimum, a movement that began as unconsciously class-bound and race-bound has now become consciously class-bound and race-bound. At a maximum, a movement that intially mobilized around taken-for-granted class and race worldviews has now begun to mobilize women from very different backgrounds and worldviews. In either case, this new awareness of class and race opens up dramatic potential for a more broadly based movement. More than most social movements, the women's movement has attempted to hear and respond to criticisms that it has failed to represent diversity among its constituents. In this sense, its ideological and theoretical diversity constitutes an important learning mechanism by which the movement can benefit from past practice, reformulate theory and analysis, and seek more effective practice. Realizing this potential requires genuine representation of all groups of women within movement organizations and the movement more generally. Without such a presence, the rhetorical acknowledgment of race and class issues may continue, but the movement will still represent the priorities of some groups of women and not others.

Many of these processes are illustrated by the reproductive politics of the contemporary women's movement. Throughout U.S. history, black fertility has been closely monitored and controlled by dominant groups. Under slavery, this often meant encouraging high fertility among black women to augment a cheap labor force. By the twentieth century, however, the concern of dominant groups had shifted toward limiting the fertility of subordinate groups. Expressed in fears of race-suicide at the turn of the century, these goals were concretized in state legislation and public policy directed at population control. "Ironically, racial prejudice caused the South to take a leading role in the incorporation of birth control into public health services" as one means of limiting black population growth (D'Emilio and Freedman 1988: 247). These efforts assumed their most coercive form in the practice of involuntary sterilization, which actually increased throughout most of the century: "by the 1960s, . . . medical professionals found ways of sterilizing far larger numbers of women whose fertility patterns offended their values" (D'Emilio and Freedman 1988:255). The history and scope of these efforts provides considerable evidence to support interpretations of birth control as a plot to exterminate members of minority groups (Gordon 1976:398).

It was in this socio-historical context that the contemporary women's movement articulated the demand for access to abortion, and it is not surprising that this goal was perceived by many minority group members as an additional strategy in a campaign of population control directed against them. If legal abortion represented a new weapon in the arsenal of dominant interests seeking to limit minority fertility, then opposition to abortion could be framed as a racially progressive stance vital to protecting minority interests. Like many other debates, this one appeared to pit the interests of (white) women against those of blacks, and the impasse was not transcended until women of color made it clear that reproductive freedom entailed more than access to abortion. For many poor and minority women, the most pressing reproductive issue was not necessarily the right to terminate an unwanted pregnancy but rather the right to have children in the face of societal pressure or coercion not to do so. More generally, the energy devoted to securing the right to abortion appeared to many minority and working-class women to sidestep more fundamental economic issues of how to adequately provide for children in a period of growing female impoverishment. These insights were responsible for broadening the demand for abortion to the goal of reproductive self-determination, and for recognizing the broader socioeconomic context that so often impinges on the reproductive choices of women.

Despite the evolution of a more inclusive approach to reproductive freedom within the contemporary women's movement, the subsequent politics of these issues have continued to be refracted through the lenses of class and race. Antiabortion forces mobilized quickly after the 1973 Supreme Court decisions, and by 1976 the Hyde Amendment was passed, prohibiting the use of federal money to fund abortions. Congress subsequently barred the financing of abortion with tax dollars, so that "by 1978, the number of federally funded abortions had fallen from 295,000 to 3,000" and by "1979, only nine states still paid for abortions" (D'Emilio and Freedman 1988:348). For all practical purposes, these actions made a woman's social class the determinant of whether abortion was a viable option; middle-class and wealthier women could afford them while poorer women could not. Given the history of population control efforts directed toward poor and minority women, this would be a highly ironic outcome if not for the fact that the ultimate goal of the antiabortion forces is to eliminate access to abortion for all women. It has simply proven more difficult to limit the options of middle-class women than those of poor and minority women. There is also very recent evidence that the women's movement is still not immune to population control strategies that are at least implicitly racist, as evidenced by NOW pronouncements about the danger of overpopulation both at home and abroad (see Bader 1989).

If one compares the resiliency of class and race barriers around the contemporary women's movement, it appears that the movement has accommodated some of the concerns of working-class women more readily than it has those of black and other minority women. Put differently, it has proven easier to move toward class diversity within the contemporary movement than it has to move toward racial diversity. Several factors account for this difference. One is the probability that white, middle-class women subjectively feel closer to white, working-class women (and vice versa) than they do to minority women of any class background. A second factor is that the movement's long-standing concern with economic opportunity and independence can be framed in a way that reflects important priorities of working-class women. Economic issues in the women's movement have often been framed in terms of the aspirations of middle-class women for careers, but they can and have been reframed to include such issues as the feminization of poverty, the inadequacy of social welfare programs, the rigidity of sex-segregated labor markets, and the prevalence of sexual ha-

rassment in the workplace. Such a reframed agenda speaks to situations confronting virtually all working women. While the movement has not reflected and
probably never will reflect a traditional working-class consciousness and perspective on women's issues, the centrality of the movement's economic agenda is
an important bridge that can link the concerns of middle-class and working-
class women within the contemporary women's movement.

Another factor that has promoted some cross-class links has been the
movement's challenge to conventional notions of class for describing the situation of women. The sociological concept of class has traditionally been used to
locate families within systems of stratification on the basis of husband's income,
occupation, and status. The implicit assumptions that all women are married,
stay married, and unproblematically derive their class position from their husband have been questioned by feminist scholars for obscuring the differences
between women and men within a given class and the similarities among women
across classes. The theoretical critique that conventional class categories are not
adequate for analyzing the position of women has been dramatically underscored by the very uneven impact of rising divorce rates on the economic life-
chances of women and men (Weitzman 1985). For women with limited or nonex-
istent labor market skills and experience, divorce can produce immediate and
extreme changes in "class" position. In an important sense, women are not as
firmly anchored as men in the (traditionally conceived) social class system, and a
large majority of women are in or are only one step removed from situations of
extreme economic vulnerability. The long-standing feminist goal of economic
self-reliance thus has continuing relevance in the contemporary women's movement, and has allowed the movement to forge some important links across con-
ventionally defined class categories.

The relative receptivity of the contemporary movement to white, working-
class women as compared to minority women suggests a parallel with the later
stages of the woman suffrage movement. After the turn of the century and under
the influence of prominent settlement house leaders, the suffrage movement
cultivated strategic alliances with working-class women who had developed
their own rationale for the vote and who were active in working-class suffrage
leagues. In this instance, the political vulnerability of all women due to
disenfranchisement provided a basis for a cross-class alliance among white
women to pursue a goal that most women nonetheless sought for class-specific
reasons. In the contemporary movement, the economic vulnerability of many
women may provide a similar basis for a cross-class alliance to seek measures
that will reduce such vulnerability. The lack of the right to vote was a potent
symbol of women's political vulnerability and provided a powerful mobilizing
issue in the suffrage movement, however. No equally potent symbol of women's

economic vulnerability has served to mobilize the contemporary movement. As a result, the cross-class alliances and commonalities have not yet been established as strongly as they were in the final days of the suffrage campaign. Nonetheless, the economic grounds for such an alliance are deeply rooted and have already promoted within the women's movement a more inclusive economic agenda that speaks to the conditions of diverse women.

The same suffrage movement that moved toward cross-class alliances with working-class white women moved dramatically away from cross-race alliances with black women during the later stages of the suffrage campaign. The contemporary movement has also had difficulty finding common ground and bases for alliances with women of color. The contemporary movement has not taken as explicitly racist a stance as the suffrage movement did when it accepted the rationale of white southern suffragists for maintaining white supremacy, but it has not been able to build bridges across the divide of race to the extent that it has been able to do so across the divide of class. This failure is all the more striking given that black women have had consistently more favorable attitudes toward the women's movement than white women have; in 1970, 60 percent of black women were favorable versus only 37 percent of white women; in 1980 the relative figures were 77 versus 65 percent (Ferree and Hess 1985:82). The failure of cross-race alliances is also striking given that the movement's emerging economic agenda, which speaks to the situation of working-class women, applies with even greater force to the situation of women of color, who are disproportionately poor and economically disadvantaged. Given the new rhetorical awareness of issues of race within the movement, this situation can no longer be explained simply on the basis of unconscious racism. While conscious racism continues to be a factor, the relative dearth of cross-race alliances within the contemporary women's movement tells us something important not just about the attitudes of movement participants but also about the strategic choices that have been made within the movement, and about the interlocking nature of systems of domination based on class, race, and gender, which make such alliances very difficult to envision, create, and sustain.

One cause of this difficulty has been the historical tendency for women's movements to rely on an analogy between race and sex as a means of conceptualizing women's condition. Although this analogy can be illuminating, it is subject to a number of dangers and difficulties. As noted earlier, the analogy implicitly tends to assume that all blacks are men and all women are white, thereby obscuring the distinctive position of black women as members of both groups. In addition, the analogy often obscures vital differences between black women, black men, and white women in their respective histories, levels of consciousness, types and degrees of oppression, constancy of resistance, and the

like (Chafe 1977). During the late 1960s, when the demise of the black movement coincided with the rise of the women's movement, black women were especially incensed at the ease with which some white women characterized
themselves as "niggers" and appropriated the analysis and rhetoric of the black
movement for their own purposes (Giddings 1984: 308). Surveying the entire
history of women's movements, Bell Hooks finds "endless" comparisons and
analogies equating the two groups, which always functioned to exclude black
women from the equation. Beyond this, Hooks argues that the use of the analogy
in fact constituted an "appeal to the anti-black-male racism of white patriarchal
men . . . to protect the white female's position on the race/sex hierarchy"
(Hooks 1981:143–144). In Hooks's analysis, the subtext in the analogy of race
and sex involves white women appealing to white men to raise their status above
that of black men, thereby preserving dominant racial hierarchies. The historical
popularity of this analogy, combined with frequently superficial interpretations
of it, has been one factor that has alienated black women from the mainstream
women's movement.

Black women have also been alienated from the mainstream women's
movement because they have traditionally seen racism as a more important factor in their lives than sexism. In Joseph and Lewis's argument, "it has not been as
necessary or as possible to institutionalize sexism as a repressive measure
against Black women in the same way as it has been to use it against White
Women. Black women can be kept in their places via racism alone. Hence, Black
women correctly state that they are affected by racism more than by sexism"
(1981:278). As a result, "most Black women who spoke out reflected Frances
Ellen Harper's view that the race must rise in order for Black women to do so"
(Giddings 1984:309). Chafe concurs that "black women have perceived racial
oppression as much more basic to their lives than sex oppression" (1977:54).
This perception has been historically reinforced, as it were, from two directions.
On one hand, women's movements have traditionally been led by relatively privileged, white, middle-class women whose advantages on the basis of race and
class have made it difficult for black women to identify closely with them, even
on the basis of some gender commonalities. On the other hand, the racism that
the dominant society has directed at both black women and black men has made
racial unity between black women and black men an urgent necessity for black
survival. This is not to deny the role of sexism on the part of black men nor to
deny that black women perceive and resist such sexism. But it is to say that on
balance, black women are much more likely to gravitate toward black men than
toward white women as their closest allies in struggles for social change.

This is most evident in black women's rejection of those strains of radical
feminism that assert a fundamental dichotomy between all men as oppressors

and all women as victims and move in the direction of separatism (Ferree and Hess 1985:164–165). Joseph and Lewis state simply, "Black women cannot operate with a philosophy whose dynamics include separation, rejection, or exclusion of men" (1981:29), and "one of the ultimate forms that White feminist racism or racist feminism could take might be to argue that all men are oppressors" (1981:281). Dill argues that the radical feminist insistence on the primacy of patriarchy necessitates a choice for black women between their identity as women and their identity as blacks, which precisely reflects the patriarchal tactic of divide-and-conquer (1983:136). The ability to utilize divide-and-conquer strategies, in turn, is a function of the interlocking nature of multiple systems of domination, which promotes such priority debates whenever two or more sources of oppression occur together. Ideological insistence or felt needs to choose between race, class, or gender can thereby reinforce the power of all three systems of domination by undercutting resistance against any one. Bell Hooks has taken this criticism the farthest by arguing that it is reactionary rather than radical to claim that all men are the enemies of all women. The reactionary nature of this claim arises because it is an attempt to universalize the experience of some women, and also because such a perspective will make a politically effective, mass movement of women virtually impossible (1984:33–34). Although separatism has never been the dominant ideology of the contemporary movement, its periodic prominence has contributed to black women's reluctance to become involved in that movement.

Black women have also been critical of the concept of sisterhood. Bell Hooks and Bonnie Dill argue that the concept of sisterhood presumes common, shared forms of oppression as the universal experience of all women. In Dill's argument, sisterhood ultimately reduces to bourgeois individualism or to a politics of personal experience, neither of which have been very appealing to black women. Both versions of sisterhood promote a lifestyle politics of self-fulfillment with a strong individualist strain. For these writers, the concept of sisterhood, which was originally part of the ideology of the women's liberation sector, was always a close relative of the liberal feminism of the women's rights sector; what both shared was an underlying premise of individualism and what both promoted was individual opportunity and mobility on the one hand or personal transformation and self-fulfillment on the other hand (Dill 1983; Hooks 1981, 1984). What is missing from all these variants of feminist ideology is a recognition of the need for a collectively oriented struggle by a mass movement of people against structurally rooted sources of institutionalized sexism and patriarchal power. The tendency for feminism to fall back into individualist ideologies and goals is not surprising given the continuing predominance within the movement of white, middle-class activists whose immediate interests may best be served by such strategies. But it is also not surprising that a movement with such an orientation has had difficulty attracting women from other class and racial backgrounds.

The common thread in all of these critical black perspectives on the contemporary women's movement concerns how that movement has falsely universalized its own experience and failed to recognize the profound diversity that race and class impose on the lives of women. The perspectives of black women are thus essential to any future broadening of the women's movement. Such perspectives require a reappraisal of some of the core insights of the women's movement. The notion that paid work can and will liberate women looks very different from the long history of oppressive working conditions faced by black women. The claim that the family is the central patriarchal institution looks very different from the standpoint of black women who have struggled to maintain family and often found in family a source of support and a basis of resistance. It is this failure to recognize diversity that has historically kept black women away from the mainstream women's movement even though black women have supported many of that movement's goals. Over the last decade or so, all of these issues and questions have been raised and debated within the movement, and there are important signs in feminist theory and political practice that the movement now has the potential to broaden its base significantly beyond its traditional roots in the white middle class.

In the view of many of the writers cited here, the most productive direction for such a broadening of the movement involves coalition politics. The dream of a unified and universal women's movement contains the seeds of its own reversion to a movement that speaks with a particular class and race accent, because a unified and universal movement cannot do justice to the diversities that class and race impose on women's experience. As Joseph and Lewis argue, coalition politics don't require that all groups "identify" with one another, but rather that they listen to one another and by listening find the issues and goals on which there are common ground and prospects for progress (1981). One model for such progressive coalitions is to be found in the cross-class alliance of the later suffrage movement, in which working-class women and their organizations developed a working-class rationale for woman suffrage and moved into a productive coalition with the mainstream suffrage movement in pursuit of a common goal for class-specific reasons. This model is rich in negative as well as positive lessons, however, for the same coalition politics that produced a cross-class alliance for woman suffrage collaborated in the racist exclusion of black women and the interests of blacks more generally in access to the franchise. This does not invalidate the model as a guide to forming alliances and coalitions across lines of class and race where diverse women have common or class- and race-specific reasons for pursuing similar goals. But it does serve as a final reminder that even if coalition politics are a fruitful strategy, the potential always exists in a society with interlocking systems of domination for coalitions working for some oppressed groups to simultaneously work against other oppressed groups.

Conclusions

The dynamics of race and class in women's movements must be seen in the broader context of a social order consisting of three interlocking systems of domination based on class, race, and gender. Every individual is simultaneously a member of each of these systems, producing complex combinations of structural locations. For each of these locations, there are equally complex sets of interests based on intersecting privileges and disadvantages associated with one's class, race, and gender. Social movements that emerge against this complex backdrop of structural location and associated interests may challenge some part of that overall social order, but they always bear the imprint of the very social order that the movement confronts. We have already seen one form of this imprint in analyzing the origins of women's movements. Class and race systems of domination tend to concentrate subordinate group members together and apart from dominant group members. This creates the initial networks, identity, and consciousness that are vital to the emergence of movements based on class or race. Gender systems of domination, by contrast, disperse subordinate group members throughout the social order but in close connection with dominant group members. This makes it more difficult for the initial networks, identity, and consciousness vital to the origins of social movements to be established. This is part of the reason why women's movements have historically tended to follow on the heels of other movements that could mobilize more easily.

The model of interlocking systems of domination and associated interests is also useful for understanding the class and race composition of women's movements as they mobilize to challenge aspects of gender stratification. The truism that women's movements tend to be white, middle-class movements follows the structural logic of this model because white, middle-class women are relatively privileged by race and class and thereby experience the clearest and most readily identified forms of discrimination on the basis of gender. This makes such women the most likely candidates for recruitment to women's movements because, aside from the resources they may possess, gender is the system of domination that has the greatest negative impact on them. The same structural location may also promote mobilization into antifeminist countermovements by women who value their class and race privileges and perceive traditional gender arrangements as an intrinsic part of these privileges. Thus, feminist movements and countermovements both tend to be dominated by white, middle-class women. At the very least, the situation is more complicated for women who face discrimination on the basis of class and gender, race and gender, or class, race, and gender. For straightforward structural reasons, working-class women, women of color, and working-class women of color are less likely recruits to women's movements because gender defines only one of two or three systems of domination that affect them. Beyond this, when such women choose priorities among these struggles, they are more likely to identify with class-based or race-based movements than they are with gender-based movements. This also follows straightforward structural logic in that subordinate groups based on class or race already have common networks, identities, and consciousness that make the mobilization of class and racial movements initially more likely than the mobilization of gender movements. Thus, the same structural factors that make middle-class white women the most likely recruits to a women's movement make non-middle-class nonwhite women less likely recruits to such a movement.

This static, structural analysis is important because it identifies factors that constrain certain actions and enable other actions. But it is only part of the story, because action is also a function of more fluid, situational, contextual, and idiosyncratic factors that create a more complex mosaic than one could ever predict on the basis of structural logic alone. Movement mobilization is not just a dependent variable resulting from structural constraints; it is also an ongoing, interactive process with its own developmental dynamics, which insure that movements will always have a more complex profile than structural factors would predict. Nonetheless, the weight of structural constraint seems evident even when one recognizes movement mobilization as a fluid and ongoing process. Following movement mobilization over time often reveals what may be the most pernicious effects of interlocking systems of domination, because it becomes clear that challenging one system can be consistent with maintaining another. Indeed, recruitment into a movement challenging one system of domination may be premised precisely on maintaining another system of domination, as occurred in the case of white southern suffragists who sought the right to vote as a means of maintaining and strengthening white supremacy in the South.

The danger that a movement challenging one system of domination will simultaneously reinforce another system is greatest when the movement is directed by those who experience only one form of domination. For both structural and experiential reasons, white, middle-class women may not only perceive gender as the major source of inequality in the social world but may also consciously or unwittingly embrace tactics that reinforce class and race domination while challenging gender domination. For parallel reasons, racial movements directed by middle-class men or class movements led by white men may adopt tactics that reinforce class and gender or racial and gender forms of domination respectively. Even when movements against one system of domination do not actively reinforce other systems, they may simply ignore them. This has perhaps been the most common posture of the women's movements examined here, and it results from the peculiar forms of class and race "unconsciousness" that often inform the worldview of groups that are partially dominant and partially subordinate. One of the privileges of being a member of a relatively dominant class or racial group is the ability to deny that class or race really matter. Middle-class activists or white activists are likely to have blind spots when it comes to understanding the deeply rooted nature of class and race systems of domination. These blind spots are reinforced by other dominant belief systems stressing individual effort, equality of opportunity, upward mobility, and related values that exaggerate prospects for individual change, obscure structural obstacles to social change, and deny the collective nature of the subordinate group and the system of domination itself.

There would appear to be three ways in which movements challenging one system of domination might avoid reinforcing or ignoring other systems of domination. One would be to cultivate heterogeneous movement groups so that the perspectives and interests of those who experience multiple forms of domination explicitly inform movement strategy and tactics. A second would be to encourage coalition strategies in which homogeneous groups actively seek common or overlapping interests around which they can work together without danger of losing the distinctive identities of each group. A third way would be conscious efforts at "ideological stretch"; that is, explicitly cultivating ideological and theoretical reflection that would transcend one's structural location and its narrowly defined interests to analyze how interlocking systems of domination rely on the subordination of one group to reinforce the subordination of another group. Women's movements are richly illustrative of all these possibilities because they have at various times reinforced, ignored, or challenged other systems of domination while also experimenting with the options of heterogeneous groups, coalition strategies, and "ideological stretch."

The history of women's movements may be viewed through the lens of class to reveal many of these possibilities. The woman's rights movement began as a class-bound, class-"unconscious" movement that ignored working-class women but then briefly attempted to build a cross-class alliance when it split with the abolitionist movement after the Civil War. From there to the end of the century, the movement largely ignored working-class women while a new middle-class consciousness emerged in the suffrage movement's leadership ranks. After the turn of the century, there were important efforts at organizational alliances and coalition politics, which created an effective, cross-class, mass movement in support of the right to vote. The contemporary movement began in a similarly class-bound, class-"unconscious" way, but fostered the emergence of working-class feminist organizations, which then created the potential for alliance-building and coalition politics around common economic concerns. There continues to be a tension in the contemporary movement between a careerist version of feminism and a more broadly oriented cross-class agenda. Nonetheless, considerable progress has been made in identifying issues that effect working women from diverse class backgrounds; these issues include comparable worth, the feminization of poverty, sexual harassment, and child-care needs. While the mainstream movement still speaks with a middle-class accent, its multi-issue agenda reflects some of the interests and needs of women from differing class backgrounds as well.

Reading the same history through the lens of race reveals less diversity in movement positions and less success at cross-group alliances. The women's rights movement had roots in the abolitionist movement but nonetheless maintained a race-bound view of blacks, and of black women in particular. The complicated political maneuverings of the post–Civil War period activated the latent racism of many in the women's movement, which then receded into a profound indifference until the turn of the century. The later phase of the suffrage struggle again activated the latent racism of many in the suffrage movement, as the leading movement organizations accepted a strategy that linked woman suffrage with white supremacy. The contemporary movement began in a race-bound way that largely ignored black women once again, and has developed in somewhat contradictory fashion. Many have become more receptive to the participation of black women, but remain somewhat perplexed by their lack of participation. This perplexity has given way to a slowly dawning awareness that many of the priorities and some of the ideologies that inform the movement have limited its appeal to, and sometimes explicitly alienated, women of color. This new awareness, fostered in large part by the response of black women to the women's movement, has led to new dialogues between diverse women; these dialogues have the potential to build cross-race bridges and meaningful coalitions that will recognize difference and diversity as well as common concerns.

This overview suggests that women's movements have always had difficulty transcending their white, middle-class roots, although they have been somewhat more successful in transcending class barriers than race barriers. While this reality is often presented as a criticism of the movement, it is important to note that few movements have been better and many have been much worse at transcending (or even recognizing) such barriers. Women's movements may never be able to resolve this tension, because they are always likely to speak with a white, middle-class accent while implicitly claiming all women as their constituency. But this tension can itself be a source of strength and renewal, because it continually invites reflection, dialogue, and criticism, which all seek to clarify both the differences and the commonalities characterizing women as a social movement constituency. There is no more diverse constituency, and no movement has greater potential to reverberate through every aspect of social life and to challenge all of the interlocking systems of domination that make up the existing social order. One important resource the movement possesses that may help it move in this direction is the richness and diversity of its ideological traditions. This diversity can be an important learning mechanism, allowing the movement to explore the dialectical relation between theory and practice in fruitful and innovative ways. Future movement success depends on attaining and maintaining this ideological diversity, for this may well be the key to activating the diverse and potentially enormous constituency of the women's movement.

Chapter
five

Opposition
and
Countermovements

[handwritten marginalia: "Q: movement not an group in this regard"]

Social movements often provoke opposition. Indeed, the emergence of explicit opposition to a social movement is often the best indicator that the movement is succeeding, because only then do established interests and privileged groups feel compelled to defend their position and counter the challenge posed by the social movement. By this standard, women's movements must be judged very successful, for they have provoked substantial opposition and major efforts to defend the status quo. Although opposition to social movements is fairly common, opposition to women's movements is distinctive because it often consists predominantly of other women. Most social movements are opposed by people from other social groups: property-holders resist labor movements or powerful whites oppose racial movements. The expected *[handwritten: (mainly)]* analogue would be that men would oppose women's movements. Although there has been no shortage of antifeminist men to fulfill this expectation, men are often outnumbered by women in active opposition to women's movements. Thus, women have historically been the only major group to organize against their own emancipation (Chafetz and Dworkin 1987a:41; Conover and Gray 1983:9), providing an especially interesting example of movement opposition.

This tendency for some women to oppose movements that speak on behalf of women has been understood in various ways. Movement activists sometimes characterize female opponents as irrational and deluded victims of a false consciousness that prevents them from seeing their true interests as women. While this depiction is not without merit, the opposition of some women may be quite "rational" on several grounds. For one, women who are privileged on the basis of class, race, or other statuses may perceive that they have more to lose than to gain from the implementation of a feminist agenda, and therefore oppose women's movements. For another, the identities of many women may be so profoundly shaped by dominant notions of family, femininity, and motherhood that a feminist agenda can only be experienced as a frontal attack on one's identity, and opposition to such a movement becomes a defense of self. Finally, the structure of a patriarchal society puts many women in positions of relative dependency and vulnerability while creating the appearance of male protection. For some, a women's movement threatens to remove the protections and heighten the vulnerability; opposition to a women's movement may thus be a rational and self-interested response to the perceived danger of even greater vulnerability. While a sophisticated theory of patriarchal power may ultimately be able to explain female opposition to women's movements as further evidence of that patriarchal power, it does not follow that such opposition can simply be dismissed as an irrational form of false consciousness. Taking such opposition seriously is vital to understanding the dynamics of women's movements, and important to grasping the relations between movements and countermovements more generally.

Social movement theory is rather underdeveloped when it comes to analyzing opposition to social movements, so it is helpful to begin with some broad distinctions between different types of opposition. At the most general level, movements may be said to be "opposed" by cultural inertia and tradition, which often make it difficult to accomplish any type of planned social change. If and when movements are able to overcome cultural inertia, they may then encounter a range of social control efforts that attempt to blunt the movement's impact. For Smelser, the ineffective operation of social control is seen as a prerequisite for the emergence of a fully developed social movement (1963), but even when movements do emerge they often find themselves in an ongoing battle with various agents of social control. These agents may represent the state in its role as the guarantor of sociopolitical order, and these efforts may range from gentle forms of cooptation to explicit exercises in repression. Social control agents may also represent particular institutional sectors that are specifically threatened by the agenda of a movement and seek to defend their interests and privileges against the challenges of outsiders. Finally, the most specific form movement opposition may take is that of a countermovement that emerges in direct response and opposition to an existent social movement.

The analysis of countermovements requires a further distinction between conservative, reactionary, or right-wing movements on the one hand and countermovements on the other hand. There is a long tradition of research depicting right-wing movements as reactions to the social changes these movements oppose (for example, Lipset and Raab 1970). Depending on the issues involved, these movements may appeal to political, economic, social, or religious conservatives, and they often have important linkages to elites in established institutions (Lo 1982). Although countermovements (CMs) often share many of these characteristics, there is general agreement that CMs are better defined as movements that arise in specific opposition to a prior social movement (SM) and its agenda (Mottl 1980; Zald and Useem 1987; Lo 1982). Although CMs are often conservative, this definition permits cases where conservative movements spark progressive countermovements, as exemplified by recent mobilizations in response to the renewed power of the Ku Klux Klan and other racial hate groups. Theorists of CMs also concur that the appropriate unit of analysis is precisely the interaction that occurs between SMs and CMs. Mottl speaks of the "movement conflux" created by the dialectical interaction of SMs and CMs, stressing that both are elements of a common reform process (1980). Zald and Useem also call for an interactional focus to understand "loosely coupled conflict" between SMs and CMs (1987). This interactional focus implies that neither the original SM nor the subsequent CM can be adequately understood apart from the relational dance each movement conducts vis-à-vis the other.

Building on this relational conception of SM-CM dynamics, these authors have proposed several hypotheses. Movements that achieve visibility or have impact create the conditions for CM mobilization, which becomes more likely if the initial SM appears to be accomplishing its goals. CMs are typically oriented to challenges from below and are often motivated by a perception of socioeconomic decline on the part of their participants. The likelihood and type of mobilization that a CM undergoes depends on its structural location, access to resources, and opportunity structures; CMs will mobilize more rapidly and effectively if they can build on preexisting organizations and recruit leadership from elites in those organizations. CMs often appeal to established societal myths to oppose change and preserve the status quo. As a mobilizing strategy, they often use a single, powerful idea to arouse enthusiasm, create commitment, and mobilize followers. Once both movements are well established, SMs and CMs engage in loosely coupled spirals of conflict and mobilization as the strategies and tactics of one side condition those of the other side. Much activity may be devoted to neutralizing or discrediting the opposition, although strategic options can also include damaging actions, information gathering, restricting resources, projecting negative images, and preemptive moves. Finally, SM-CM conflict may become superimposed with conflict between various govermental levels, with different sectors of the state taking divergent positions in the SM-CM dance (Mottl 1980; Zald and Useem 1987; Lo 1982). Most of these hypotheses have been formulated without specific reference to women's movements, so the latter provide an additional test case of these hypotheses and an opportunity to refine and expand them.

Additional hypotheses derive from prior research into the specific dynamics of feminist and antifeminist movements. Chafetz and Dworkin claim that antifeminist CMs often rest on two sources of organized opposition. Vested-interest groups are typically male dominated and oppose change-oriented movements on the basis of class interest, while voluntary grass-roots associations are typically female dominated and oppose change-oriented movements on the basis of status politics. Vested-interest groups opposing feminism include both religious and economic interests, whereas voluntary grass-roots associations draw on a constituency of "role-encapsulated" women who sense a status threat from feminist women who have benefited from role expansion. When feminist movements begin to achieve some success, that very success triggers the development of preexisting diffuse sentiment into an organized antifeminist movement. Vested-interest groups mobilize first in response to economic threats; voluntary grass-roots associations follow somewhat later in response to status threats. Although the voluntary associations may attract more publicity, Chafetz and Dworkin argue that the vested-interest groups provide the initial impetus and the resource base for organized antifeminist CMs. They suggest that organized antifeminist movements will generally receive overt support from religious organizations and covert support from economic-interest groups (Chafetz and Dworkin 1987a, 1987b). Since many discussions of opposition to women's movements focus on the seeming paradox of women's opposition, Chafetz and Dworkin's attention to male-dominated vested-interest groups that oppose feminist movements provides a needed corrective to our view of such CMs.

The relatively few attempts to compare opposition to the woman suffrage movement and to the contemporary women's movement support Chafe's observation that "the consistency of anti-feminist arguments constitutes one of the most striking facts of the entire debate in America over woman's place" (1972:231). One study of the rhetoric of antifeminist women in both centuries found a common concern with preserving traditional arrangements concerning gender, sexuality, and family. Whereas contemporary antifeminists discuss sexuality more openly than antisuffragists did, both groups agree that the breadth and depth of differences between the sexes renders goals like suffrage or the ERA meaningless or dangerous. Both groups detect in feminism a dangerous threat to the position of women, the sanctity of marriage, and the stability of families. Both groups perceive strong links between feminism and radicalism, foreign ideologies, Marxism, and/or secular humanism. Finally, both groups feel that women are already able to exercise a distinctly feminine power, which is threatened by a feminist agenda (Frenier 1984). Marshall concurs that both CMs used similar rhetoric, but argues that anti-ERA forces were organizationally more effective than antisuffragist groups at mobilizing needed resources (1985). Beyond organizational effectiveness, there were other important differences in mobilization rates, climates of opinion, and symbolic strategies which account for the success of the anti-ERA forces and the ultimate failure of the antisuffrage groups (Marshall and Orum 1986).

The following analysis compares the role of opposition and countermovements in the cases of the woman suffrage movement and the contemporary women's movement. In ideological terms, this survey reveals a great deal of continuity over time. Explicit opposition to women's movements has always been rooted in a defense of separate spheres and sex-specific roles, and has consistently detected a broad and pervasive threat to the family, the nation, and social order in women's movements. In organizational terms, differences between the two periods are more evident. Contemporary antifeminist organizations have been more effective at marshalling resources, enlisting support, and obstructing the goals of the women's movement than their nineteenth-century counterparts. Modern antifeminist organizations are also embedded in a dense network of right-wing conservative groups. These ties have provided important resources to countermovement organizations, but they have also reproduced traditional schisms among conservative groups within contemporary antifeminism, thereby limiting the groups' effectiveness.

The Woman Suffrage Movement

One pattern of countermovement mobilization that is evident in the opposition to woman suffrage is the tendency for CMs to mobilize only when the initial movement presents a creditable threat to the existing social order. In keeping with this principle, there was little sustained countermovement organization until the 1890s, when suffrage forces began to win concrete if limited victories in various states and localities. As the tempo of the suffrage campaign accelerated after the turn of the century, so did the ferocity of the countermovement opposing woman suffrage. Before the 1890s, however, expressions of opposition to woman suffrage influenced the movement. Before the Civil War, opponents invoked dominant ideological notions of separate spheres and woman's place to ridicule women's rights. There was also resistance to the inclusion of women's rights in the agendas of other social movements, especially abolitionism. Immediately after the war, opposition became more concrete in partisan battles over Reconstruction. Finally, the post–Civil War period saw the first mobilization of an antisuffrage countermovement, which occurred on an ad hoc basis to resist legislative proposals that would have granted women the right to vote.

Ideological notions like the doctrine of separate spheres, the "cult of true womanhood," and the legal notion of coverture in marriage formed a cultural backdrop that early opponents of women's rights used against the movement. If men and women were to specialize in the public and private spheres respectively, then woman suffrage represented an unjustified intrusion of women into the public sphere and a corresponding neglect of the private sphere. If women were to aspire to true womanhood, understood as domesticity, piety, purity, and submissiveness, then voting rights threatened to unsex women and turn them into men. If the interests of wives were subsumed under the rights of husbands in keeping with Blackstone's principles, then (married) women had no need of the vote or other legal and civil rights, which properly belonged to heads of households. A common thread in these arguments was that the differences between the sexes were profound, numerous, and unalterable. Given the strict dichotomy between feminine and masculine and the assignment of women and men to very different roles in the social order, it was easy for opponents of women's rights to portray these goals as ludicrous, unnatural, and irrational perversions of a natural order. The antebellum women's rights movement had to devote considerable energy to legitimating its goals in the face of these challenges.

Another form of antebellum opposition to women's rights involved resistance by some abolitionists to the inclusion of these issues in their agenda. Many theorists have called attention to the interaction between movements and countermovements; this dynamic was evident in the very origins of the women's rights movement. From the late 1830s onward, that movement coalesced through a dialectic of opposition in which even the presence of women was initially opposed by some reform organizations. This opposition helped to thematize gender as a mobilizing issue and contributed to an explicit and conscious women's rights ideology. As women began to articulate this ideology from abolitionist platforms, opponents challenged the tactical appropriateness (if not the fundamental legitimacy) of pursuing women's rights in this way. This opposition became a catalyst for a number of independent women's rights conventions in the dozen years before the Civil War. My earlier analysis of movement origins concluded that the abolitionist movement both nurtured and constricted the development of the women's rights movement. From the perspective of this chapter, that constriction can be understood as a form of opposition that ultimately contributed to the emergence of an independent women's movement.

While the antebellum movement faced ideological opposition from the overall culture and organizational opposition from specific reform movements, a new kind of opposition emerged immediately after the Civil War. Battles over postwar Reconstruction brought the women's rights agenda into the midst of partisan political conflict between Republicans and Democrats. In this struggle, Republicans marginalized women's rights while implementing their Reconstruction agenda. Democrats temporarily courted some suffragists to embarrass the Republicans, but had no genuine interest in supporting women's rights. In this way, the sentiment for woman suffrage was manipulated and ultimately ostracized by both major parties because neither perceived any substantial benefits from supporting that cause. Ellen DuBois's analysis of the 1867 Kansas campaign for black and woman suffrage, in which even the supposed Republican allies of woman suffrage formed an "Anti-Female Suffrage Committee," is a potent illustration of the partisan political system's rejection of woman suffrage in this period (1978:79–104). Up to this time, then, the women's movement was confronted by ideological opposition from the dominant culture, organizational opposition from other reform movements, and tactical opposition from the partisan political system. While all these were potent obstacles to movement success, they were also somewhat oblique forms of opposition when compared to the direct challenge of a countermovement.

The earliest signs of a direct countermovement challenge appeared around 1870. On the national level, an antisuffrage petition was presented to Congress by a group of elite women opposed to any extension of voting rights to women (O'Neill 1969:57; Flexner 1975:305). On the state level, a classic example of countermovement mobilization occurred in Illinois. During 1869 and 1870, Illinois held a constitutional convention to draft a new state constitution. From January to April of 1870, the convention received a number of prosuffrage petitions with a total of 1,600 signatures, and it decided to submit the issue of woman suffrage (and Negro suffrage) to a popular vote. In April, the convention received a single massive antisuffrage petition with 1,381 signatures. In response, they reversed their earlier decision to submit the issue to the voters. The convention eventually wrote Negro suffrage into the new constitution on their own initiative, but did not do so for woman suffrage (Buechler 1986:103). While little is known about this specific incident, it foreshadowed some important movement-countermovement dynamics. For one, while there had been organized prosuffrage groups in Illinois for at least a year, there was no organized antisuffrage group. For another, the convention drew back at the first sign of controversy and opted to preserve the status quo. This was an early instance of what would become a familiar pattern: an eleventh-hour, ad hoc mobilization of antisuffrage sentiment that effectively defeated the sustained, organized efforts of prosuffrage forces to win the right to vote for women.

The prospects for winning suffrage waned after 1870, and so did counter-movement activity. By most accounts, the suffrage movement became dormant from 1870 to 1890. There were no major successes, and in many locales the movement suffered from declining membership and shrinking resources. Despite hard times, the movement persisted: state organizations survived, annual conventions met, and Stanton and Anthony began writing what became a massive, six-volume history of the suffrage movement. These activities contributed to movement maintenance by preserving vital networks until the movement could become more effective. During this period of movement maintenance, resistance to the goals and ideology of the suffrage movement was more subtle than the direct challenge of a countermovement, but had more profound effects because it came at a time when the movement was at a low ebb and was highly vulnerable to such resistance. This resistance was rooted in the rapid growth of a diverse array of women's organizations during the last three decades of the nineteenth century. Sorosis, the Young Women's Christian Association, the Association of Collegiate Alumnae, the Women's Christian Temperance Union, the American Social Science Association, and the women's club movement all attracted significant numbers of relatively well-to-do women at a time when the suffrage movement was fighting hard simply to maintain itself.

The thread that linked these organizations was the ideology of social feminism, and once again the temperance movement provides the best example of how this orientation implicitly challenged the equal rights ideology of the woman suffrage movement. For instance, the prosuffrage arguments of temperance advocates often received a warmer reception than those of equal rights suffragists, because their underlying social feminism was more consistent with dominant cultural notions of sex differences. In addition, new recruits to the suffrage movement in this era were more likely to advocate social feminist than equal rights rationales for the vote. Finally, the leadership of the suffrage movement at local and state levels often overlapped with the leadership of temperance forces. In all these ways, the rise of social feminism exemplified by the temperance movement helped to tip the ideological balance within the suffrage movement from equal rights to social feminism. While the temperance movement was not a countermovement, it nonetheless challenged the underlying rationale of the suffrage movement and contributed to the transformation of that movement (see Buechler 1986:117–130 for a more detailed version of this argument). As we shall see later, it also earned the suffrage movement a formidable foe in the liquor and brewing industries, whose opposition to woman suffrage matched their resistance to temperance and prohibition.

Sustained mobilization and organization by antisuffrage countermovements occurred only after 1890. Before examining this process, an overview of antisuffrage ideology is in order. The most central beliefs uniting all antisuffrage forces were that the sexes were fundamentally different from each other and that the division of society into separate spheres was a natural and desirable reflection of these sex differences. Antisuffragists believed that women and men were suited for very different tasks and had very different sensibilities, and that each sex should thereby exercise control over and responsibility for its respective sphere. Based on this worldview, antisuffragists presented themselves as the real defenders of womanhood, motherhood, and the family — a claim that was consistent with the idea that women had special responsibility for the private sphere. From this perspective, the vote threatened to eliminate the special protections women enjoyed as representatives of the home and the private sphere. Antisuffragists believed that the ballot would be a burdensome, destructive influence that would corrupt women and drag them into the unwholesome arena of partisan political struggle. Antisuffragists feared that the vote would unsex women and turn them into the "mannish" suffragists they so strenuously opposed. Perhaps most important, antisuffragists believed that the ballot would undermine true womanhood, the sanctity of marriage, and the stability of the family (Frenier 1984; Howard 1982; Kraditor 1965; Marshall 1985).

Antisuffrage ideology may be read as one side in a debate over sexual politics. However, the traditional positions that antisuffragists advocated were linked to a much broader conservative worldview that transcended sexual politics. One bridge to this worldview was the premise that the family, not the individual, was the basic unit of society. "To a true conservative, woman suffrage represented not merely a quantitative change in the size of the electorate but a qualitative change in the nature of society toward a more atomized and anomic form of social life" (Buechler 1986:21). The family was not the only institution linking antisuffragism to broader conservative themes. Antisuffragists also depicted themselves as defenders of the nation and the country against a variety of looming threats. The second most common theme in *The Woman's Protest*, a leading antisuffragist publication, was fear that socialist insurgency would be strengthened because woman suffrage would empower industrial workers and the foreign born. "Race suicide" constituted another danger that would be heightened by granting voting rights to women (Marshall 1986:334). Woman suffrage thereby became an ideological lightning rod that attracted diverse fears about everything that threatened social order during a time of rapid social change.

These links between antisuffragism and a broader conservatism were exemplified in the biography of Caroline Corbin, an avid antisuffragist who founded the Illinois Association Opposed to the Extension of Suffrage to Women in 1897. Eleven years earlier, Corbin had attended a talk by Eleanor

Marx and Edward Aveling. In response to a question about the impact of social-ism on marriage, Karl Marx's daughter "frankly acknowledged there would be no obligations for a man and woman to remain together . . . and that a man could at any time put away an old wife for a younger one, or a sickly wife for a healthy one" (Corbin, n.d.[a]). Corbin became convinced that socialism was the major threat to the sanctity of marriage and the stability of the family, and began a career advocating these views. The increasing prominence of woman suffrage in the 1890s provided a convenient focal point for this activity, and Corbin's anti-suffrage organization became an important vehicle for promulgating conserva-tive views. In a widely circulated pamphlet titled "Industrial and Political Independence of Women," Corbin argued that the nation's need for population growth required high fertility, which precluded women working outside the home (Corbin, n.d.[b]). In "Why the HomeMakers Do Not Want to Vote," she defended the notion of separate spheres by arguing that women workers would undercut male wages and family stability (Corbin, n.d.[c]). For Corbin, defense of separate spheres and the traditional family necessitated active opposition to the twin threats of socialism and woman suffrage.

Helen Johnson's *Woman and the Republic* (1897) also exemplifies the links between conservatism and antisuffragism. Johnson's premise that woman suf-frage and women's progress are antithetical is supported in subsequent chapters, which challenge all the major rationales advanced in favor of the right to vote. She argues that woman suffrage is antidemocratic and antirepublican, that suf-frage is a privilege not a right, and that voting must ultimately be backed up by force and might. Johnson refutes prosuffrage arguments based on the consent of the governed and the representation of taxpayers. She chastises woman suffra-gists for dividing and undermining such reform efforts as abolitionism and tem-perance. She criticizes suffragists for seeking to undermine the contractual nature of marriage, claiming that suffragists want all the advantages of single and married women with none of the disadvantages of either. She claims that the vote is not required to improve women's occupational opportunity, economic status, educational access, or professional mobility. She accuses suffragists of hostility to religion, of inciting the battle of the sexes, and of undermining the home and the family. Throughout all these arguments, however, is the underly-ing premise that suffrage is born out of socialism, anarchism, and other danger-ous political elements that must be resisted at all costs if social order is to be preserved.

One of the ironies of this opposition is that by the time antisuffragists for-mulated arguments linking woman suffrage to radical causes, the suffrage move-ment had repudiated most of these goals. The suffrage movement posed the most radical challenge to social order before and just after the Civil War, when it was allied with other social movements seeking fundamental change. By the 1890s, it was becoming a specialized, single-issue movement for the vote and explicitly rejected radical social change (Buechler 1986). Antisuffrage arguments had a certain plausibility, however, because no one could be sure of the impact of the measure if it passed. Suffragists traditionally claimed that the vote would bring massive changes, and antisuffragists opposed suffrage precisely on this basis. By the turn of the century, however, suffragists were just as likely to argue that the vote would not change any "desirable" features of society, and would simply extend a political voice to women who could help strengthen dominant social institutions and groups. Antisuffragists displayed the same rhetorical flexibility, arguing that woman suffrage wouldn't change anything and therefore was not worth the trouble. The fact that both sides could argue their positions from opposite premises suggests that nobody was sure about the effects of woman suffrage. It also suggests that the issue served as a symbolic template for diverse concerns and anxieties on both sides.

The temptation to view antisuffragist ideology as fundamentally irrational and hysterical (which it occasionally was) should be resisted because it obscures the accuracy and the self-interestedness of many antisuffragist positions. On balance, antisuffragists were closer to the mark when they argued that woman suffrage would change little than suffragists were when they predicted sweeping change. In the later stages of the suffrage struggle, antisuffragists pointed to numerous states that had enfranchised women and substantiated their claim of minimal impact. Some antisuffragists thus saw the issue more clearly than some suffragists (O'Neill 1969). In addition, many antisuffrage leaders came from privileged backgrounds, and their opposition is consistent with a model of rational, class-conscious political struggle by women identifying more closely with their class position than with their gender group. While it may be correct that antisuffragism expressed "a sense of powerlessness beyond traditional roles" (Howard 1982), the traditional roles of elite and privileged women were valued enough by their occupants to motivate many to actively oppose woman suffrage and its uncertain consequences. The same rational, self-interested logic applies to all the constituencies and organizations that had some vested interest in the status quo and opposed woman suffrage because it posed a potential if uncertain threat to that interest.

The more difficult task is to explain the conflict between women who came from similar class backgrounds but were on opposite sides of the suffrage debate. Marshall argues that this requires us to recognize both class interest and status politics in the antisuffrage campaign. "The status issue centered around the defense of the homemaker lifestyle, which antifeminists perceived as threatened by suffragist efforts to integrate public and private spheres, thereby reducing the social distance believed necessary for men's continued bestowal of status privileges to women" (Marshall 1986:328). From the perspective of status politics, antisuffragist efforts to maintain separate spheres and a corresponding decorum and modesty concerning femininity was a rational defense of status against an unknown and threatening alternative. However, antisuffragism was also motivated by a class interest in protecting against the expansion of women's paid and unpaid labor. Antifeminists believed that suffrage would ultimately force more women into the labor market without alleviating their domestic responsibilities, creating or exacerbating a double burden of work for women and heightening competition and antagonism between the sexes in the labor force. Class interest and status politics thereby combined in motivating some women to oppose suffrage. In Marshall's view, the fact that this ideological stance dovetailed with capitalist interests (not to mention patriarchal ones) does not mean that antisuffragists were falsely conscious or acting irrationally. Indeed, this dovetailing is another instance of the mutually reinforcing character of multiple systems of domination based on class, status, and gender.

The impact of antisuffragism on prosuffrage ideology is difficult to ascertain. While antisuffragism may not have won many new converts, it often set the parameters of subsequent debate because suffragists felt compelled to counter all antisuffrage arguments. Since these were often based on inconsistent or contradictory premises (that the vote would change nothing or everything), the attempts of suffragists to counter these arguments created inconsistencies and contradictions in prosuffrage ideology as well. Each side thus seized on the other's inconsistencies to bolster their own position, and both sides brought considerable ingenuity to constructing and deconstructing these arguments. On balance, antisuffragism did not create significant changes in prosuffrage ideology, if only because the suffrage movement underwent its major ideological transformations before its direct confrontation with antisuffragist forces (Buechler 1986). As noted earlier, suffrage forces eschewed radical causes well before they came under sustained attack by antisuffragists for such links. However, antisuffrage ideology did bolster transformations in suffrage ideology that had been taking place since the Civil War, and made it unlikely that an increasingly cautious movement would revive its earlier rationales for the vote. The greatest impact of antisuffragism derived not from the logic of its arguments but from the fact that it was defending rather than challenging the status quo. As such, antisuffragism did not need to win the debate to be effective; it merely needed to mystify the issues and neutralize the opposition to prevent a suffrage victory. In this effort, antisuffrage ideology had some modest if temporary success.

The various strands of antisuffrage ideology were promulgated by antisuffrage organizations beginning in the 1890s. In keeping with the principle that countermovements tend to mobilize only when initial movements pose a creditable threat, there was little need for antisuffrage organization before this decade, and a growing need after this decade as the suffrage cause became more respectable and its prospects for success improved. The Massachusetts Association Opposed to the Further Extension of Suffrage to Women was organized in 1890 and became a national clearinghouse for antisuffrage activity in the various states where such organizations eventually formed. In Illinois, where suffrage forces began winning minor victories in the form of limited female suffrage in 1891, Caroline Corbin founded the Illinois Association Opposed to the Extension of Suffrage to Women in 1897. In New York, an attempt to put woman suffrage into the revised state constitution sparked the formation of an antisuffrage organization in 1895. Other state organizations followed, culminating in the formation of the National Association Opposed to Woman Suffrage (Flexner 1975; Howard 1982).

Organized countermovement activity peaked from 1911 to 1916, when the exclusively female membership of the national antisuffrage organization grew to 350,000 and the number of state antisuffrage organizations grew to twenty-six. The national organization was originally headquartered in New York, but subsequently moved to Washington, D.C., in 1917 to oppose the federal suffrage amendment more effectively. The organization published the only national antisuffrage publication, *The Woman's Protest,* on a weekly basis; it provided persistent reminders of all the leading antisuffrage themes by rigorously defending the concept of separate spheres and a gender-based division of labor, warning against socialist insurgency and race suicide, linking antifeminism to defense of home and country, and warning that woman suffrage would destroy motherhood, femininity, the home, and thereby all social order. During World War I, the publication was renamed *The Woman Patriot,* and it appeared under the masthead "For Home and National Defense, Against Woman Suffrage, Feminism and Socialism." This peak period of antisuffrage organization corresponded with some major defeats of woman suffrage referenda. In 1915 alone, such measures lost in New York, New Jersey, Pennsylvania, and Massachusetts (Marshall 1986; Howard 1982).

The leaders of antisuffrage organizations have been variously described as "women of irreproachable social position" and "ladies of means and social position" (Flexner 1975:305–306); as "clubwomen, conservative, earnest social reformers" (O'Neill 1969:57); as "wealthy, socially prominent women with considerable experience in philanthropic work" (Marshall 1986:331); and as "women of high social station, the wives of wealthy businessmen or politicians, the daughters of important families" (Howard 1982:464). To the extent that antisuffragist leaders came from more privileged backgrounds than suffragists, there was a distinct class dimension to the conflict over woman suffrage. It is important to remember, however, that by this stage of the suffrage campaign, many upper-class, elite women had joined ranks with the suffrage cause as well. In DuBois's analysis, "from an elite perspective, the antisuffrage argument was more consistent than the prosuffrage one" because woman suffrage ultimately meant greater political democracy, which could threaten elite privilege (DuBois 1987a:39). Given this logic, the puzzle was not why elite women would oppose woman suffrage but rather why they would support it. DuBois suggests that the prosuffrage stance of some elite women was ultimately rooted in a presumption that they could provide political leadership for all women, and that working-class women in particular would defer to them. Hence, the complex intersection of class and gender meant that both pro- and antisuffragism were rational positions for elite women to assume, depending on their reading of the opportunities and dangers of an enfranchised female populace (DuBois 1987a).

Like all social movements, antisuffrage countermovements had to resolve various mobilization dilemmas in order to establish effective movement organizations. Given that the major constituency for such movements was women, many of the mobilization problems confronting the suffrage movement also confronted the antisuffrage movement. To the extent that women were structurally isolated and confined to a private, domestic sphere, they were a difficult constituency for both sides to mobilize. However, antisuffrage forces faced the additional countermovement paradox of needing to bring women out of traditional, nonpolitical roles in order to bolster the ideology that women should remain confined to precisely such roles. One way that antisuffragists dealt with this paradox was to call for a "quiet campaign" that remained appropriately ladylike and presented itself as an educational effort in keeping with traditional female moral reform rather than a political battle that would provoke conflict and partisan struggle. As a result, antisuffrage tactics "tended to be subtle and individualistic, such as leaving antisuffrage cartoons and pink roses on the desks of state legislators" (Marshall 1985:352). Counterbalancing this difficulty were two relative advantages that antisuffragists enjoyed. First, the predominantly elite and privileged leadership had relatively easy access to substantial resources that could be used to facilitate movement mobilization. Second, the antisuffrage movement never was, and never needed to be, a mass movement in order to be effective. In many instances, a small delegation appearing before a legislative committee was sufficient to neutralize greater numbers of prosuffrage women, who had the more difficult task of changing rather than defending the status quo.

While antisuffrage organizations delayed woman suffrage, more substantial opposition was encountered from vested-interest groups threatened by woman suffrage. There were important regional variations in the types of vested-interest groups mobilized to oppose woman suffrage (Flexner 1975:305). In the South, those who sought to maintain white supremacy strenuously opposed woman suffrage as a potential threat to their dominance. In the Midwest, opposition was especially likely from brewers and distillers, who associated woman suffrage with prohibition. In the East, industry and business were likely opponents of woman suffrage. This array of antisuffrage forces illustrates Chafetz and Dworkin's model of antifeminist countermovements, which includes voluntary grass-roots associations and vested-interest groups (1987a). In keeping with their model, most explicitly antisuffrage associations tended to be female dominated, while virtually all of the vested-interest groups were male dominated. In at least some cases, these opponents colluded to oppose the suffragists, who "believed that a trail led from the women's [antisuffrage] organization into the liquor camp and that it was traveled by the men the women antis employed" (Catt and Shuler 1923:276).

At various points, the suffrage campaign was vigorously opposed by organized religion, political machines, diverse business interests, southern Democrats, and southern women (Flexner 1975:309–318). But the best-known and most consistent opposition came from the liquor and brewing industry. The industry Catt and Shuler referred to as the "invisible enemy" organized as early as 1862 into a Brewers' Association to protect the trade. They point to this group's obstruction of suffrage legislation and referenda as early as the 1870s in various states (1923:111–112ff). In their view, the association feared woman suffrage even more than they feared prohibition, because the latter was subject to much easier repeal than the former. Hence, liquor opposition grew in tandem with progress toward suffrage. By the 1890s this was readily apparent to most suffragists, who began to distance themselves from the temperance movement precisely because of the additional opposition this association attracted (Bordin 1981). Despite this effort, liquor opposition to suffrage contributed importantly to the defeat of suffrage initiatives in a great number of state campaigns from the 1890s through the 1910s (Flexner 1975). The ability of this opposition to win or literally steal elections led most suffragists to reject state campaigns as a futile tactic, particularly because their strongest campaigns tended to attract the greatest opposition (Catt and Shuler 1923).

One of the best accounts of suffrage opposition argues that the vote was delayed by "the control, the deflecting, and the thwarting of public sentiment, through the trading and the trickery, the buying and selling of American politics" (Catt and Shuler 1923:viii). In their analysis of the final push for a woman suffrage amendment after 1915, they identify four forces: suffragists, liquor interests, antisuffragists, and prohibitionists. They characterize antisuffragists as well-to-do women defending their privileges and claim that neither suffragists nor liquor opponents credited antisuffragists with much influence. The only real success of antisuffrage forces that they acknowledge was their ability to win equal time in legislative hearings on suffrage initiatives; the worst damage they acknowledge was that the antisuffragists provided legislators with a convenient rationale for opposing suffrage. Whereas antisuffragist and liquor forces complemented one another and occasionally colluded, suffragists and prohibitionists maintained at best a benevolent neutrality, with prohibition vastly complicating the attempt to win woman suffrage. Catt and Shuler conclude that woman suffrage was delayed by "politics," which, in addition to these forces, included underlying male resistance, party inaction, and public indifference.

Both the general opposition and the specific countermovements to woman suffrage took diverse forms over the seven-decade struggle to win the right to vote. The entire suffrage campaign occurred against a backdrop of cultural inertia and ideological justification of separate spheres. The early movement encountered both resistance and support from abolitionism, tactical opposition during Reconstruction, and brief flurries of explicit, ad hoc countermovement mobilization around 1870. The relative demise of suffrage and rise of temperance represented another kind of resistance by promoting more instrumental and expedient suffrage rationales increasingly divorced from the broad radicalism of the early suffrage movement. By 1890, antisuffrage ideology was explicitly linking suffrage to a myriad of threats to social order, and antisuffrage forces were mobilizing ongoing countermovement organizations. As the tempo of the suffrage campaign increased, so did the determination of the antisuffrage crusade, producing many difficult and expensive battles in various states. These struggles finally gave way to a federal amendment whose ratification returned the battle to the states and revived one last ferocious antisuffrage barrage until ratification was successfully completed. The ex post facto characterization of these forces as victors and losers obscures the longevity of the battle over suffrage, the elaborate dance between movement and countermovement, and the uncertainty of the outcome until the very last state had ratified the woman suffrage amendment.

The Contemporary Women's Movement

For the purpose of studying its opposition, the contemporary women's movement may be divided into three phases. The first, from the mid-1960s through the early 1970s, was marked by little organized, overt opposition. This helps explain the relative ease with which the movement won passage of the Equal Rights Amendment (ERA) and the *Roe* v. *Wade* Supreme Court decision on abortion. In keeping with the principle that CMs tend to mobilize only after the initial movement achieves some success, CM organization began during a second phase in the early 1970s. By the end of the 1970s, there was an obvious, organized network of antifeminist groups articulating a CM ideology that challenged the premises and rejected the goals of the contemporary feminist movement. A third phase began in 1980 with the election of Ronald Reagan, the emergence of the New Right, and the political and cultural influence attributed to conservatism. In this period, it became clear that the antifeminist CM would successfully block ratification of the ERA, and that some of these groups would continue to mobilize in opposition to abortion. From the mid-1970s to the present, there has thus been an ongoing movement-countermovement dialectic between the contemporary women's movement and the various CM groups that have challenged that movement.

Available knowledge about antifeminist CMs tends to be skewed in two ways. Much media publicity and scholarly research has focused on the ERA campaign, with episodic attention to reproductive rights. It is clear that the ERA became a crucial symbol of the women's movement whose importance escalated far out of proportion to its probable concrete effects. The symbolic dimension of the ERA is reminiscent of the woman suffrage amendment, which some proponents and most opponents saw as promising or threatening massive social change. Both campaigns suggest that specific legislative proposals for broad changes in the status of women whose consequences are relatively unknown solidify major fault lines between profeminist and antifeminist forces. Despite these similarities, there are some obvious and ironic differences in outcomes. The suffrage campaign ultimately succeeded, although there was little evidence of popular support for the amendment until the end of the struggle. The ERA campaign lost in 1982 and appears dormant for the foreseeable future, despite the fact that public opinion consistently supported the amendment at least until the very last days of the ratification process. In any case, the symbolic importance the ERA assumed for protagonists was mirrored by the publicity and research that followed this struggle. The result is that we know a great deal about opposition to the ERA, but relatively little about other instances of opposition to the contemporary women's movement.

The other way in which our knowledge of contemporary opposition is skewed concerns the almost exclusive emphasis on voluntary, grass-roots organizations instead of vested-interest groups. If Chafetz and Dworkin's characterization of the former as female dominated and the latter as male dominated is correct, then our skewed knowledge about these groups exaggerates female opposition and obscures male opposition. In their own review of the evidence, Chafetz and Dworkin point to organized religion as an important opponent that has provided considerable financial resources. However, much of this opposition has involved sponsoring antifeminist CMs that more closely approximate voluntary, grass-roots organizations. Discussing economic associations, they point to several instances of vested-interest-group opposition but concede that "the actual evidence is scant" (Chafetz and Dworkin 1987a:47–48). In a rare examination of economic vested-interest groups, Langer argues that corporations that face economic threats from the ERA's probable effects on women's wages and employment status have been quietly active in opposing the ERA. Langer draws parallels between liquor opposition to suffrage and business opposition to the ERA, while conceding that the secrecy of such opposition means that "the case is circumstantial" (Langer 1976).

Antifeminist CM ideology and rhetoric reveal a number of continuities and similarities with an earlier generation of antisuffragists. Contemporary antifeminist ideology is fundamentally rooted in beliefs about extensive natural differences between the sexes. Given this perception of substantial biological, physical, psychological, and emotional differences by gender, the notion of sexual equality strikes antifeminists as a category mistake because it is nonsensical to speak of equality between such unlike entities as women and men. Based on this view of gender differences, antifeminists have positioned themselves as the defenders of traditional conceptions of gender and sexuality (Frenier 1984) and an updated version of the cult of true womanhood (Marshall 1985). As in antisuffragism, this defense of traditional gender differences and true womanhood is closely associated with support for the traditional family and the sanctity of the home (Marshall and Orum 1986). The master concept linking antifeminist themes in explicit opposition to feminist ideology is a fundamental belief in the appropriateness of separate spheres for women and men with distinctive rights, duties, obligations, tasks, and sensibilities for each gender and sphere. For antifeminists, the women's movement challenges the basis of familial and social organization in which family life is rooted in an exchange of women's homemaking and mothering for men's financial support (Chafetz and Dworkin 1987b).

Given the dominant themes of contemporary antifeminist ideology, it is tempting to view feminist and antifeminist ideologies as simply mirror images of one another. There are important differences between the two belief systems, however. Mueller and Dimieri (1982) distinguish the belief systems of feminist, proactive, challenging groups and antifeminist, reactive, defending groups along three dimensions: constraint (individual consistency of beliefs and preferences); consensus (degree of agreement within a group); and position extremity (extent to which the beliefs of a group differ from general public opinion). Their research shows that proactive feminist groups exhibit greater constraint, greater consensus, and greater position extremity than reactive antifeminist groups. Put differently, proactive belief systems exhibit more consistency, more intersubjective agreement, and more polarization from mainstream beliefs than do reactive belief systems. They found this pattern for a number of feminist policy preferences, including equal pay for equal work, governmental support for day care, paternity leave, and the right to abortion. They attribute the differences to higher levels of interaction and a greater sense of group antagonism among proactive groups as compared to reactive groups. They also see reactive groups as echoing the prevailing ideology, meaning that "their beliefs should have a good deal of the looseness and contradictions associated with everyday definitions of the social world" (1982:660). Since "the belief system of a reactive movement always enjoys more cultural legitimacy than that of a proactive movement" (1982:672), they expect that antifeminist ideology will continue to display less constraint, consensus, and position extremity than will be found among proactive, feminist belief systems.

In keeping with theoretical principle and historical precedent, the actual mobilization of an antifeminist CM and the articulation of a reactive belief system did not occur until the feminist movement won important gains in congressional passage of the ERA in 1972 and the Supreme Court's *Roe* v. *Wade* decision in 1973. CMs follow movements by definitional logic, but antifeminist CMs face particular mobilizing obstacles that can further delay their appearance. As with antisuffragism, contemporary antifeminist CMs that take the form of voluntary, grass-roots organizations must mobilize precisely that sector of the population that is most heavily imbued with traditional beliefs about appropriate activities for women. Such CMs must thus identify effective strategies for persuading women to leave the home in order to defend norms that prescribe their restriction to the home (Freeman 1983; Marshall 1985). These CMs did develop such strategies by tapping latent fears about the economic vulnerability of homemakers, which motivated them to become active participants in antifeminist CMs. But the process unfolded over a period of several years in the mid-1970s, gradually gaining adherents and building momentum toward the end of that decade.

The first explicitly anti-ERA organization appeared in October of 1972, when Phyllis Schlafly founded STOP ERA. Within a year the amendment had been ratified in thirty states, but STOP ERA was targeting the remaining states for a prolonged antiratification battle, which began to show definite effects by 1974. In 1975, Schlafly founded Eagle Forum to broaden her focus from the ERA to other issues. In characteristic antifeminist CM fashion, the ERA was a convenient symbol that allowed the organization to tap a much broader set of conservative concerns; Eagle Forum described itself as "a national organization of women and men who believe in God, Home, and Country, and are determined to defend the values that have made America the greatest nation in the world" (quoted in Conover and Gray 1983:74). The organization addressed issues of school textbooks, ERA ratification, abortion rights, gay rights, school prayer, and school busing. By the later 1970s, these interrelated issues led CMs to formulate a "profamily" agenda in defense of the status quo. These concerns were crystallized by what many CM members perceived as the unfair treatment of conservative women at the 1977 government-sponsored International Women's Year Conference. "In Houston they discovered that Judeo-Christian values, the nuclear family, and other institutions had been replaced by humanism and feminism, all funded by the federal government" (Conover and Gray 1983:74). The Houston Conference, along with President Carter's liberal White House Conference on Families, illustrated how a strong social movement could pressure the state into creating political opportunities and facilitating movement objectives (Chafetz and Dworkin 1987a:50–51). However, such facilitation had the unintended and unanticipated consequence of mobilizing conservative countermovement forces in opposition to feminism.

The relative success of contemporary antifeminist CMs (compared with their antisuffragist counterparts) has been attributed in part to their greater organizational ability. In a comparative analysis of both centuries, Marshall and Orum point out that antisuffragist forces organized relatively late and always conducted a quiet campaign in keeping with notions of appropriate feminine behavior. Contemporary antifeminism, by contrast, has been more effectively organized into an oppositional force (especially on the national level) and has benefited greatly from the experience and charisma of a leader like Phyllis Schlafly. This movement has also appealed to traditional notions of femininity, but the quiet campaign of "feminine" women presenting themselves as concerned citizens has been combined with a highly organized CM that has proven very adept at gaining publicity and manipulating mass media (Marshall and Orum 1986). There is a broader explanation for this differential success as well. As Ferree and Hess point out, "opposition to the ERA began with the John Birch Society" (1985:134), and Schlafly herself has a long involvement in right-wing organizations and politics. However, Schlafly provides only the most dramatic example of a broader pattern in which most contemporary opposition has built on a preexisting network of conservative, right-wing organizations. The confrontation with feminism and the debate over the family provided this group a broader airing of their views than any previous issue. There is no evidence of a comparably well-defined, right-wing network of conservative organizations that provided a foundation for antisuffragism, despite the common rhetorical and ideological themes that link antifeminism in both centuries.

The connections between contemporary antifeminism and right-wing politics are complex and intriguing. Brady and Tedin initially distinguished between the religious right, the secular right, and the segregationist right (1976), while Conover and Gray subsequently detected secular, religious, and profamily branches within the right wing (1983). The secular branch is the oldest and identifies big government and bureaucratic regulation as major threats; the religious branch sees religion, family, and morality as threatened by humanism, liberalism, and feminism; the profamily branch seeks to defend the family against diverse threats. "Initially this sector was composed of single-issue groups such as anti-abortion and anti-ERA groups. In the late 1970s this countermovement started calling itself 'pro-family.' Such a label is a shorthand way of summarizing opposition to feminism and coopts the family as the movement's symbol" (Conover and Gray 1983:77). In general, the New Right is a defensive mobilization based on self-interest, normative appeals, and a sense of urgency, and its use of symbolic politics has been especially important in mobilizing a constituency. In this context, the ERA and abortion issues were critical because they lent themselves to highly symbolic readings and emotionally charged forms of community conflict. The result has been somewhat paradoxical: the New Right has been less influential in affecting public opinion than is commonly believed (Conover and Gray 1983:130–171; Ferree and Hess 1985:83), but it has successfully mobilized a minority of citizens into a ferocious CM with considerable impact at the level of symbolic politics.

More recent evidence suggests that the New Right is split between social conservatives and laissez-faire conservatives (Klatch 1988). Social conservatives see the world in religious terms, see gender as central and hierarchial, deny discrimination against women, and blame feminists for a range of problems. Laissez-faire conservatives see the world in libertarian terms, do not see gender as central or hierarchical, recognize discrimination but counsel individual resistance, and partially support feminism. Klatch interprets these conflicting positions by assuming that traditional gender roles "work" for socially conservative women but not for women who are laissez-faire conservatives. The result is another paradox: socially conservative women are the furthest from feminism but nonetheless act as a unitary gender group defending their interests. Women who are laissez-faire conservatives share some feminist beliefs about individualism, freedom, and the like, but deny any collective basis for action on the basis of libertarian principles. The split between these two groups is important because their views on the role of the state are quite different. Social conservatives favor using state power to pursue their agenda and expressed disappointment in President Reagan's reluctance to do so. Laissez-faire conservatives favor limited state power and resist using this power even to advance their own agenda. This fundamental tension within the right wing poses important limits to its effectiveness in achieving its goals.

The general conclusions that follow from these studies are twofold. First, they make it clear that contemporary antifeminist CMs are deeply embedded in a network of conservative, right-wing organizations that offer important resources and advantages. The presence of a skilled and charismatic leader like Schlafly has enabled antifeminist forces to take maximum advantage of the opportunities provided by their links to the right. The second lesson of these studies is that the right wing is itself divided, with different sectors advocating conflicting strategies for pursuing their objectives. With all the attention paid to the New Right, it is worth remembering that its positions represent only a minority of the population. In fact, from 1970 to 1980 the percentage of the population supporting "most of the efforts to strengthen and change women's status in society" increased from 40 to 64 percent. From 1972 to 1978, support for "women's liberation" — a provocative term likely to maximize negative responses — grew to become a majority position (Ferree and Hess 1985:81–82). "From 1970 to 1982, a majority of adult Americans consistently supported the ERA" (Mansbridge 1986:14). The lack of popular support for New Right positions makes it all the more intriguing that antifeminism has won at least one clear victory in preventing ratification of the Equal Rights Amendment. Close anlaysis of this struggle is warranted because it provides the best contemporary illustration of the interactive dance between movements and countermovements.

The Equal Rights Amendment enjoyed broad, consistent public support at the time of its congressional passage and throughout much of the subsequent debate over ratification. For all its publicity, the New Right was not especially effective at changing public opinion about the amendment. ERA supporters tended to be younger, less religious, better-educated, relatively affluent, and more likely to be unmarried and employed outside the home. Opponents tended to be white, middle-aged, middle-class, politically conservative, and strongly religious homemakers. In an extensive study using 1980 survey data, Burris found that the strongest predictors of ERA attitudes for both sexes were race, church attendance, and geographic region; nonwhites were more supportive than whites, nonchurchgoers more supportive than churchgoers, and those on the East and West coasts more supportive than those in southern and central states. Burris also found that opposition to the ERA was strongly associated with other indicators of political conservatism, including opposition to the civil rights movement and to social welfare spending (Burris 1983). In an earlier study, Huber, Rexroat, and Spitze found some similar patterns, but concluded that social background factors were not as powerful in predicting ERA attitudes as were the anticipated consequences people associated with passage of the ERA. Both sexes tended to oppose the ERA if they thought it would hurt male job opportunities, but both favored it if they thought it would improve women's job opportunities (1978). Perhaps the most significant conclusion to be derived from studies of public opinion on the ERA is that such opinion changed very little during the decade-long ratification battle. The opposition succeeded in blocking the ERA for reasons other than their ability to affect public opinion.

One explanation for the defeat of the ERA emphasizes the myriad difficulties associated with passing and ratifying any amendment to the Constitution (Berry 1986). Historical analysis of other constitutional amendments suggests that successful ones must be ratified during a period of more general reform, must rest on widespread consensus, must be rooted in a sense of urgency and necessity, must involve effective political agitation and public relations, and must not be overly threatening to those affected. To the extent that these conditions do not obtain, it is much easier for opponents to defeat a proposed amendment than for proponents to see it through to final ratification. In the case of the ERA, Berry judges its congressional approval to have been premature because the required consensus at the state level had not yet emerged. This premature and partial success lulled supporters and alarmed opponents, so that opponents were fully mobilized and well organized when proponents were just beginning to understand the kind of battle that would be required to secure ratification. As a result, the required consensus in the necessary number of states was never achieved, the struggle bogged down over rescission efforts and deadline extensions, and state legislators in nonratifying states never felt compelled to ratify the amendment.

The defeat of the ERA is also due to the fact that the campaign became a complex battle of symbolic politics on both sides. The effects of passage were unclear even to many legal experts, so that proponents and opponents projected their greatest hopes and deepest fears onto the amendment. In Conover and Gray's terminology (1983), the ERA became a higher-order, condensational symbol that cast the issue in its broadest, most expansive, and most emotionally charged form. Countermovements are especially likely to use such symbols to mobilize support and enlist sympathy because they tap dominant cultural myths that CMs depict as under attack. In reality, both sides tended to argue from basic principles, eliminating the possibility of compromise or negotiation (Mansbridge 1986). However, it became even more difficult for proponents when the debate shifted from the broadly supported principle of equal rights to the amendment's ambiguous and controversial substantive effects. For example, both sides incorrectly assumed that passage of the ERA would put military women in combat situations, a substantive effect that opponents used much more effectively than proponents (Mansbridge 1986:60–89). The formal nature, ambiguous consequences, and symbolic dimensions of the ERA thereby facilitated opposition.

The forces opposing the ERA succeeded precisely because they were able to frame the amendment not as a narrow, technical, legal issue but as a broad, substantive question of national priorities (see, for example, Hoff-Wilson 1986). In Boles's terminology, whereas proponents followed an interest-group conflict model by mobilizing as organized lobbying groups and appealing to logic, opponents followed a community conflict model by mobilizing as ordinary citizens and appealing to emotion and sentiment. The use of the community conflict model by opponents allowed peripheral issues to be used effectively to recruit followers, exaggerate fears, and escalate debate. While some proponents saw the danger of this development, many were more than willing to join in the escalation of rhetoric about the amendment. The problem was that this escalation was much more beneficial to opponents than to proponents. As Boles argues, increasing conflict over an issue introduces a bias against adopting new policies (1979:177). As Mansbridge argues, it was opposition and subsequent controversy (rather than lack of support) that doomed the ERA, because controversy leads to greater caution on the part of legislators, prevents the necessary supermajority required for ratification, and persuades decision-makers to maintain the status quo rather than initiate change. Even more fatefully, Mansbridge argues that the ERA was doomed once it became evident that women themselves were sharply divided over the amendment (1986:6).

The failure of the ERA must also be attributed to some fundamental fault lines that derive from a gendered division of labor. As Mansbridge notes, both sides had natural constituencies of working women and homemakers motivated by differing kinds of relative deprivation. For all the inflated, exaggerated, and fallacious fears that opponents voiced in the anti-ERA campaign, feminists and homemakers had some genuinely differing interests over some of the issues in the ERA debate, and homemakers perceived some real threats to their status and position (Mansbridge 1986:90–112). The opposition was effective because it was able to tap these real threats and differing interests, to articulate and embellish them in an escalating and symbol-laden opposition to the amendment, and to raise the level of controversy to a point where decision-makers found it easier to support the status quo than vice versa. The ERA's ultimate failure should not obscure the fact that during the ratification struggle, much legislation and litigation occurred that improved the position of women (Berry 1986:86–

100; Mansbridge 1986:45–59). These gains mean that the defeat of the amendment was not a straightforward defeat of mainstream feminism, because many progressive (though potentially reversible) gains were won in the context of an ultimately unsuccessful campaign. Those very gains deprived proponents of some of their most effective pro-ERA arguments, and paradoxically contributed to reframing the ERA as a symbolic issue, and hence to its ultimate defeat.

The rhetoric of the anti-ERA movement reveals that these forces believed that the amendment threatened the "traditional family"; this threat permeates the ideology and rhetoric of the New Right and other contemporary conservative CMs (Gordon and Hunter 1977/78). The appeal on behalf of the traditional family was one of the most effective recruiting tools of the anti-ERA CM, allowing it to build a mass base of followers whose goal of defending home and family was reminiscent of the temperance movement a century earlier (Ehrenreich 1982). However, the New Right's position rested on a cultural politics of sex and family with implications well beyond this rallying point. "New Right patriarchalism" involved hostile opposition to feminism, youth, sexuality, civil liberties, and gays and lesbians while advocating for the traditional family, the work ethic, and religious fundamentalism. With regard to feminism in particular, the real target of New Right hostility was not so much the concept of equality as the notion of independence for women (Gordon and Hunter 1977/78). The New Right's perception of broad and sweeping threats to social order in a liberal reform like the ERA echoes those strands of antisuffragism that also perceived a holistic challenge to social order in the liberal reform of woman suffrage a century earlier.

The ability of a single issue to tap a much broader set of fears is illustrated not only by the ERA campaign but also by the struggle over abortion and reproductive rights. Before the *Roe* v. *Wade* decision, antiabortion activism was the province of male Catholic professionals; after the decision, these groups were overwhelmed by an influx of self-recruited housewives and a proliferation of prolife groups. The typical new participant was a married mother with a high school education who was not employed outside the home. These new recruits fervently believe that the fetus is a person, although this belief has a vague and abstract quality akin to a belief in patriotism, and abortion is a foreign experience for many. Prolife activists are likely to believe that abortion is a recently developed assault on the traditional sanctity of life; that important differences exist between the sexes and their appropriate sex roles; that sex is intended for procreation; that artificial contraception is wrong; that premarital sex is wrong; that sex education and contraception promote premarital sex; that parenthood is a natural, not a social role; that motherhood is the most fulfilling role a woman can have; and that motherhood is also a full-time job. On balance, prolife ideology tends to be deeply religious and antisecular, while prochoice views typically appeal to humanistic and secular rationalism as their foundation (Luker 1984).

Whereas earlier abortion debates tended to be amoral, professional discussions about medical decision-making, the more recent abortion debates have framed the issue as a deeply moral question about the relative status of the woman and the fetus. In symbolic terms, the debate is less about fetal life than it is about the meaning of women's lives and the specific role of motherhood in those lives. As Luker's study demonstrates, both sides in the debate have made life commitments based on deeply held values that are not easily changed but are threatened by the other side of the debate. For most prolife activists, the traditional sexual division of labor has worked well, and their valorization of motherhood as a women's natural destiny is consistent with this life pattern. For many prochoice advocates, the traditional sexual division of labor has not worked, they have commitments beyond or instead of the traditional family, and they see motherhood as a private, discretionary choice. The abortion issue has became a highly condensed symbol of these differing value positions. The intensity of the debate flows from the fact that it physically involves issues of life and death and symbolically raises basic questions about the meaning of women's lives. In this sense, the arguments of both sides are profoundly "self-serving" because they embody longstanding worldviews and lifetime value commitments (Luker 1984).

By the later 1970s, right-to-life forces had won several successes that restricted many women's access to abortion. The 1976 Republican party platform had a plank calling for an amendment banning abortion; the Hyde amendment outlawing federal funds for abortion passed the same year and was upheld by the Supreme Court two years later; Congress cut abortion funding for government employees; and hearings began on the Human Life Amendment. From the mid-1970s to the early 1980s, the anti-ERA campaign and the antiabortion campaign were closely related and mutually reinforcing struggles that were successful for similar reasons. Neither campaign had public opinion on its side, but both brought an intensity of commitment, a tactical sophistication, and a willingness to engage in single-issue politics that overcame the fact that they were not advocating popular positions. The use of telecommunications was especially important because it turned the relative isolation of the housewife into a political asset rather than a liability; available evidence suggests that CM activists devoted much more time to their cause than pro-ERA or prochoice activists were able to do. These factors helped account for the success of the anti-ERA movement, and they also typify the tactics of the prolife movement, which became the major focal point of CM mobilization after the ERA was defeated in 1982 (see Luker 1984 for a more detailed account).

An adequate understanding of CM mobilization around abortion requires at least two levels of understanding. On the one hand, it is important to understand in an empathetic way how the deeply felt value commitments of each side have compelled them to partake in the struggle. On the other hand, it is vital to see the links between this single-issue activism and larger political currents in society. Concerning the latter, it is clear that issues of sexuality and reproduction have given the New Right much of its ideological legitimacy and organizational coherence (Petchesky 1981). The antiabortion movement has been a haven for right-wing backlash, and the right-to-life movement has become the model for building a mass base for conservative movements. As Petchesky observes, the antiabortion movement has never been and could never be a single-issue movement, given abortion's intricate relation to issues of family, sexuality, and the position of women. Hence, the issue provided a point of entry for a broadly patriarchal, right-wing agenda. This agenda is supportive of male supremacy, hostile to sexuality in general, and virulently homophobic. Just as abortion serves as a template for broader concerns regarding sexuality, the "defense of the family" taps a larger set of social realities: "economic pressures, class divisions, and racism are integrally tied to people's concerns about 'family autonomy' and to sexual politics" (Petchesky 1981:227). Hence, both the ERA and abortion have functioned as points of entry into a broader political and cultural debate over social organization.

This broader debate concerns the dichotomy between public and private, and the role of the state in constituting and maintaining this distinction. The concept of privatism has been one of the most important links between the newer conservative politics of family and sexuality and the older forms of social and economic conservatism. The defense of privatism and the public-private dichotomy fuels not only the antifeminist component of the New Right but also the antisocial welfare backlash that has been a prominent feature of contemporary conservative ideology. A major goal of this conservative backlash has been to reprivatize social welfare functions assumed by the state in the twentieth century, and thereby to restore a mythical world of laissez-faire markets, rugged individualism, and social Darwinism. Contemporary conservatism must therefore be seen as a defense of capitalist economics, racial domination, and patriarchal power in which the common theme of privatism supports the restoration of power in the hands of traditionally dominant groups defined by class, race, and gender (Petchesky 1981). The contemporary women's movement and the countermovement it has inspired are thus at the center of leading political struggles and ideological debates over the structure and organization of advanced capitalist society.

Many of these movement-countermovement dynamics converge on the role of the state as the patriarchal institution par excellence, because it constitutes and maintains the distinction between public and private that is at the heart of the debate. While the feminist movement may have been realizing more of its radical potential, the state has been moving in a more conservative direction, evidenced by its attack on women's reproductive rights and its hostility to social welfare programs. At the time of this writing, it is evident that access to abortion will be at the center of these struggles for the foreseeable future, and that these struggles will be conducted as much through state institutions as through direct confrontations between movements and countermovements. The movement-countermovement dance now includes a third partner in the form of the state, and movements and countermovements now devote much attention to the state, not only to achieve objectives but also to neutralize opposition. Finally, it is clear that the state is not simply a passive or neutral bystander in these struggles but has frequently played a facilitating role in the genesis of both movement and countermovement. Most obviously, the last decade has witnessed a powerful dialectic between state institutions and antifeminist countermovements in which each has fed the initiatives of the other. If these countermovements were a monolithic force, they would have been more successful; their schisms have limited their success to date. Grasping these complex relations within and between movements, countermovements, and the state will be essential to understanding the future course of events and the eventual fate of the feminist agenda in the 1990s.

Conclusions

In both centuries, antifeminist CMs mobilized only when feminist movements began to achieve notable successes. Many participants in antifeminist CMs appear to have been motivated by a sense that they are losing ground relative to the constituency of the movement they are opposing. Mobilization in antifeminist CMs has often built on preexisting organizational or social networks and has depended on elites for resources and leadership. Antifeminist CMs have consistently invoked established societal myths to express opposition to change and have often mobilized a mass following on the basis of a single, powerful idea. Once established, antifeminist CMs in both centuries engaged in loosely coupled conflict or an interactive dance with the movement they were opposing. Both sides in this dance resorted to a number of rhetorical and tactical devices to promote their positions and damage the opposition. Finally, the SM-CM dance in both centuries came to include a third partner in the form of the state, as both sides prevailed upon this institution for support of its position. In all these ways, antifeminist CMs illustrate sociological propositions about movements and countermovements (Mottl 1980; Lo 1982; Zald and Useem 1987). Beyond these illustrations, the analysis presented here suggests several clusters of issues that are especially important to understanding antifeminist CMs.

One cluster of issues concerns the opposition of some women to women's movements. Often presented as a paradox or a case of false consciousness, these readings oversimplify by obscuring the multiple identities, roles, statuses, and interests that may motivate female opposition to women's movements. Chafetz and Dworkin's notion of role-encapsulated women (1987a) nicely characterizes women who closely identify with traditional feminine roles and perceive real threats to those roles in the feminist agenda. There may be compelling arguments that in the long run all women will benefit from the implementation of a feminist agenda. However, social change always occurs in a series of short runs in which agendas are partially and unevenly implemented, and in which unintended and unanticipated consequences flourish. Lenore Weitzman's oft-cited study of no-fault divorce (1985) provides just one example of how the implementation of seemingly progressive change can produce deleterious consequences for the very group the changes were intended to help. Given this, it is more plausible to analyze female opposition as a rational response based on women's perceived interests from a multidimensional social location. A better understanding of female opposition to women's movements may emerge from cross-movement comparisons. For example, while blacks may never have "organized against their own emancipation," there have been many divergent strategies within the black community, ranging from assimilation to integration to pluralism to separatism. In some respects, the position of traditional antifeminist women resembles the racial strategy of assimilation; the parallel serves as a reminder that subordinated groups are not homogeneous and can evidence a wide range of responses to a situation of subordination.

A closely related cluster of issues concerns the applicability of theories of status politics to antifeminist CMs. Such theories developed in response to economistic theories that presumed that class interests alone motivate political activity. Weber's (1947) classic conception of status as the amount of social honor bestowed upon a particular group, as well as the modern notion of status as prestige, combine to suggest that much antifeminist sentiment may be a defensive reaction against perceived threats to the honor or prestige of women's traditional status. Again, this argument applies best to role-encapsulated women who are likely to have high psychic investments in traditional roles and to have relatively few marketable skills. To the extent that the feminist movement is perceived (accurately or not) as devaluing the traditional activities of role-encapsulated women and privileging labor force participation, the opposition of traditional women to the feminist movement follows quite logically as a case of status politics. As this example also suggests, status politics and economic interests are often closely intertwined, because the traditional roles of women also presume male breadwinners who are morally obligated to provide for the material needs of nuclear families.

A third cluster of issues concerns the role of symbolic politics in the loosely coupled conflict between SMs and CMs. Although it may be true that CMs typically mobilize around a single issue that creates commitment and arouses enthusiasm (Mottl 1980), it is also true in the case of antifeminist CMs that "single issues" like woman suffrage or the ERA have functioned as symbols of much larger aspirations and agendas on both sides. Although the issues changed from woman suffrage to the ERA, both struggles saw remarkably similar ideological confrontations over public and private spheres, the gendered division of labor, the nuclear family, and sexuality and reproduction. Suffrage and the ERA lent themselves to a symbolic politics of broad ideological differences because they functioned as higher-order, condensational symbols (Conover and Gray 1983) whose ambiguous consequences invited considerable speculation and rhetorical escalation by both proponents and opponents. One of the ironies of these campaigns is that antifeminist CMs have often perceived bigger threats to social order than were likely to occur, or even than proponents intended. However, it has been precisely the exaggerated nature of the threat to social order that has provided an effective recruiting device for antifeminist CMs.

Another cluster of issues concerns the tactical choices made by feminist movements and their antifeminist counterparts. One CM tactic has been of particular importance in the suffrage campaign and in more recent feminist struggles: denigration and stigmatization of movement proponents. Throughout the entire suffrage battle it was commonplace for suffragists to be described as mannish or masculine, with the implication that their cause violated a natural order of gender relations (Frenier 1984). In the contemporary movement, similar tactics have been used. Movement proponents have been described as "man-haters"; the movement has frequently been caricatured by the labels "women's lib" and "women's libber"; and movement participants are often the target of lesbian-baiting. The effectiveness of these tactics is reflected in the frequency with which people disavow explicit identification with the movement even as they express support for many movement goals ("I'm not a feminist, but . . . ").

While denigration of the opposition is a common tactic in SM-CM dynamics (Zald and Useem 1987), these cases are especially powerful because they appeal to fundamental myths about natural and essential differences between the sexes. The denigration of movement proponents in these ways is at the same time an affirmation of a deeply rooted ideological belief system that can provide CMs with substantial influence over bystander publics.

The heterogeneity of CM participants is another significant cluster of issues to emerge from this analysis. Every student of antifeminist CMs has detected schisms within their ranks, including differences between religious and secular groups, moral and economic interests, social and libertarian conservatives, and the like. Such divisions have long been recognized in other CMs (Lo 1982) and can be vital determinants of CM success or failure. As in social movements generally, such heterogeneity can be a source of movement strength, because it permits recruitment from diverse groups, but it more often proves to be a movement weakness, because these groups bring with them equally diverse ideologies, goals, and tactics that are difficult to reconcile into an effective movement. Another important aspect of CM heterogeneity concerns the relative balance of voluntary, grass-roots organizations and vested-interest groups (Chafetz and Dworkin 1987a). In the case of the suffrage movement, it is clear that both types of groups were prominent in opposing the enfranchisement of women, and there is reliable evidence of collusion between these different groups as well (Catt and Shuler 1923). In the case of the contemporary women's movement, there is abundant evidence of voluntary grass-roots organizations engaged in CM activity but relatively little evidence of vested-interest-group activity. Despite the scanty evidence, it remains a very plausible hypothesis that certain business and economic interests that would be greatly affected by such measures as comparable-worth legislation are playing a quiet but substantial role in opposing these proposals. If Chafetz and Dworkin (1987a) are correct that women predominate in voluntary organizations and men predominate in vested-interest groups, then it becomes all the more important to accurately assess the role of vested-interest groups, and hence active male opposition, to the contemporary women's movement.

A final cluster of issues that emerges from this analysis concerns the multifaceted relationship between SMs, CMs, and the state. As we have already seen, the state was important in facilitating the emergence of both movements and CMs at various points in time. Once feminist SMs and antifeminist CMs establish a pattern of loosely coupled conflict, their struggle is more likely to be conducted through the state than through direct confrontation with each other. The history of woman suffrage, the ERA, and abortion rights underscores the vital importance of state structure for the interaction between SMs and CMs (Lo

1982; Zald and Useem 1987). For a variety of reasons, antifeminist CMs have been least effective at the level of the federal government and most effective at the level of state governments, as exemplified by the struggles over suffrage and the ERA. The same dynamic is evident in the conflict over abortion, with CMs using states' rights arguments to chip away at federal decisions and ultimately challenging those decisions directly after cultivating strength in various states. If this characterization is correct, then it would follow that a more centralized governmental structure would produce more favorable outcomes for feminist movements. Finally, as Zillah Eisenstein has argued (1981, 1984), there is a much broader sense in which the state is inevitably implicated in these conflicts, because the state constitutes and maintains the division between public and private that is at the heart of so many of the issues involved in the struggle between feminists and antifeminists. In myriad ways, then, understanding the role of the state is vital to comprehending SM-CM conflict.

Some social movements disappear almost as quickly as they appear, while a very few achieve a quick and overwhelming success. In such cases, CMs are unlikely to arise. In more typical cases, however, SMs persist for some time, achieve partial successes, and go through cycles of mobilization and demobilization. In these situations, CMs are likely to emerge to challenge movement initiatives and defend existing social practices. In these cases, SMs have the advantage of timing because their offensive, change-seeking mobilization precedes the defensive, change-resisting mobilization of CMs. CMs, however, have what might be called the advantage of inertia, in that it is generally easier to prevent change than it is to bring it about. When an SM's advantage of timing is countered by a CM's advantge of inertia, the outcome is a complex, interactive chain of events that may resemble debates, chess, or guerrilla warfare (Zald and Useem 1987). Sociological attention to SM-CM dynamics has been long overdue, and the study of antifeminist CMs provides a powerful example of the need to study and theorize these movement-countermovement dynamics.

Chapter
six

Endings
and
Futures

Assessing the ending of past movements and the future of contemporary movements raises the same questions of definition and periodization that arise in discussions of movement origins. To identify origins and endings is to define and periodize episodes of collective action by placing boundaries around those actions which constitute the movement and those which do not. These problems of definition are readily evident in the case of the contemporary women's movement. A plausible claim can be made that this movement experienced a rather typical movement life cycle, from origins and energetic mobilization in the late 1960s to a mass movement in the early 1970s to institutionalization, fragmentation, decline, and defeat as indexed by the failure of the Equal Rights Amendment. This account's plausibility rests on defining particular issues and organizations as central to the movement while discounting others. A rather different scenario can be constructed by attending to the longevity of social movement communities and the survival of certain SMOs. This more plausible reading requires analysis not of the ending of the contemporary women's movement but of its transformations during the 1980s and its possible futures during the 1990s.

The case of the suffrage movement appears more straightforward, because this movement achieved its major goal, defining the end of the movement in unambiguous fashion. This simplistic reading obscures several important questions, however. One concerns whether the vote really accomplished what most suffragists hoped it would, since many had come to view the vote as a means to further ends. Another concerns whether the various groups in the suffrage coalition viewed their success as the end of their struggle, or whether they proceeded to other agendas and goals that have been obscured by the attention paid to the suffrage victory. The relative nature of definitions of movements, success, and failure can be appreciated by a somewhat fanciful thought experiment. If the National Woman's Party had been successful in pursuing the Equal Rights Amendment in the 1920s, our perceptions of this period would be drastically different. We would see an "equal rights movement" rather than a "suffrage movement," and see the ballot as a stepping-stone to the ERA. The very definition of who the central actors were and what the vital issues were are thus defined on the basis of movement outcomes. Hence, seemingly simple events like the ERA defeat in 1982 or the suffrage victory in 1920 are better seen as benchmarks in ongoing movement activity than as definitive end points in the form of failure or success.

If cases of failure and success are not as simple as they appear, it must also be recognized that most outcomes involve something between success or failure. The traditional view of movement outcomes involves a life-cycle model. According to this model, all movements are expected to follow a standard, evolutionary pattern of origins, mobilization, and growth, followed by neutralization, demobilization, and decline. The main determinants of the cycle are presumed to be internal to the movement, with external events accelerating or retarding the timing of the inevitable evolutionary cycle. These natural history or life-cycle models are relatively pessimistic about the outcomes of social movements; the presumption is that most movements will simply collapse and leave few traces or, at best, will become institutionalized and bureaucratized, accommodating themselves to a power structure they once challenged (Lang and Lang 1961; Jenkins 1983). McAdam (1983) refers to this as the classical model of movement decline, in which movements undergo oligarchization of leadership, conservatization of goals, and institutionalization of the movement. Central to the life-cycle or classical model is the presumption that the important determinants of movement outcomes are internal to the movement and its organizations, and that these internal determinants follow an inevitable course toward predetermined outcomes (Weber 1947; Michels 1961).

More recent trends in social movement theory suggest that movement outcomes are more a function of external events and factors. These newer perspectives have also recognized that the outcomes of movements are more varied than the inevitable collapse or bureaucratization forecast by the traditional or classical models. In McAdam's version of resource mobilization theory, the essential factor is the level of resources an external party provides to a movement. Just as the provision of such resources can spark mobilization in the first place, resource withdrawal will precipitate movement decline. However, this externalist logic also implies that if movements can maintain, expand, or supplement such external resources, they may continue indefinitely rather than face an inevitable life-cycle decline. McAdam argues that the internal focus of the classical model and the external focus of the resource mobilization model are both one-sided, and he proposes a "political-process" model to capture the dynamic interplay between internal and external factors. In this model, the key factors influencing movement outcomes are organizational strength, the structure of political opportunities available to the movement, and the response of other groups to the movement's challenge. Applying the classical, resource-mobilization, and political-process models to a study of the civil rights movement reveals that conservatization is not an inevitable outcome, that resource levels do not simplistically determine movement activism, and that movement fates are a function of the dialectical relation between external and internal processes (McAdam 1982, 1983).

The complex interplay of forces recognized by the political-process model makes possible a number of movement outcomes. Movements that do not simply fail may nonetheless be repressed or coopted, and movements that succeed often involve compromise, negotiation, or absorption (Miller 1983). Even success involves two distinct dimensions: movements may win new advantages, or they may win acceptance, or both, or neither (Gamson 1975). Movements that win both advantages and acceptance may be judged full successes, while movements that win neither can be classified as failures. Movements that win acceptance but no new advantages can be said to be coopted, while those that win new advantages but no acceptance can be said to be preempted. Gamson's typology is of particular interest because it guided research into a large number of movements in the United States and allowed him to detect certain patterns of movement outcomes. In general, he found that successful movements were bureaucratically organized, had narrow goals, used selective incentives, had sponsorship, used unruly methods, and made claims during times of sociopolitical crisis. Coopted movements tended to have large memberships and formalized structures, and to make their demands during wartime, whereas preempted movements tended to be small, centrally controlled, and less active during crisis periods (Jenkins 1983:543). Gamson also found a consistent pattern whereby groups that sought to displace powerholders had very low rates of success, while groups that sought to influence but not displace powerholders were much more likely to be successful.

The application of these theoretical positions to particular movements remains a complicated undertaking. Movements seeking a limited number of clearly articulated goals pursued by well-defined organizational structures are easier to assess because one can turn to organizational documents for goal statements and measure movement success or failure (or something in between) by examining efforts to win legislation, gain representation, and the like. For all these reasons, as well as the advantage of hindsight, the woman suffrage movement can be classified as a success because it won legislative passage of its major goal as defined by leading movement organizations. Assessing outcomes in the contemporary women's movement is qualitatively more difficult for several reasons. The movement is seeking several different levels of goals; measuring accomplishment of some of these goals is inherently difficult; the movement consists of multiple, shifting, and frequently noncentralized organizational structures; and the movement is ongoing even as it is being studied. For these reasons, no definitive statement of movement outcomes is possible for the contemporary movement, though it is possible to speculate on likely futures for this movement.

The following analysis compares the ending of the woman suffrage movement with the current status and probable futures of the contemporary women's movement. In the case of the suffrage movement, success resulted from a combination of movement initiatives and a sociopolitical context that facilitated passage of the amendment. The meaning and consequences of that success are the subject of considerable debate and widely divergent interpretations, however, particularly given the seeming dissolution of the movement in the subsequent debate over the ERA. This complex history is subject to both "pessimistic" and "optimistic" readings, which are discussed later in this chapter. The contemporary movement may appear to be in a similar state of dissolution, but there are a number of reasons to believe that ongoing mobilization will occur. Some of these reasons are rooted in background factors that are conducive to maintaining a large pool of potential recruits for a women's movement; others involve proximate causes like ideological and organizational diversity, which has the potential to sustain the movement even in an inhospitable climate. Among other things, the movement's future depends importantly on how it responds to the debate about equality and difference, for this will be critical in orienting future feminist efforts.

The Woman Suffrage Movement

The ratification of the Nineteenth Amendment granting women the right to vote was the culmination of a seventy-two-year struggle that began at the Seneca Falls convention. It is tempting to view this retrospectively as an inevitable outcome, but the temptation should be resisted. There was nothing inevitable or automatic about the suffrage victory of 1920, and it is not difficult to imagine a scenario in which woman suffrage could have been deferred once again. The inevitability thesis also obscures the tactical and strategic moves undertaken by the woman suffrage movement during the campaign. If the granting of the vote appears inevitable in retrospect, it is largely due to the efforts of suffragists in normalizing the idea of women exercising the franchise. The inevitability thesis also conceals the distinctive socio-historical circumstances in which the victory occurred, and these are vital to understanding why success occurred at this time rather than at some other time.

Among suffragists themselves, there is ample evidence of pessimism as late as 1916 (Flexner 1975:284). Despite the pessimism, however, some important changes had occurred in the movement since the turn of the century. Perhaps most important was the fact that it broadened its base of support in the early twentieth century. Settlement house workers recruited immigrant groups and educated ethnocentric suffragists about the need for cultural diversity in the suffrage movement. Organizations like the Women's Trade Union League built cross-class bridges between working-class women and upper-class "allies," helping to cultivate working-class support for woman suffrage. The women's club movement drew elite women into public service and provided additional rationales for the right to vote. This fostered a genuinely cross-class movement for woman suffrage for the first time, as the class-specific motives of working-class, middle-class, and upper-class women led many of them to support a common goal (Buechler 1986). The major exception to this broadening support concerned black women; the exception was not that black women weren't interested in the vote but rather that the mainstream suffrage movement consistently rejected black women to retain the support of white, southern suffragists. Hence, as we saw in Chapter Four, class barriers proved much more permeable than race barriers in the later suffrage movement.

These new constituencies were accompanied by greater organizational and ideological diversity within the movement. When the Congressional Union split from the National American Woman Suffrage Association in 1914 and later became the National Woman's Party, it redirected and reinvigorated the suffrage battle in a vital way. Despite their rivalry and because of their very different tactics, each organization made important contributions to the suffrage cause. Beyond the suffrage associations themselves, many other organizations endorsed woman suffrage in the later days of the suffrage battle (Flexner 1975). The movement's growing organizational diversity was matched by increasing ideological flexibility. Mainstream suffrage organizations took great pains to develop prosuffrage arguments that spoke to the highly differentiated situations of early-twentieth-century women, noting that whatever one's particular life circumstances might be, women would be better off with the right to vote than without it (Buechler 1986). At the most abstract level, the ideological diversity of the later suffrage movement was evident in its ability to accommodate pro-suffrage arguments premised on the similarities as well as the differences between women and men. By the 1910s, then, the lack of the vote was becoming the essential common thread that tied together otherwise diverse constituencies, organizations, and ideologies into a powerful, cross-class, mass movement for woman suffrage (Cott 1986).

The development of a mass movement for woman suffrage both facilitated and necessitated a more strategic approach to influencing powerholders. While the NWP used militant tactics to win suffrage, Carrie Chapman Catt formulated a detailed, state-by-state strategy to build momentum and focus pressure on the U.S. Congress (while also planning for the ratification battle that would have to follow passage of a suffrage amendment). The major deviation from Catt's plan was that the movement succeeded earlier than she anticipated (Flexner 1975). The timing of the suffrage victory was importantly related to the involvement of the United States in the First World War. The patriotic rationales for entering the war provided suffragists with some of their most powerful rhetorical arguments for woman suffrage, as they questioned fighting for democracy abroad before it was fully established at home. At the same time, women argued that their contribution to the war effort merited recognition from powerholders in the form of woman suffrage. The combination of militant agitation by the NWP and persistent pressure by the NAWSA gradually moved President Wilson and the Democrats from moderate opposition to neutrality to support for woman suffrage, yielding a congressional victory in 1919.

The right to vote was won only when a cross-class, multiconstituency alliance of women generated an organizationally and ideologically diverse mass movement that was strategically directed to important political pressure points within a larger wartime context that created new political opportunities for victory. In some accounts of these events, the accent falls very heavily on the wartime context of the suffrage victory, amounting to what Katzenstein calls the social-control paradigm of electoral politics. In this view, the extension of the vote to women was merely "an expedient ploy to secure women's support for the war effort" (Katzenstein 1984:11). This reading implies an omnipotent ruling group and denies the efficacy of collective action for the franchise. However, as Katzenstein points out, it is doubtful that the vote would have been granted even as a social control ploy in the absence of an organized women's movement pushing for such reform. Further, this account does not explain prewar victories in a minority of states or postwar ratification in a majority of states. Katzenstein concludes that it would be a simplistic misrepresentation to see this campaign as either a pure victory for feminist forces or a pure case of social control and coop-tation by the state.

A broader frame for interpreting the significance of the suffrage victory is provided by the concept of the "domestication of politics" (Baker 1984). From this perspective, "the social separation of the sexes and women's informal methods of influencing politics [and] domesticity provided the basis for a dis-tinct nineteenth-century women's political culture" (1984:625). The suffrage struggle was long and bitter precisely because it challenged the separateness of the sexes and their spheres, and victory brought an end to nineteenth-century womanhood and women's political culture by putting women and men on a more equal political footing and undermining the social and cultural bases for a dis-tinctive women's sphere. At the same time, however, the suffrage victory domes-ticated politics because it was accompanied by growing state involvement in and responsibility for social policies and programs that had formerly been the prov-ince of women's voluntaristic activity in social service organizations. The domes-tication of politics undermined women's political culture and the power of appeals to an abstract, nineteenth-century concept of womanhood at the same time that it accelerated state intervention into the private domain and increased opportunities for individual women.

As a common female political culture disintegrated upon winning the vote, differences between former allies in the suffrage coalition came to the fore. This was readily evident in women's actual voting behavior, which divided along con-ventional lines of class, ethnicity, and party preference. Hence, the women's bloc vote that some suffragists sought never materialized. Fragmentation of the suf-frage coalition also led to organizational transformation as the National Ameri-can Woman Suffrage Association was replaced by the civic-oriented, non-partisan League of Women Voters. Flexner ponders whether the League "may not have short-circuited the political strength of the most gifted suffragist women. Certainly it planted firmly in the minds of a goodly number of politicians the idea that the ladies were not really interested in politics — as politicians un-derstood the term — but rather in 'reform,' which was quite another matter" (1975:340). This interest in reform was symbolized by another postsuffrage or-ganization, theWomen's Joint Congressional Committee, which formed to pur-sue legislation concerning child labor and infant and maternity care. The organization's time of greatest effectiveness was immediately after women won the vote, when the potential for a female bloc vote was still unknown, but the group disintegrated shortly thereafter (Flexner 1975:338).

Whereas the mainstream suffrage forces lost their raison d'être upon win-ning the vote, the National Women's Party immediately went to work on other issues they saw as logical extensions of women's newfound voting rights. Under Alice Paul's leadership, the NWP turned to women's remaining legal disabilities and sought strategies to eliminate them and institute complete legal equality between the sexes. This orientation to "pure feminism" in the 1920s set the NWP apart from virtually all other women's organizations as it continued to seek formal equality for an abstract, undifferentiated "Woman." This focus meant that the NWP divorced woman's legal status from the complexities of women's social, sexual, and reproductive roles, and also meant that class and race differences were ignored in the name of a generic womanhood. This approach constituted what Cott calls a "peculiar radical elitism" in which white, upper-middle class, professional women demanded far-reaching legal change in the name of an abstract womanhood with little reflection upon the variable impacts such change might have on concrete groups of differently situated women (1987:76).

The NWP arrived at this position only after intense political debate in the early 1920s. At various points, it was proposed that the NWP become involved in disarmament, birth control, or the pursuit of voting rights for black women. In each debate, however, Alice Paul defined these as diversionary, peripheral issues that would dilute the drive for legal equality between the sexes. While there is evidence of racism as well as elitism in Paul's position on these and other issues, her "outlook was at least as much due to her conception of the viability of single-issue politics as it was to racism" (Cott 1984:54). The same single-issue orientation that the NWP had successfully brought to the suffrage battle was now redirected to legal equality for women. For a brief time, this strategy supported so-called blanket bills that would remove all existing legal inequalities between the sexes at a single stroke. However, this proposal quickly gave way to advocacy of an Equal Rights Amendment to the Constitution that would achieve the same goals more definitively. In the ERA, the NWP found the perfect vehicle for its purely feminist orientation and its single-issue politics, and the organization devoted itself to this new cause with the same determination and fervor it had brought to the suffrage battle.

The importance of the NWP in this historical period arises from the fact that it was the only organization to maintain a purely feminist focus on the issue of sexual equality. This orientation stands out in sharp relief against the goals of most other women's organizations in this period, which tended to subordinate women's rights to other causes. At the same time, the NWP's orientation, reflecting its rather distinctive constituency, made it difficult to build a mass base for its program. NWP members assumed women should have jobs or careers; they were ambivalent toward marriage and motherhood; and they were distrustful of men. These assumptions created a sense of urgency around the goal of legal equality, but they also made it difficult to recruit broad support among wives, mothers, and workers (Becker 1985). These differences were acutely reflected in the ERA debate of the early 1920s, which pitted the pure feminism of the NWP against the social feminism of virtually all other surviving women's organizations. Among the opponents of the ERA were the League of Women Voters, the U.S. Women's Bureau, the Women's Trade Union League, and the Consumer's League; these groups presumably agreed with Carrie Chapman Catt's claim that having secured the right to vote, further purely feminist programs were unnecessary (Becker 1985).

The central issue in the ERA debate was its probable impact on protective legislation for women. Although the NWP sought exemptions for maternity legislation and mother's pensions, it specifically challenged the differential impact of protective labor legislation on the sexes because it recognized how easily such legislation could promote discrimination against female workers. The NWP's stance attracted two major opponents. First, the ERA was opposed by social feminists who had worked very hard to secure protective labor legislation for women in the first place and saw the amendment as a step backward rather than forward. Second, the proposal was also opposed by the American Federation of Labor and various other union groups that also supported protective legislation. Whereas unions were quick to defend such legislation as a victory of past labor struggles, NWP members were equally quick to point out that the sex-differentiated nature of the legislation made it harder for women and easier for men to find work in some branches of industry. Though the debate was heated, "neither side acknowledged the real ambiguities and complications of the workings of sex-based protective legislation at the time" (Cott 1984:61).

The postsuffrage decade of the 1920s is frequently characterized as a standoff between pure feminist advocates of the ERA and social feminist defenders of protective labor legislation. Critics of the NWP's position were correct that it failed to appreciate how marriage, motherhood, and child care could put women in positions of vulnerability that the ERA could not address and might exacerbate. Critics of social feminists were correct that protective legislation could become a powerful tool against women in the labor force, and that there was a vital need for continued work on women's rights and sexual equality. Other positions in the debate during the 1920s transcended some of these polarities, but they were not able to attract a substantial following. One example was the program advanced by Crystal Eastman, which combined feminist, pacifist, socialist, and cultural concerns to advance the feminist movement after the suffrage victory; the program was debated but voted down at the 1921 NWP convention. Another example was the stance taken by Harriot Stanton Blatch, who rejected the discrimination of protective legislation as well as the vagueness of the ERA in the name of an alternative program based on the German tradition of socialist feminism (DuBois 1987b). Although they never became popular, the presence of these alternatives undermines caricatures of the 1920s as simply a two-sided debate between advocates of the ERA and of protective labor legislation.

Any definitive assessment of the suffrage movement must consider how earlier interpretations of the movement have defined key events and shaped collective perceptions of what the movement was, what happened to it, and whether it was a success or a failure. One conventional account of the suffrage movement recognizes the winning of the ballot but by and large regards the movement as a failure because the ballot didn't change any of the other pressing issues that had, at various times, been part of the women's movement agenda. In this pessimistic reading, the struggle for the ballot consumed a tremendous amount of energy, the victory didn't accomplish much concrete change, and the postsuffrage battle over the ERA fragmented a movement that won a formal goal but failed to bring substantive changes to the society. There are implicit traces of this interpretation in every account of the suffrage movement (for example, Flexner 1975; Kraditor 1965) because no competent history can fail to note the striking difference between the lofty aspirations of many suffragists and the mundane realities of what women did and did not do with the ballot.

The most explicit version of this reading of the suffrage movement is to be found in the work of William O'Neill (1969). He concurs with many others who perceive a fundamental radicalism in the early women's rights movement because it challenged the structure of the family and the limitations of women's domestic and marital statuses. Over time, however, this radical critique of domesticity faded as the movement came to concentrate on the vote. As a result, winning the ballot was a hollow victory because it had become detached from a larger, feminist critique of social and domestic order. O'Neill explains this change in two ways. On the one hand, he suggests that the radicalism of the early movement was tamed through social control exercised by the larger society. On the other hand, he faults the movement's own analysis and ideology for not retaining its earlier and more radical approach to women's position. These partial explanations pose further puzzles, however. The social control directed at the movement was greatest in its earliest days, and yet it retained its radicalism throughout this early phase. Moreover, the movement's analysis did not merely become diluted over time, but rather reflected the changing orientations of differently situated leaders in new socio-historical conjunctures. O'Neill's analysis amounts to an ex post facto, defeatist reading of events in which the movement was more than radical enough to attract social-control efforts, which tamed it, but not radical enough to maintain its original and incisive criticism of the sources of women's subordination. In this account, the "failure" of the movement seems predestined (see Buechler 1986:22–24 for a fuller account).

O'Neill's reading of the movement frames his analysis of the postsuffrage period as a time of decline and disintegration. The postwar return to normalcy and the decline of reform saw both social feminists and radical feminists revert to type, meaning that the former remained trapped in their acceptance of the domestic system while the latter proved ineffective at waging instrumental political battles. Such disintegration appears inevitable in O'Neill's account because the lack of voting rights was the only thread that held the suffrage coalition together. In paradoxical fashion, then, winning the vote may have done more harm than good to women's political unity, which was quickly lost once the vote was secured. The vote, in turn, didn't mean much because women were unable to organize bloc voters along gender lines. Given the relatively quick incorporation of women into the existing party system, there is some basis for O'Neill's claim that women may have had more indirect power over politicians before they had the vote (because no one knew how they would use it) than they did after they had it when the lack of a female voting bloc became readily evident. A related problem concerned the overselling of the vote in the later days of the suffrage campaign as the panacea for a host of social ills. Once again, the realities of voting were no match for the great expectations many suffragists had of the ballot; it did not prove to be the key to accomplishing all other goals (O'Neill 1969).

My own work on the suffrage movement offers a different explanation for movement transformation and the postsuffrage era. The movement can be roughly divided into three periods: a radical period from the 1840s to about 1870, a period of transformation from 1870 to the 1890s, and a specialized movement for the vote from the 1890s to 1920. Movement transformations occurred as a result of class formation and organizational dynamics. In class terms, the middle movement was led by increasingly class-conscious, middle-class women seeking to harmonize and stabilize a conflict-ridden society, and the later movement saw many elite and professional-managerial women enter leadership positions. The ideology of the later movement (including its acceptance of many traditional notions of gender) was a function of class-specific interests and gender ideology, which were transposed into the movement through a new leadership. In organizational terms, the middle movement saw a major challenge to suffrage organizations by the growing popularity of temperance groups, which brought more traditional views of gender into the suffrage movement; the later movement made a self-consious effort to build streamlined, specialized, single-issue organizations to win the vote by whatever means possible (Buechler 1986).

This emphasis on specialized, single-issue organizations is essential to understanding the tactical battle that won the vote. But the danger is that it obscures the diversity of women's organizations, interests, and activities in the early twentieth century, or recognizes this diversity only as it related to the suffrage campaign. Thus, there is an inherent tendency for accounts of the suffrage campaign (including my own) to marginalize the emergent forms of women's activism that went beyond suffragism to include cultural radicalism, socialism, anarchism, pacifism, and a host of other causes. Although all these diverse groups were supportive of the struggle to win the vote for women, none regarded it as the penultimate goal of women's political activism. Thus, the claim that "the movement" oversold the vote applies by and large to the elite leaders of the mainstream suffrage organizations, and not to the other constituencies, who supported suffrage but didn't overestimate its value. To take merely one example, a number of working-class women and organizations became part of the suffrage coalition in the closing days of the struggle, but they certainly did not see the vote as the most important tool for resolving the problems they faced as women workers. The theme of overburdened expectations and deflated hopes before and after suffrage was won reflects the distinctive perspective of mainstream suffragists, not the varied views of the diverse groups that constituted the mass movement for suffrage in the final days of the campaign.

The growing recognition of these other groups challenges the standard perception of the suffrage victory as the fundamental divide in women's political activity. The most explicit such argument may be found in the recent work of Nancy Cott (1987), who claims that conventional accounts of suffragism have obscured the emergence of modern feminism, which began around 1910 and persisted through the 1920s. From the perspective of traditional suffragism, 1920 is the last chapter in a long story; from the perspective of modern feminism, 1920 is merely the midpoint of a multidecade movement. This distinctly modern feminism was defined by its opposition to sex hierarchy, its view of women's condition as socially constructed, and its stress on gender group identity (1987:4). Compared to suffragism, feminism was broader in intent but narrower in following, and it was grounded in a number of paradoxes concerning equality and difference, individuality and solidarity, and unity and diversity. Feminists advocated suffrage, but only as part of a broader social and cultural revolution. While there is a real danger of reading the present back into the past, Cott offers a persuasive case that the feminists of the 1910s and 1920s had as much in common with present-day feminists as they did with their contemporaneous suffragists. In this view, suffragism was a nineteenth-century movement, grounded in one set of premises, that happened to persist until 1920; feminism is a twentieth-century movement, with different assumptions, that began in 1910 and persists to the present. These movements shared some goals during their decade-long coexistence, but they nonetheless had distinct identities.

Much of Cott's evidence thereby points to continuities between the 1910s and 1920s in women's political and social activism. The National Woman's Party provides one example as it shifted its support from the vote to the ERA after winning suffrage. Beyond the NWP, however, Cott underscores women's preference for voluntaristic rather than electoral politics, as evidenced by their steadily increasing participation in organizations throughout the 1920s. The growth of old organizations and the creation of new ones reflected the diversity, differentiation, and specialization of the women who joined and led them. The increasing organizational involvement of women has been marginalized in traditional accounts of the postsuffrage era, which focus only on electoral politics. In Cott's view, the lack of an effective women's voting bloc was overdetermined; general declines in voting, active hostility to the idea of a women's vote, a partisan political system, and women's own heterogeneous preferences each undermined the possibility of a female bloc vote. Confronted with these realities, women did not retreat but rather redirected their activity into voluntaristic politics. While this evidence effectively counters the traditional view of the demise of women's activity after 1920, it skirts questions about the political focus of this activity. At times, Cott's conception of and evidence for feminist activity seems to include virtually all public action by women and doesn't always distinguish between activity that may have reinforced rather than challenged traditional notions of gender. Nonetheless, when compared to the traditional, defeatist reading of the end of the suffrage movement offered by O'Neill, Cott reveals a rich tapestry of feminist activism that survived the winning of the vote but has been obscured by the conventional focus on electoral politics.

The case for continuity in women's activism is also made in Rupp and Taylor's (1987) analysis of how the post-1920 movement "survived in the doldrums" until a broader mass movement reemerged in the 1960s. Rupp and Taylor stress the continuity of women's movements from the 1840s to the 1980s, but characterize the 1940s and 1950s as a virulently antifeminist period in which a feminist presence was only maintained through an "elite-sustained movement." The National Woman's Party was at the center of this elite movement, surrounded by numerous other groups that contributed to movement survival. The ideology of the NWP during these decades frequently deviated from current feminist expectations, but it nonetheless constituted a vital link between earlier and later mass movements. The NWP and related organizations operated as what Aldon Morris calls "movement halfway houses: established organizations that lack a mass base and are relatively isolated from the larger society because of their activity on behalf of social change. Such organizations lack broad support but are able to mobilize a variety of resources that a developing mass movement can use" (Rupp and Taylor 1987:186). As we have seen, the NWP played a direct role in the origins of the "second wave" of feminism during the 1960s, thereby linking the two waves of feminism.

These interpretations challenge both the pessimism and the definitiveness of traditional accounts of the suffrage movement. According to this newer scholarship, by the time the suffrage movement "ended" it had become intertwined with a multiplicity of other feminist issues and goals, which survived with considerable vigor through the 1920s and with determined tenacity through the inhospitable 1940s and 1950s. This perspective demonstrates that the ending of a movement is at best elusive, because all definitions of endings are highly sensitive to which actors, organizations, and issues are taken to constitute the movement in the first place (see Taylor 1989a). The closer one looks, the more there appears to be an irreducible gap between the fixity of analytical categories and the fluidity of movement processes. Each attempt to definitively resolve the paradox of movement endings is vulnerable to competing readings, which emerge with slight alterations in focus. One lesson to emerge is that the search for movement endings can never be completely successful, for the straightforward reason that movements are not objects with endings as much as they are processes with both histories and futures.

The Contemporary Women's Movement

The woman suffrage movement had a specific goal that it pursued through well-defined organizations in a campaign that can be examined with the luxury of hindsight. Nonetheless, a definitive statement about the outcome of that movement is difficult to formulate because of the other goals, multiple organizations, and diverse constituencies that became part of the drive for suffrage and persisted to varying degrees after the vote was won. The contemporary women's movement is more difficult to interpret because of its pursuit of multiple goals through very diverse organizational forms, which continues at the time of this writing. In some respects, the ERA is analogous to the vote, and the pursuit of both has yielded unintended consequences. The success of the suffrage campaign demobilized the mass movement because victory deprived it of its one common thread. The failure of the ERA campaign helped remobilize the contemporary movement because it appeared to symbolize feminism in retreat at a time of conservative ascendancy. The role of failed campaigns in reinvigorating movements is merely one example of the complex dynamics of the contemporary movement, which preclude definitive statements but invite judicious speculation on the movement's trajectory in the next decade.

One important determinant of the future course of the women's movement concerns the organizational forms it can sustain in pursuit of various goals. Movement vitality and effectiveness will depend on its ability to sustain a mix of organizational forms. The structure of the contemporary movement has been described as amorphous, noncentralized, segmentary, polycephalous, and reticulate. This structure is well suited to a movement consisting of diverse groups of varying size and scope, competing and shifting leaders, a plethora of campaigns and goals, and a loose network of ties that bind these various branches together (Taylor 1989b). Such structures are often criticized as ineffective for accomplishing specific, instrumental goals (such as passage of the ERA), but they can provide several distinct advantages to a movement. Decentralized, segmentary groups have a high adaptive capacity in the face of opposition because they are difficult to suppress or coopt. Such structures are also open to innovations that can maintain and reinvigorate movements. Such networks can more readily bridge the public and the personal by revealing the political in both. For all these reasons, the structural and organizational characteristics of the contemporary movement may contribute to its persistence and longevity.

Within this mix of organizational forms, some have made the transition from social movement to interest group and are in a position to translate movement efforts into policy outcomes (Costain, 1982). The ERA campaign was especially important in training a new generation of politically experienced women who can work as insiders or outsiders on given campaigns; these gains in the form of institutionalized participation may ultimately be more important than winning specific, substantive rights, because the former brings ongoing access to power centers and is likely to increase mobilization, whereas winning substantive rights can often produce demobilizing consequences (Ferree and Hess 1985:177–178). The danger that those who work as interest group insiders in policy circles will be institutionalized, coopted, and rendered ineffective is partially offset by ongoing mobilization of movement participants who remain outside such official channels. These outsiders provide the specter of a more radical alternative, which can create political space in which to win concessions on the policy level. The decentralized social movement community that persists outside of mainstream organizations has had considerable success in avoiding what some depict as the inevitable waning of protest in formal organizations (Piven and Cloward 1977). By retaining informal, segmented, and decentralized organizational forms, the contemporary movement has avoided some of the dangers of cooptation and institutionalization while maintaining pressure on dominant institutions for progressive change.

Movement organizations and communities will retain their vitality only through ongoing recruitment of participants and mobilization of resources.

There is reason to think that this will be encouraged by dominant, macro-structural social trends. Whereas the suffrage movement's pursuit of equality cut against the grain of most women's daily lives, the contemporary movement's call for equality is solidly grounded in the experiential realities of an increasing number of women in the society. Describing the 1960s and 1970s, Chafe claims that "for the first time ideological protest and underlying social and economic changes appeared to be moving in a similar direction" (1977:119). The most important of these changes involves the steady increase in women's labor force participation, creating an ever-larger recruiting ground and mobilization pool for the movement. Klein concurs that growth in support for feminism is a long-term, structurally grounded trend evident not only in women's increasing labor force participation but also in changes in the nature of the family, the definition of motherhood, and women's educational attainment (1984). There is mounting evidence that women in nontraditional positions are the most likely recruits to a feminist movement (Klein 1984; Plutzer 1988); combined with evidence that more women are finding themselves in such positions, the potential for ongoing feminist recruitment and mobilization seems promising. If this potential can be combined with the organizational strengths depicted previously, the prospects for movement development through the next decade will be much enhanced.

Future mobilization depends in part on the movement's ability to frame women's situations in terms of feminist ideology. Contemporary feminist ideology is as diverse as the movement's organizational forms, and this pluralism can be a source of movement strength as long as it does not promote excessive factionalism and preclude effectiveness. Ferree and Hess identify four broad strands of contemporary feminist ideology (1985:42) and argue that most aspirations of the contemporary movement are related to one of these four orientations: career feminists seek desegregation of the labor force; liberal feminists pursue equal rights; socialist feminists challenge the intertwining of capitalism and patriarchy; and radical feminists redefine the nature of community (1985:141–166). The combination of ideological pluralism and organizational diversity (and the tendency of each to reinforce the other) can promote factionalism and fragmentation, which can be a serious weakness in specific, single-issue campaigns such as the ERA, where greater movement unity and coordination might have led to a different outcome. In the long run, however, pluralism and diversity are likely to be sources of movement strength, signifying that it has transcended the boundaries and viewpoints of any single group of women to encompass a broader spectrum of women's concerns.

In addition to this diversity, there is some reason to think that feminist ideology contains an inherent dynamic that leads from liberal, mainstream views to radical, transformative perspectives. If we define liberal feminism as a mainstream effort to redistribute persons within an existing structure and radical feminism as a transformational politics that seeks to redistribute rewards and change dominant structures, there may be reason to think that "the most important trend in feminist ideology today is the increased radicalization of the contemporary movement. This shift is evident at both the individual and the organizational levels" (Taylor 1989b:476). Part of the radicalizing dynamic of feminist ideology is that it links various social issues together so that whatever one's point of entry, the connections between issues and the need for broad social transformation become apparent. It is also true that feminist ideology blurs the traditional distinction between reform and revolution and that the combined challenge of separate ideological strands has potentially revolutionary consequences for modern society (Ferree and Hess 1985:173). Finally, there may well be a "radical future of liberal feminism," because the latter contains a contradiction between the patriarchal, individualist assumptions of traditional liberalism and the egalitarian, collectivist assumptions of feminism (Z. Eisenstein 1981). As a result, there is a strong potential for those who start as liberal feminists to move to more radical positions over time.

Arguments about the inherently radicalizing tendencies of feminist ideology must be located in a social context that includes other ideological dynamics as well. Most modern social movements have had an ambivalent relationship with the mass media. One the one hand, such media make possible levels of publicity, recruitment, and mobilization that would have been inconceivable in earlier social movements. On the other hand, the dynamics of these media can be quite effective at coopting radical ideologies and reproducing dominant relationships. Chomsky and Herman (1988) propose a propaganda model of mass media in which messages pass through a series of "ideological filters" before transmission to the general public. The effect of these filters is to eliminate or transform oppositional content and transmit only those messages that are compatible with the status quo. A somewhat broader notion of ideological and cultural filters helps describe the transmission of feminist ideas through mass media channels. These filters do not preclude transmission of feminist ideas; to the contrary, some aspects of feminist ideology are consistently conveyed and depicted in a positive light. But the filters insure that only the most cooptable feminist ideas are transmitted. Hence, the mass media offers a caricature of feminism as liberal, individualist, procapitalist, upwardly mobile, consumerist, and careerist because these strands of feminist ideology taken in isolation do not threaten as much as they reinforce the status quo. This counterfeminist process is all the more effective because it invites "populist" critiques of feminism as selfish and hostile to children, men, and families.

The mass media provide a counterpoint to the radicalizing tendencies of feminist ideology by their caricature of liberal feminism and their complete denial of the more radical and transformational aspects of feminism. The effect becomes even more pernicious through the now-familiar image of the newly liberated superwoman, which can reinforce new forms of female subordination through a dual burden of work. As the media coopt the feminist goal of economic independence and wed it to the evolving needs of an advanced capitalist economy, they have also stigmatized explicit identification with the women's movement. Although many women support many parts of the feminist agenda, most reject the label of "feminist" because most believe feminists are antimale, antimarriage, and antimotherhood, and many homophobically equate feminism and lesbianism (Schneider 1987). The power of the media to coopt feminism has an important generational dimension as many young women take the gains of the women's movement for granted and derive their impressions of the movement from media-filtered images. Hence, the "optimistic" reading of the movement's future based on underlying socioeconomic trends and the radicalizing trajectory of feminist ideology must be set beside the "pessimistic" reading based on the ability of the mass media and other institutions to coopt, marginalize, and stigmatize the movement, thereby neutralizing new generations of potential participants.

Further evidence of media efforts at movement cooptation may be found in frequent references to the current period as a "post-feminist" era. Most uses of this term reveal more about the hopes of movement opponents than the realities of the contemporary movement. The term "postsuffrage" is meaningful because enfranchisement required concrete legislative action, which occurred at a particular moment. No analogously specific action provides any comparable meaning to the term "post-feminist," because the goals of this movement have been much broader (hence, the defeat of the ERA in 1982 did not initiate a "post-feminist" era). If the term has utility, it is in the sense that Judith Stacey imputes to it: "use it not to indicate the death of the women's movement, but to describe the simultaneous incorporation, revision, and depoliticization of many of the central goals of second wave feminism" (Stacey 1987:8). This conception acknowledges ongoing feminist politics as well as the resistance of existing structures and dominant groups to many parts of the feminist agenda. This concept also allows us to see movement effects across a broader range of the population. Stacey's study of "post-feminist" attitudes in Silicon Valley (described in Chapter Three of this book) reveals fascinating cases of women who appropriated various feminist insights and combined them with other viewpoints in an effort to make sense of their lives. This study is a reminder that many of the movement's central ideas have been very widely diffused (as well as diluted) throughout the general population in ways that preclude simplistic judgments about a "post-feminist" era.

Judgments about "post-feminism" also presume a certain definition of the movement. Since the term "feminism" often refers to white, middle-class activists who are members of formal movement organizations with explicit ideological standpoints, that is usually the implicit frame of reference when assessing the current status of the movement. If one broadens the referent of the term to include all forms of resistance to institutional and interpersonal sexism, then the frame for judging the status of the movement is quite different. The distinction underscores the importance of "How Community Ties Shape 'Feminist Politics'" (Stall 1988), because a great deal of resistance to sexism is embedded in a broader context of community ties and social bonds that is not well understood by dominant ideologies of either liberal or radical feminism. Many women who neither belong to feminist organizations nor identify with feminist ideology engage in forms of feminist struggle. Such women may have appropriated ideas from the organized movement, although it is equally likely that the rise of the movement has simply allowed us to see age-old antisexist struggles for what they have always been. A final difficulty in assessing the status of the movement is that many feminists have now joined other activist groups (peace, antiracist, disarmament, ecology) and carried their feminist politics with them (Bader 1988). If this is accurate, then it is even possible to interpret declines in exclusively feminist organizations as a sign of the movement's strength, because it indicates that activists have branched out into related issues and movements to which they bring a well-defined feminist perspective.

Among the many internal debates that animate modern feminism, the tension between seeking equality or recognizing difference is perhaps most vital to the future of the movement. This polarity is inherent in feminism itself, arising from the dual identity of feminists as human beings who make equality claims and as women who assert differences from men. Such paradoxes of feminism (Cott 1987) will not be definitively resolved, but movement choices to pursue equality or defend difference in particular campaigns will be critical to movement outcomes. In an earlier era, this issue arose in the effort to win suffrage, as some argued for the vote on the grounds of justice and equality while others pointed to women's differences from men as the most important reason they needed the vote. The ultimate success of the suffrage movement was due in part to its ability to argue for the vote on the grounds of both equality and difference, suggesting that these two standpoints are not always incompatible. But the subsequent split over the Equal Rights Amendment during the early 1920s was the more typical case, in which equal rights feminists promoted the ERA while social feminists defended protective labor legislation, and the equality versus difference debate reemerged.

This debate has its counterpart in the history of legislative and judicial action concerning the status of women in the United States. In Hoff-Wilson's characterization, one side of the debate involves political feminists who seek equality, equal rights, individual rights, equality of opportunity, and access to a male public sphere on the basis of an assimilationist concept of justice that will produce "equality in sameness." The other side involves relational or familial feminists who seek equity, relational rights, group rights, equality of results, and defend a private female sphere on the basis of a pluralist concept of justice that will produce "equality in difference" (Hoff-Wilson 1987:15). The approach of political feminists is important in eradicating lingering legal disabilities, which continue to put women at certain disadvantages relative to men, but the danger is that the resulting equality will be based on a male standard and will integrate women into a male-defined world that will still leave them in a vulnerable position. The approach of relational feminists is important in revealing how formal equality may leave women at a substantive disadvantage by failing to recognize sexual differences, but the danger is that sexual difference will be interpreted in an essentialistic or biologistic way that implicitly supports patriarchal notions of separate spheres, privileges, advantages, and powers for the sexes.

This debate is at the heart of a number of current controversies. One concerns the goal of comparable worth as the next step beyond equal pay and affirmative action in redressing women's economic inequality. Comparable worth seeks a revaluing of women's traditional wage work that will put it on a more equitable footing with traditionally male forms of wage work; as a policy, it embodies the perspective of relational feminism toward the goal of equity. Such an approach has recently come under criticism from equal rights feminists who argue that "paying above-market wages for 'women's work' . . . ensures that women stay in those jobs for good, instead of striking out into largely male fields" (quoted in Hoff-Wilson 1987:29). Sexual violence in pornography is another issue that has sharply divided the feminist community along these ideological lines. Some feminists, supported by arguments about sexual difference, predatory males, and vulnerable females, have advocated ordinances banning pornography as a violation of women's civil rights. Other feminists have argued, on the basis of an equal rights approach, that such laws will inevitably violate First Amendment free speech rights, which must take priority (Hoff-Wilson 1987:33). Such debates reveal the ideological vitality of the current movement, but they can have demobilizing consequences in a conservative and reactionary climate. At a time when all forms of feminism are under attack, the movement's ability to resolve or transcend these issues will be an important determinant of its continuing effectiveness.

Legal decisions reflecting these debates have offered women "equally unattractive interpretations" of "equal treatment as unequal individuals (when judged by male standards) or special treatment as a protected (and thus implicitly inferior) group" (Hoff-Wilson 1987:36). Nowhere is this more evident than in public policy surrounding pregnant women in the workplace. In 1978, Congress enacted the Pregnancy Discrimination Act, requiring that pregnant workers be treated exactly like other workers concerning their ability or inability to work. An attempt to outlaw discriminatory treatment of pregnant workers, this policy exemplified an equal rights approach blind to reproductive differences among workers. However, the federal law appeared to conflict with laws in several states that recognized the particular needs and special character of pregnant women and exemplified a sexual difference approach to the issue (Vogel 1987). In subsequent debate, the drawbacks of both positions became more evident. The equal-rights approach can easily yield unequal results because of reproductive differences, whereas the special-treatment approach can provide a basis for unfavorable as well as favorable treatment. In a carefully nuanced argument, Vogel concludes that a gender-neutral approach is a better strategy (and contains fewer pitfalls) than a special treatment approach in the current political climate. At the same time, she encourages further exploration of an "incorporationist" approach that transcends these polarities by recognizing sharply circumscribed special rights that would apply only to well-defined physiological sex differences, avoiding the traditional traps of prior special-treatment approaches (Vogel 1987). In all these arenas, the women's movement must confront the central question posed by Wendy Williams: "Do we want equality of the sexes — or do we want justice for two kinds of human beings who are fundamentally different?" (cited in Hoff-Wilson 1987:36).

The sometimes arcane debate between advocates of equality and difference became interlaced with more practical concerns about work and family that attracted renewed attention after the defeat of the ERA. Although Friedan's call for *The Second Stage* (1981) of the women's movement was widely criticized in feminist circles for abandoning the goal of women's independence, similar arguments found a more receptive audience just four years later as Friedan pondered "How to Get the Women's Movement Moving Again" (1985). For Friedan, the problem was that work continued to be structured for men and homes continued to be structured for women; until both were restructured, it would be impossible for women to "have it all," and the feminization of poverty would increase. Friedan's call for a new politics of home and family underscored that "having it all," had become "both a personal compulsion and a social responsibility, either to prove that feminism 'worked,' or that it's irrelevant." "The 'having it all' malaise is the new feminist mystique that must be exposed to make more women see that their individual problems have a social cause" (Walsh 1985:13). An effective response requires an explicit economic agenda for radical change, including subsidized child care, parental work leaves, pay equity, income supports, comparable worth, and an expanded public sector (Walsh 1985). Such an agenda promises progressive change because it bridges work and home in ways that can improve women's status in both.

The most concrete examples of programs that include at least some of these policies are the social democracies of western Europe. The benefits of such programs are detailed by Hewlett (1987), who argues that "the social feminists in Western Europe have achieved more for working women by demanding special privileges than the equal-rights feminists in America have by taking an uncompromising stand on sex-blind laws and social policy" (cited by Wickenden 1986:24). Hewlett's advocacy of western European social democracy reflects a criticism of the contemporary women's movement in the United States for its focus on personal independence, equal rights, and social freedom, and its reputed reluctance to address the needs of most women as wives and mothers as well as workers (Walsh 1986). In a parallel critique, Wickenden claims that NOW's focus on equal rights has sidestepped the most "intractable" issue of women's economic plight and that its emphasis on the ERA has diverted attention from vital issues concerning class, race, jobs, day care, and the like (1986). In a spirited response, Connell defends NOW by claiming that work and family issues have been at the heart of the movement's agenda from the beginning, and that the worsening situation of many women results from economic crises, conservative governments, and the power of the New Right rather than any failure on the part of equal rights feminism to identify important issues (1986).

This debate crystallizes the ideological quandary of equality and difference in the contemporary movement. It is strongly reminiscent of the struggle that occurred when the ERA was first introduced in the early 1920s, with social feminists arguing for special privileges on the basis of sexual difference while equal rights feminists insisted on equality as the only standard for improving women's status. In the current debate, the advocacy of western European social-democratic models emphasizes sexual difference, and especially the manner in which reproductive differences put women at a disadvantage in both spheres. The appeal of the social-democratic model is strengthened by the fact that the United States has lagged far behind all other advanced capitalist democracies in fashioning decent and adequate social welfare policies, but there is a complex irony in using these programs as a model. They were instituted not as a response to feminist pressure from organized women's movements but rather as a pronatalist response to labor shortages and a desire to limit in-migration. Hence, the policies were designed to strengthen women's reproductive roles out of nationalist concerns about population patterns. This irony poses two important questions for the women's movement. First, have these policies benefited women beyond reinforcing their traditional reproductive roles and despite their nonfeminist origins? Second, what are the prospects for implementing similar agendas in the United States on the basis of an explicitly feminist politics that must acknowledge but not reify women's reproductive role?

Like its origins, the future of the contemporary women's movement will be a function of background conditions and proximate causes. More than in the past, however, background conditions will remain conducive to ongoing feminist activism. Increasing conflicts between capitalism's need for women's secondary labor and the patriarchally defined institution of motherhood are critical here (Z. Eisenstein 1984). Attempts by the state to reconcile these conflicts in the past have endorsed limited forms of liberal feminism, but this strategy of cooptation was abandoned during the 1980s in a frontal attack on all forms of feminism. The ongoing efforts of the state to mediate conflicts and contradictions between capitalism and patriarchy may well exacerbate rationality and legitimation crises in the state (Habermas 1975). In addition, there are a number of deeply rooted, socio-structural trends in the economy and labor force, in marriage and the family, and in other social institutions that will continue to provide new generations of women with the kinds of nontraditional roles and experiences that appear to foster feminist consciousness (Chafe 1977; Klein 1984).

If the background conditions likely to provoke a feminist response have become a constant, then the future of the women's movement will turn on the proximate causes that define its mobilizing potential. All of the elements that have been part of this analysis are relevant to this question. The movement's future will turn on the salience of gender as a basis of group identity and the politicization of that identity. The contemporary movement's organizational and ideological diversity bode well for its ability to adapt, survive, and grow even in a hostile climate. A central question is whether this diversity will allow the movement to recruit across race and class lines more effectively than it has in the past. Another potential obstacle concerns the persistence of countermovements, although opposition can provide another basis for (initially defensive) mobilization. Finally, the experiential basis of feminist politics provides additional reason to think that the movement has a promising future. Rossi argues that this produces a multigenerational cycle of recurring feminist mobilization as new generations not only take past gains for granted but discover and mobilize around new limitations that are part of their experience. Steinem offers a related generational analysis (see Ferree and Hess 1985:180–181) that suggests that as women age, they are likely to become more rather than less radical, thereby forming an ever-larger pool of potential movement recruits. Compared to other social movements, all these factors bode well for the ongoing mobilization of the contemporary women's movement.

As we enter the 1990s, it is clear that many of the conflicts between feminists, antifeminists, and the state are condensing around the state's effort to regain control over the reproductive freedom of women. For both theoretical and historical reasons, the issue of reproductive self-determination is central to women's movements. In theoretical terms, effective control over one's own body and fertility is an essential prerequisite for achieving the goals of autonomy and independence that have been at the center of women's movements for almost two centuries. In historical terms, the issue of reproductive freedom has been an important component of all the vital phases of women's mobilization, from the voluntary motherhood campaigns of the nineteenth century to the birth control movement of the early twentieth century to the current mobilization for reproductive self-determination. It is equally clear that when women's movements lose their vitality, reproductive politics become deradicalized and divorced from feminist principles, as occurred in the birth control movement from the 1920s to the 1960s. In such periods, reproductive issues are controlled by nonfeminist or antifeminist professionals whose decisions often work against the vital interests of various groups of women.

These theoretical and historical realities combine with the specific movement-countermovement dynamics of the 1980s to put reproductive issues at the center of the political agenda in the 1990s. Public opinion on abortion has assumed a rather well-defined middle-of-the-road position, and it will be very difficult for either prolife or prochoice advocates to capture full public support for their position (Luker 1984). Public opinion may not be the final arbiter in this discussion, however. Antiabortion forces have escalated their tactics to include civil disobedience, public disruption, and periodic bombing of abortion clinics. Judicial appointments have brought a more conservative viewpoint to the bench. As a result, the prospects for rigidly antiabortion legislation and policy, which would be out of step with mainstream opinion, have increased greatly. The 1989 Supreme Court decision in *Webster* v. *Missouri Reproduction Services* is a critical first step here because a narrow majority of the Court let stand every restrictive provision of the Missouri antiabortion statute. The immediate effect is to prohibit abortion altogether in any "public facility" in Missouri. The decision may have opened the door for a subsequent reconsideration and rejection of the *Roe* v. *Wade* decision, and it has increased the likelihood that other states will enact similarly restrictive antiabortion statutes in the interim (Dworkin 1989).

For the foreseeable future, the factors conducive to ongoing feminist mobilization will be pitted against the increasing momentum of the antiabortion campaign in a battle that promises to vitally affect the lives of women in the 1990s and beyond.

Conclusions

The woman suffrage movement and the contemporary women's movement are cases of long-lived movements pursuing multiple goals through diverse organizational structures with varied ideological beliefs. One means of understanding such movements is the traditional life-cycle model that envisions all movements as following a natural history of origins, growth, decline, and death. However, the outcomes of women's movements have not been primarily determined by the internal dynamics central to a life-cycle model, nor did these movements follow an inevitable and unambiguous path to failure or institutionalization as envisioned by this model. Another model for understanding movement outcomes places primary emphasis on the availability of external resources, but the outcomes of women's movements were not a simple function of the level of external resources, as envisioned in some versions of resource-mobilization theory. The best fit between these movements and abstract models of movement outcomes is the political-process model, in which the interaction between internal and external factors is central to the course of the movement (McAdam 1983).

Three specific factors cited by McAdam have been central in the suffrage movement and in the contemporary movement. Organizational strength was clearly related to outcomes in both cases. In women's movements, it is particularly clear that organizational strength often depends upon organizational diversity; women's movements succeeded when they encompassed a wide range of organizational forms that included social movement communities as well as formal movement organizations. The structure of political opportunities has also been central to outcomes in both cases. In the suffrage movement, wartime conditions created important opportunities after the Civil War and during and after World War I. In the contemporary movement, the period of reform sparked by other social movements during the 1960s and early 1970s was vital to many early successes. Finally, the responses of other groups have had a major impact on the outcomes in both cases. The suffrage movement won the vote because it built a broadly based coalition of supportive groups, won support from Wilson and the Democratic party, and neutralized antisuffragist forces by offering multiple rationales for why women needed the vote. The fortunes of the contemporary movement have also been importantly affected by other groups, including government facilitation of the early movement as well as effective antifeminist mobilization around the Equal Rights Amendment. In both movements, organizational strength, political opportunities, and group responses have not only been vital to outcomes but were dialectically related to one another as well.

Further attempts to apply models of social movement outcomes to women's movements underscore the limitations of the models and the richness of women's movements. Both the movements in this study achieved multiple outcomes that defy the simple categorizations of most theories. The suffrage movement clearly succeeded in winning the right to vote, and in doing so it closely resembled the profile of successful social movements that employ bureaucratic organization, seek narrow goals, enjoy sponsorship, use unruly methods, and make claims during periods of crisis (Gamson 1975). But the paradox of the suffrage movement was that its veteran leaders and many members expected that women's gender identity would determine their use of the ballot. This expectation was understandable given the salience of gender identity during the campaign and given the specific gender commonalities that white, upper-middle-class suffragists themselves shared. Winning the vote undermined the salience of gender identity, deprived women of their common condition of disenfranchisement, and revealed the particularities of class, race, and other statuses. For those who sought a unitary female voice via woman suffrage, the movement won the means but the means did not lead to the desired end. Hence, the outcome of the suffrage movement was both a success and a failure, but not simply either/or, because of the varied aspirations of different movement actors.

If the ballot cannot simply be characterized as a success or a failure, it can be put in broader perspective as part of a process that undermined the traditional separation of spheres and assignment of each gender to a respective sphere. Voting rights made women full and equal members of the political community regardless of how they used the vote and thereby overcame their exclusion from the public sphere. After a century of circuitous efforts to influence public affairs indirectly through education and persuasion, the right to vote created legitimate space and direct influence for women as members of the voting polity. Women's entry into this polity reflected the "domestication of politics," whereby a whole new set of issues became a legitimate part of the political agenda (Baker 1984). To a considerable extent, the women's movement laid the foundations for state intervention into formerly private domains, as government was compelled to take greater responsibility for social policy and societal welfare. The boundary between spheres became permeable in both directions; as women entered the public sphere, government entered the private sphere in unprecedented ways. The typical emphasis on how much women disagreed about these issues once the vote was won (as in the ERA debate of the early 1920s) too often obscures this major shift in the political agenda in this period. By the 1920s, women and men were debating issues that had not even been part of the political agenda a mere twenty years before. Hence, the success/failure of the suffrage campaign was embedded in broader sociopolitical changes that partially eroded the traditional division of society into separate spheres for women and men.

The contemporary women's movement has been even more diverse than the suffrage movement, as evidenced by its multiple goals, organizations, and ideologies. As noted, the political process model that emphasizes the interplay of internal and external factors in determining movement outcomes is especially useful for analyzing the outcomes of the contemporary movement. However, the movement's diversity and ongoing character preclude any single statement of movement outcomes and necessitate recognition of multiple outcomes. The contemporary women's movement has experienced failures, cooptation, institutionalization, and successes. The movement as a whole does not fit any of the profiles identified by Gamson (1975), because they all presume greater bureaucracy, centralization, and formal structure than can be found in this movement; those parts of the movement that are the most bureaucratized, centralized, and formalized have been most prone to institutionalization, however. A good deal of movement rhetoric and ideology has been coopted by mass media, which have publicized only those elements of feminism that suit commercial purposes and dominant interests. The movement has experienced failures in specific initiatives such as the Equal Rights Amendment as well as in its most visionary and revolutionary goals (as articulated in the late 1960s and early 1970s). Finally, the movement has experienced successes in campaigns for specific legislation, in changing social attitudes about gender, and in promoting transformations in the lives of many women.

The diversity of movement outcomes results from the movement's multiple goals, which in turn derive from the holistic character of sexual inequality. In contrast to some other forms of domination, sexual inequality is woven throughout the public and private sides of all social institutions. As women gain access to these institutions, there is a certain inevitability to their resistance. A common theme in this resistance is its challenge to the duality of public and private as the root of sexual inequality. For advocates of sexual equality, the goal has been to undermine this duality and to equalize the statuses of women and men in the process. For advocates of sexual difference, the goal has been to valorize the distinctive voices of women (traditionally limited to the private sphere) as the basis for transforming society in keeping with a different set of social values. As different as these goals have sometimes appeared, they share a basic challenge to the traditional division of society into public and private as the foundation of sexual inequality.

This challenge provides a vital link between the woman suffrage movement and the contemporary women's movement. In their own socio-historical contexts, each movement has confronted forms of sexual inequality that derived from this principle of social organization. The suffrage movement succeeded in gaining access to the public sphere while also forging connections between public institutions and private lives. The contemporary women's movement has built on these successes and extended the struggle into new arenas. At the most abstract level, these movements may thus be seen as phases in a larger, continuing challenge to sexual inequality. The existence of such inequality has been a constant feature of this society, as has the resistance of some women to it. While the existence of and resistance to sexual inequality have been constant, the effectiveness of the resistance has varied more sharply over time. It has been effective in direct proportion to the vitality of the movements women have organized as collective endeavors to change the patriarchal organization of social life.

Bibliography

Allen, Robert. 1975. *Reluctant Reformers*. New York: Doubleday.

Bader, Eleanor. 1988. "Will Feminism Regain Its Militancy?" *Guardian*, 16 March: 2, 9.

———. 1989. "Echoes of Racism Infuse NOW Strategy." *Guardian*, 13 September: 2.

Baker, Paula. 1984. "The Domestication of Politics." *AmericanHistorical Review* 89: 620–647.

Balser, Diane. 1987. *Sisterhood and Solidarity: Feminism and Labor in Modern Times*. Boston: South End Press.

Banks, Olive. 1981. *The Faces of Feminism*. New York: St. Martin's.

Barnes, Donna. 1987. "Organization and Radical Protest: An Antithesis?" *Sociological Quarterly* 28:575–594.

Beach, Stephen. 1977. "Social Movement Radicalization: The Case of the People's Democracy in Northern Ireland." *Sociological Quarterly* 18:305–318.

Becker, Susan. 1985. *The Origins of the Equal Rights Amendment*. Westport, CT: Greenwood Press.

Berry, Mary Frances. 1986. *Why ERA Failed*. Bloomington, IN: Indiana University Press.

Black, Naomi. 1989. *Social Feminism*. Ithaca, NY: Cornell University Press.

Boles, Janet. 1979. *The Politics of the Equal Rights Amendment*. New York: Longman.

Bordin, Ruth. 1981. *Woman and Temperance*. Philadelphia: Temple University Press.

Bouchier, David. 1978. "The Deradicalization of Feminism." *Sociology* 13:387–402.

Brady, David, and Tedin, Kent. 1976. "Ladies in Pink: Religion and Ideology in the anti-ERA Movement." *Social Science Quarterly* 56:564–575.

Breines, Wini. 1980. "Community and Organization: The New Left and Michels' 'Iron Law.'" *Social Problems* 27:419–429.

Buechler, Steven M. 1986. *The Transformation of the Woman Suffrage Movement*. New Brunswick, NJ: Rutgers University Press.

_____. 1987. "Elizabeth Boynton Harbert and the Ideological Transformation of the Woman Suffrage Movement." *Signs* 13:78–97.

Bunch (Charlotte) Papers. n.d. Box 2, File 64, Schlesinger Library, Cambridge, MA.

Burris, Val. 1983. "Who Opposed the ERA? The Social Bases of Feminism." *Social Science Quarterly* 64:305–317.

Carden, Maren. 1978. "The Proliferation of a Social Movement." Pp. 179–196 in *Research in Social Movements: Conflict and Change*, vol. 1, ed. Louis Kriesberg. Greenwich, CT: JAI Press.

Catt, Carrie Chapman, and Shuler, Nettie Rogers. 1923. *Woman Suffrage and Politics*. Seattle: University of Washington Press [1969].

Chafe, William. 1972. *The American Woman*. New York: Oxford.

_____. 1977. *Women and Equality*. New York: Oxford.

Chafetz, Janet Saltzman, and Dworkin, Gary. 1986. *Female Revolt*. Totowa, NJ: Rowman and Allanheld.

_____. 1987a. "In the Face of Threat: Organized Antifeminism in Comparative Perspective." *Gender and Society* 1:33–60.

_____. 1987b. "Action and Reaction: An Integrated, Comparative Perspective on Feminist and Antifeminist Movements." Paper presented at the American Sociological Association meetings.

Chicago Women's Liberation Union Papers. n.d.(a). "Constitution." Chicago Historical Society, Chicago, IL.

_____. n.d.(b). Various documents. Chicago Historical Society, Chicago, IL.

_____. n.d.(c). "Structure and Membership of the CWLU." Box 5, Chicago Historical Society, Chicago, IL.

Chomsky, Noam, and Herman, Edward. 1988. *Manufacturing Consent*. New York: Pantheon.

Connell, Noreen. 1986. "Feminists and Families." *Nation* 16/23 August: 106–108.

Conover, Pamela Johnston, and Gray, Virginia. 1983. *Feminism and the New Right*. New York: Praeger.

Corbin, Caroline. n.d.(a). "One Woman's Experience of Emancipation." Illinois State Historical Society, Springfield, IL.

_____. n.d.(b). "Industrial and Political Independence of Women." Illinois State Historical Society, Springfield, IL.

_____. n.d.(c). "Why the HomeMakers Do Not Want to Vote." Illinois State Historical Society, Springfield, IL.

Costain, Anne. 1982. "Representing Women: The Transition from Social Movement to Interest Group." Pp. 19–37 in Ellen Boneparth, ed., *Women, Power and Policy*. Elmsford, NY: Pergamon.

Cott, Nancy. 1978. *The Bonds of Womanhood*. New Haven: Yale University Press.

_____. 1980. "Liberation Politics in Two Eras." *American Quarterly* 32:96–105.

_____. 1984. "Feminist Politics in the 1920s: The National Women's Party." *The Journal of American History* 71:43–68.

_____. 1986. "Feminist Theory and Feminist Movements: The Past Before Us." Pp. 49–

[handwritten: sees most certainity between 2 waves, not just in NWP]

62 in Juliet Mitchell and Ann Oakley, eds., *What Is Feminism?* Oxford: Basil Blackwell. *[handwritten: HQ1420.C67]*

———. 1987. *The Grounding of American Feminism*. New Haven: Yale University Press.

Davies, James. 1962. "Toward A Theory of Revolution." *American Sociological Review* 27:5–19.

Davis, Angela. 1983. *Women, Race and Class*. New York: Vintage.

D'Emilio, John, and Freedman, Estelle. 1988. *Intimate Matters: A History of Sexuality in America*. New York: Harper and Row.

Dill, Bonnie. 1983. "Race, Class and Gender: Prospects for an All-Inclusive Sisterhood." *Feminist Studies* 9:131–150.

Donovan, Josephine. 1985. *Feminist Theory*. New York: Ungar.

DuBois, Ellen. 1978. *Feminism and Suffrage*. Ithaca: Cornell University Press. *[handwritten: escape from clerical cults.]*

———. 1987a. "Working Women, Class Relations, and Suffrage Militance: Harriot Stanton Blatch and the New York Woman Suffrage Movement, 1894–1909." *The Journal of American History* 74:34–58.

———. 1987b. "Harriot Stanton Blatch and Feminist History in the 1920s: Daughter to the Past." Paper presented at the 7th Berkshire Conference.

Dworkin, Ronald. 1989. "The Future of Abortion." *The New York Review of Books*, 28 September: 47–51.

Dye, Nancy Schrom. 1973. "Creating a Feminist Alliance: Sisterhood and Class Conflict in the New York WTUL, 1903–1914." *Feminist Studies* 2:24–38.

———. 1975. "Feminism or Unionism? The New York WTUL and the Labor Movement." *Feminist Studies* 3:111–125.

Ehrenreich, Barbara. 1982. "Defeating the ERA: A Right-wing Mobilization of Women." *Journal of Sociology and Social Welfare* 9:391–398.

Eisenstein, Hester. 1983. *Contemporary Feminist Thought*. Boston: G. K. Hall.

Eisenstein, Zillah. 1981. *The Radical Future of Liberal Feminism*. New York: Longman.

———. 1984. *Feminism and Sexual Equality*. New York: Monthly Review Press.

Engels, Frederick. 1884. *The Origin of the Family, Private Property, and the State*. New York: Pathfinder Press [1972].

Epstein, Barbara. 1981. *The Politics of Domesticity*. Middletown, CT: Wesleyan University Press.

Evans, Sara. 1979. *Personal Politics*. New York: Knopf. *[handwritten: - n supportive religious subculture for status]*

Evans, Sara, and Boyte, Harry. 1986. *Free Spaces*. New York: Harper and Row. *[handwritten: white ?]*

Ferree, Myra Marx, and Hess, Beth. 1985. *Controversy and Coalition: The New Feminist Movement*. Boston: G. K. Hall/Twayne. *[handwritten: ct i with]*

Fireman, Bruce, and Gamson, William. 1979. "Utilitarian Logic in the Resource Mobilization Perspective." Pp. 8–44 in Mayer N. Zald and John D. McCarthy, eds., *The Dynamics of Social Movements*. Cambridge, MA: Winthrop.

Firestone, Shulamith. 1970. *The Dialectic of Sex*. New York: Morrow.

Flexner, Eleanor. 1975. *Century of Struggle*. Cambridge, MA: Harvard University Press.

Fox-Genovese, Elizabeth. 1979. "The Personal Is Not Political Enough." *Marxist Perspectives* 2:94–113.

Freeman, Jo. 1972/3. "The Tyranny of Structurelessness." *Berkeley Journal of Sociology* 17:151–164.

———. 1975. *The Politics of Women's Liberation*. New York: McKay.

———. 1979. "Resource Mobilization and Strategy." Pp. 167–189 in Mayer N. Zald and John D. McCarthy, eds., *The Dynamics of Social Movements*. Cambridge, MA: Winthrop.

———. 1983. "On the Origins of Social Movements." Pp. 8–30 in Jo Freeman, ed., *Social Movements of the Sixties and Seventies*. New York: Longman.

———. 1984. "The Women's Liberation Movement." Pp. 543–556 in Jo Freeman, ed., *Women: A Feminist Perspective*. 3rd ed. Palo Alto, CA: Mayfield.

Frenier, Mariam. 1984. "American Anti-feminist Women: Comparing the Rhetoric of Opponents of the Equal Rights Amendment with that of Opponents of Women's Suffrage." *Women's Studies International Forum* 7:455–466.

Friedan, Betty. 1963. *The Feminine Mystique*. New York: Dell.

———. 1981. *The Second Stage*. New York: Summit.

———. 1985. "How to Get the Women's Movement Moving Again." *New York Times Sunday Magazine*, 3 November: 26/106.

Friedan (Betty) Papers. 1973. 20 May, Box 46, File 1661, Schlesinger Library, Cambridge, MA.

———. 1976. "Womansurge '76 Statement of Purpose." Box 49, File 1765, Schlesinger Library, Cambridge, MA.

———. 1977. Napolitan to Friedan, 29 October. Box 45, File 1608, Schlesinger Library, Cambridge, MA.

———. n.d. Box 47, File 1701, Schlesinger Library, Cambridge, MA.

Frye, Marilyn. 1988. "Some Reflections on Separatism and Power." Pp. 62–72 in Sarah Hoagland and Julia Penelope, eds., *For Lesbians Only*. London: Onlywomen Press.

Gamson, William. 1975. *The Strategy of Social Protest*. Homewood, IL: Dorsey Press.

Gerlach, Luther, and Hine, Virginia. 1970. *People, Power, Change*. New York: Bobbs-Merrill.

Giddings, Paula. 1984. *When and Where I Enter*. New York: Morrow.

Gordon, Linda. 1976. *Woman's Body, Woman's Right*. New York: Grossman.

Gordon, Linda, and Hunter, Allen. 1977/78. "Sex, Family and the New Right: Antifeminism as a Political Force." *Radical America* 12:9–25.

Gurr, Ted. 1970. *Why Men Rebel*. Princeton: Princeton University Press.

Habermas, Jurgen. 1975. *Legitimation Crisis*. Boston: Beacon.

Harrison, Cynthia. 1980. "A 'New Frontier' for Women: The Public Policy of the Kennedy Administration." *The Journal of American History* 67:630–646.

Hersh, Blanche. 1978. *The Slavery of Sex: Feminist-Abolitionists in America*. Urbana: University of Illinois Press.

Hewitt, Nancy. 1986. "Feminist Friends: Agrarian Quakers and the Emergence of Woman's Rights in America." *Feminist Studies* 12:27–49.

Hewlett, Sylvia. 1987 *A Lesser Life*. New York: Morrow.

Hoff-Wilson, Joan, ed. 1986. *Rights of Passage: The Past and Future of the ERA*. Bloomington, IN: Indiana University Press.

———. 1987. "The Unfinished Revolution: Changing Legal Status of U.S. Women." *Signs* 13:7–36.

Hole, Judith, and Levine, Ellen. 1971. *Rebirth of Feminism*. New York: Quadrangle.

Hooks, Bell. 1981. *Ain't I a Woman? Black Women and Feminism*. Boston: South End Press.

———. 1984. *Feminist Theory: From Margin to Center*. Boston: South End Press.

Howard, Jeanne. 1982. "Our Own Worst Enemies: Women Opposed to Woman Suffrage." *Journal of Sociology and Social Welfare* 9:463–474.

Huber, Joan. 1976. "Toward a Sociotechnological Theory of the Women's Movement." *Social Problems* 23:371–388.

Huber, Joan, Rexroat, Cynthia, and Spitze, Glenna. 1978. "A Crucible of Opinion on Women's Status: ERA in Illinois." *Social Forces* 57:549–565.

Jacoby, Robin. 1975. "The Women's Trade Union League and American Feminism." *Feminist Studies* 2:126–140.

Jenkins, J. Craig. 1977. "Radical Transformation of Organizational Goals." *Administrative Science Quarterly* 22:568–586.

———. 1983. "Resource Mobilization Theory and the Study of Social Movements." *Annual Review of Sociology* 9:527–553.

Johnson, Helen. 1897. *Woman and the Republic* New York: D. Appleton.

Jonasdottir, Kirsten. 1988. "Oligarchy and/or Goal Transformation: The Case of the National Organization for Women." Paper presented at the Midwest Sociological Society meetings.

Joseph, Gloria, and Lewis, Jill. 1981. *Common Differences: Conflicts in Black and White Feminist Perspectives*. Garden City, NY: Doubleday.

Katzenstein, Mary. 1984. "Feminism and the Meaning of the Vote." *Signs* 10:4–26.

Kauffman, L. A. 1984. "NOW for Something Completely Different." *The Progressive* March:31–34.

King, Mary. 1987. *Freedom Song: A Personal Story of the 1960s Civil Rights Movement*. New York: William Morrow.

Klatch, Rebecca. 1988. "Coalition and Conflict Among Women of the New Right." *Signs* 13:671–694.

Klein, Ethel. 1984. *Gender Politics: From Consciousness to Mass Movement*. Cambridge, MA: Harvard University Press.

Kraditor, Aileen. 1965. *The Ideas of the Woman Suffrage Movement*. New York: Columbia University Press.

Lang, Kurt, and Lang, Gladys. 1961. *Collective Dynamics*. New York: Crowell.

Langer, Elinor. 1976. "Why Big Business is Trying to Defeat the ERA." *MS* May:64/108.

Leach, William. 1980. *True Love and Perfect Union*. New York: Basic.

Lipset, Seymour, and Raab, Earl. 1970. *The Politics of Unreason*. New York: Harper and Row.

Lo, Clarence. 1982. "Countermovements and Conservative Movements in the Contemporary U.S." *Annual Review of Sociology* 8:107–134.

Luker, Kristin. 1984. *Abortion and the Politics of Motherhood*. Berkeley and Los Angeles: University of California Press.

McAdam, Doug. 1982. *Political Process and the Development of Black Insurgency*. Chicago: University of Chicago Press.

_____. 1983. "The Decline of the Civil Rights Movement." Pp. 298–319 in Jo Freeman, ed., *Social Movements of the Sixties and Seventies*. New York: Longman.

_____. 1989. "Gender Differences in the Causes and Consequences of Activism." Paper presented at the American Sociological Association meetings.

McCarthy, John D., and Zald, Mayer N. 1973. *The Trend of Social Movements*. Morristown, NJ: General Learning Press.

_____. 1977. "Resource Mobilization and Social Movements." *American Journal of Sociology* 82:1212–1241.

McGlen, Nancy E., and O'Connor, Karen. 1983. *Women's Rights: The Struggle for Equality in the Nineteenth and Twentieth Centuries*. New York: Praeger.

Mansbridge, Jane. 1986. *Why We Lost the ERA*. Chicago: University of Chicago Press.

Marshall, Susan. 1985. "Ladies Against Women: Mobilization Dilemmas of Antifeminist Movements." *Social Problems* 32:348–362.

_____. 1986. "In Defense of Separate Spheres: Class and Status Politics in the Antisuffrage Movement." *Social Forces* 65:327–351.

Marshall, Susan, and Orum, Anthony. 1986. "Opposition Then and Now: Countering Feminism in the Twentieth Century." Pp. 13–34 in Gwen Moore and Glenna Spitze, eds., *Research in Politics and Society*, vol. 2. Greenwich, CT: JAI Press.

Melder, Keith. 1977. *Beginnings of Sisterhood*. New York: Schocken.

Michels, Robert. 1961. *Political Parties*. New York: Free Press.

Miller, Frederick. 1983. "The End of SDS and the Emergence of Weatherman: Demise Through Success." Pp. 279–297 in Jo Freeman, ed., *Social Movements of the Sixties and Seventies*. New York: Longman.

Moraga, Cherrie, and Anzaldua, Gloria, eds. 1981. *This Bridge Called My Back: Writings by Radical Women of Color*. Watertown, MA: Persephone Press.

Mottl, Tahi. 1980. "The Analysis of Countermovements." *Social Problems* 27:620–635.

Mueller, Carol. 1983. "Women's Movement Success and the Success of Social Movement Theory." Working Paper #110, Wellesley College Center for Research on Women.

Mueller, Carol, and Dimieri, Thomas. 1982. "The Structure of Belief Systems Among Contending ERA Activists." *Social Forces* 60:657–675.

National Organization for Women. 1988. *Issues Policy Manual*. Washington, DC: National Organization for Women.

National Organization for Women Papers. 1966. "Statement of Purpose." Schlesinger Library, Cambridge, MA.

_____. 1979. San Francisco *Examiner* article, 16 October. Carton 4, Schlesinger Library, Cambridge, MA.

_____. n.d.(a) "Lesbian Rights." Carton, 54, Schlesinger Library, Cambridge, MA.

_____. n.d.(b) Carton 27, Schlesinger Library, Cambridge, MA.

Oberschall, Anthony. 1973. *Social Conflict and Social Movements*. Englewood Cliffs, NJ: Prentice-Hall.

Olson, Mancur. 1968. *The Logic of Collective Action*. New York: Schocken.

O'Neill, William. 1969. *Everyone Was Brave*. Chicago: Quadrangle.

Petchesky, Rosalind. 1981. "Antiabortion, Antifeminism, and the Rise of the New Right." *Feminist Studies* 7:206–246.

Piven, Frances Fox, and Cloward, Richard. 1977. *Poor People's Movements*. New York: Vintage.

Plutzer, Eric. 1988. "Work Life, Family Life and Women's Support of Feminism." *American Sociological Review* 53:640–649.

Rosenfeld, Rachel, and Ward, Kathryn. 1985. "The Rise of the U.S. Women's Movement after World War II: A Competition Approach." Paper presented at American Sociological Association meetings.

Rosenthal, Naomi, Fingrutd, Meryl, Ethier, Michele, Karant, Roberta, and McDonald, David. 1985. "Social Movements and Network Analysis." *American Journal of Sociology* 90:1022–1054.

Rosenthal, Naomi, and Schwartz, Michael. Forthcoming. "Spontaneity and Democracy in Social Protest." In *Organizing for Change*, vol. 2, ed. Bert Klandermans. Greenwich, CT: JAI Press.

Rothschild, Matthew. 1989. "Third Party Time?" *The Progressive* October:20–25.

Rothschild-Whitt, Joyce. 1979. "The Collectivist Organization: An Alternative to Rational-Bureaucratic Models." *American Sociological Review* 44:509–527.

Rupp, Leila J., and Taylor, Verta. 1987. *Survival in the Doldrums*. New York: Oxford.

Ryan, Barbara. 1989. "Ideological Purity and Feminism: The U.S. Women's Movement from 1966 to 1975." *Gender and Society* 3:239–257.

Sacks, Karen. 1976. "Class Roots of Feminism." *Monthly Review* 27:28–48.

Schneider, Beth. 1987. "Feminist Disclaimers, Stigma and the Contemporary Women's Movement." Paper presented at the American Sociological Association meetings.

Schwartz, Michael, Rosenthal, Naomi, and Schwartz, Laura. 1981. "Leader-Member Conflict in Protest Organizations." *Social Problems* 29:22–36.

Sinclair, Anthony. 1965. *The Emancipation of the American Woman*. New York: Harper and Row.

Smelser, Neil J. 1963. *Theory of Collective Behavior*. New York: Free Press.

Smith-Rosenberg, Caroll. 1975. "The Female World of Love and Ritual." *Signs* 1:1–29.

Snow, David, and Benford, Robert. 1988. "Master Frames and Cycles of Protest." Paper presented at American Sociological Association workshop on social movements.

Spinster, Sidney. 1988. "The Evolution of Lesbian Separatist Consciousness." Pp. 97–121 in Sarah Hoagland and Julia Penelope, eds., *For Lesbians Only*. London: Onlywomen Press.

Stacey, Judith. 1987. "Sexism by a Subtler Name? Postindustrial Conditions and Postfeminist Consciousness in the Silicon Valley." *Socialist Review* 96:7–28.

Stall, Susan. 1988. "How Community Ties Shape 'Feminist Politics.'" Paper presented at the Midwest Sociological Society meetings.

Strasser, Susan. 1982. *Never Done*. New York: Pantheon.

Tax, Meredith. 1980. *The Rising of the Women*. New York: Monthly Review Press.

Taylor, Verta. 1989a. "Sisterhood, Solidarity and Modern Feminism: A Review Essay." *Gender and Society* 3:277–286.

———. 1989b. "The Future of Feminism: A Social Movement Analysis." Pp. 473–490 in Laurel Richardson and Verta Taylor, eds., *Feminist Frontiers*. Reading, MA: Addison-Wesley.

Terborg-Penn, Rosalyn. 1978. "Discrimination Against Afro-American Women in the Woman's Movement." Pp. 17–27 in Sharon Harley and Rosalyn Terborg-Penn, eds., *The Afro-American Woman: Struggles and Images*. Port Washington, NY: Kennikat Press.

Tilly, Charles. 1978. *From Mobilization to Revolution*. Reading, MA: Addison-Wesley.

Vogel, Lise. 1987. "The Pregnancy Discrimination Act and the Debate over Special Treatment." Paper presented at the American Sociological Association meetings.

Walsh, Joan. 1985. "Feminism's New Frontiers." *In These Times*, 11–17 December:12–13.

———. 1986. "Family Ties: Feminism's Next Frontier." *The Progressive* September:21–23.

Ward, Kathryn, and Rosenfeld, Rachel. 1986. "The Contemporary Women's Movement: An Empirical Test of Competition Theory." Paper presented at the American Sociological Association meetings.

Weber, Max. 1947. *From Max Weber*. New York: Oxford University Press.

Weitzman, Lenore. 1985. *The Divorce Revolution*. New York: Free Press.

Welter, Barbara. 1966. "The Cult of True Womanhood." *American Quarterly* 18:151–174.

West, Guida, and Blumberg, Rhoda Lois, eds. Forthcoming. *Women and Social Protest*. New York: Oxford University Press.

Whittier, Nancy E., and Taylor, Verta. 1989. "Social Movement Culture and Identity Transformation." Paper presented at the American Sociological Association meetings.

Wickenden, Dorothy. 1986. "What NOW?" *The New Republic* 194:19/25.

Zald, Mayer N., and Ash, Roberta. 1966. "Social Movement Organizations: Growth, Decay and Change." *Social Forces* 44:327–340.

Zald, Mayer N., and McCarthy, John D. 1980. "Social Movement Industries: Competition and Cooperation Among Movement Organizations." Pp. 1–20 in Zald and McCarthy, eds., *Research in Social Movements*, vol. 3. Greenwich, CT: JAI Press.

Zald, Mayer N., and Useem, Bert. 1987. "Movement and Countermovement Interaction: Moblization, Tactics, and State Involvement." Pp. 247–271 in Mayer N. Zald and John D. McCarthy, eds., *Social Movements in an Organizational Society*. New Brunswick, NJ: Transaction Books.

Author Index

Subject Index